ARE YOU OK IN THERE?

A Guide for Family Mental Health Carers

Jane Lawrence

The Book Guild Ltd

First published in Great Britain in 2020 by
The Book Guild Ltd
9 Priory Business Park
Wistow Road, Kibworth
Leicestershire, LE8 0RX
Freephone: 0800 999 2982
www.bookguild.co.uk
Email: info@bookguild.co.uk
Twitter: @bookguild

Typeset in 11pt Minion Pro

Printed and bound by CPI Group (UK) Ltd, Croydon, CR0 4YY

ISBN 978 1913551 094

British Library Cataloguing in Publication Data.
A catalogue record for this book is available from the British Library.

Dedicated to all the
mental health carers that I met over the years.
You certainly are an impressive bunch!

CONTENTS

INTRODUCTION

THE AUTHOR

I fell into working in mental health by accident really, although my family is not without its casualties; most families I suspect can find one or two. I lived my life without much thought for these peoples' troubles and largely ignored the difficulties they faced. It never crossed my mind that the way I behaved could impact on these distressed family members, that I could possibly be of some help. Of course, that was a long time ago and much has improved, we are all far more aware of the issues around mental health these days.

I trained as a Social Worker and worked for Social Care for a while. The frustration of trying to develop new ideas in the face of a huge organisation was too much for me so I have spent most of my working life in the third sector, in voluntary organisations. I preferred to be a middle-sized fish in a smaller pond.

I spent many years in services with fancy names such as Wellbeing Centre or Community Hub, working with people who had severe mental health issues. These places offered support to get back into socialising or trying new skills, to move towards being as independent as possible. I have been involved in people's crisis times when there was anguish, anger, despair and occasionally violence towards others or more frequently towards themselves, and sometimes me. Mostly the work was with people who were in a quieter place and getting back to living their lives.

You would not believe how many games of Uno I have played in order to have really uninteresting conversations about the weather with people, in the belief that this was good practice for them in engaging with slightly scary people like me. I have been sighing inwardly as the same person asks to talk to me for the ninth time that day to go over the same repetitive conversation, they had not got the slightest interest if I had a view on the situation. I have spent hours trying to sort out someone's income and expenditure, trying to explain why they are constantly in debt. This may not sound very technical, but professionals have pretty much got the same tools that families have: time and patience.

But I wasn't family, I was a professional and the relationship is different. The people I saw were usually the sort of individuals who lived at home or in a flat close by home, and really needed long-term support from relatives and friends – but this wasn't always there for them.

I believe that the reason so many families end up distancing themselves from someone they care deeply about is that they are just overwhelmed by their level of need, their moods and their behaviour. Above all they feel alone in trying to cope with all this, often expecting that they should know what to do but essentially just lurching from moments of hope to moments of despair without anything to compare it to. They get little information, not much (or often no) support and minimal appreciation or thanks.

When I worked with people within the mental health system I thought little about all this. I said goodbye at 5.30 pm and went home to my own challenging family life but these challenges were 'normal', they could be understood and moaned openly about at the school gates or with friends. They were textbook whines that we all recognised: how rude our kids were, how our partners didn't understand, what we got paid, etc.

Then, by accident or fate, or whatever controls these things, I went for a job in carer support. I had to look up the word 'carer' before the interview. I knew a bit about mental health issues and more about how they affected people but nothing about the families, partners and friends who were there in the background. After I had met my first twenty or so carers, I got back up off the floor and have become pretty involved in this carers' world for about fifteen years.

This has involved going to lots of meetings, often being the only person there who had even considered the family's perspective. My job involved trying to get professionals to recognise that they had some responsibility to involve and support this tired and bad-tempered mum or this red-eyed and worried husband. I have spent a lot of time sat in rooms or coffee shops with carers until our coffee was curdled, talking about their concerns and fears for the person they cared so much about, and their doubt as to whether they were doing the right things.

My colleague and I constructed a small booklet a few years ago and printed five hundred copies with our small service budget. It was taken up by the local mental health trust and they have been paying to have it published so they have something relevant to give to families. I am sure that many NHS and voluntary organisations duplicate our little booklet across the UK. I wanted ours to be as honest as possible while offering positive information and realistic encouragement.

That booklet sowed the seeds of this book, which can probably be described as part fact, part opinion, part rant and part nag.

I find that humour is one useful tool in trying to work with some depressing aspects of this world. This approach is not meant to detract from just how incredibly tough some days are, maybe it's just my way of dealing with what I have heard about some other people's lives.

I have enormous admiration for most of the carers I have met, although they are all quite different. Maybe it is because when it all kicked off, they stood firm(ish) and fought on. Not that I would judge anyone who stopped supporting their relative, partner or friend, sometimes it is a necessary if heart-breaking decision.

This all sounds extremely negative; I should also say that there were many positive moments, lots of laughs and stories with happy endings. It just happened that I was more likely to be involved in the worst bits.

ABOUT THE BOOK

Each topic is in a separate section. This is because family carers don't always have a lot of time to sit and read, even if they could find the energy. They probably want to look at the parts that are relevant to them right now rather than wade through a lot of unnecessary stuff but this means that if it is read it in bigger chunks there may be some repetition. This is all part of the plan and not done to annoy.

The information is largely relevant for families, friends, partners and older children supporting someone over 18 years old who has a mental health issue, but there are bits that will be relevant to supporting younger people. The major differences would be that the confidentiality issues won't be the same and parents of 'minors' tend to be involved in treatment planning to a greater degree than they are with people over eighteen.

The book doesn't cover some conditions simply because they are too complex and they require highly specialist information; these include dementia, ADD/ADHD and Autism Spectrum Disorder (ASD). The latter has been researched a lot more in recent years, but there appears to be a long way to go until the details are really understood. People may frequently be diagnosed with ASD and another mental health diagnosis together, there seems to be a great deal of common ground. ASD is currently understood as being caused mostly by how a brain is working, rather than trauma or life experiences. Probably.

Dementia is fundamentally different from most other mental health diagnoses as it is a deteriorating condition, where certain systems in the brain gradually stop functioning; it inevitably becomes worse. Most other mental health issues tend to be fluctuating, they vary considerably over time.

There may be bits of the book that do turn out to be useful, even supporting someone with one of the diagnoses that isn't covered in any detail. These may be the options around what can be done in particular situations, plus the need to look after yourself. So, if you have got this book for Christmas because your mum has Alzheimer's then I'm sorry, but please don't give it to the charity shop without a skim through.

There is quite a bit of the book which is focussed on people experiencing those severe conditions where people may be out of touch with reality or putting themselves in situations that involve high levels of risk. Most mental health carers will never have to deal with these worrying situations, although they are more common than many people seems to think. Reading sections that are not currently relevant should be regarded of passing interest but not currently anything to be concerned about.

Lastly there is some information as to why carers should look after themselves. I do realise that this will be the least read bit of the book but the bottom line is, in order to be in the best place both mentally and physically to carry on supporting the cared-for person this is not an optional activity. It may take some time to realise this; perhaps it only gets attention when a physical or mental health issue arises for the carer too.

My hope is that this book will provide a bit more information and a few suggestions on how to approach tricky situations which might help reduce the stress that comes with a caring experience.

WHAT IS A CARER?

A carer is someone who offers support to another person which that person could not manage without.

Most people strongly object to the title of 'carer'. I have heard many times 'I'm just his mum' or 'I married her, and this is just part of the job'. Usually a family member or friend will find themselves gradually taking on a variety of support tasks for another person. It seldom happens overnight, it often starts as an extension for what they would do for them anyway. Sometimes it begins in an emergency when there is no time to think about what they are getting involved in.

The term 'carer' is used interchangeably with the word 'family' in this book but that is intended to include friends, older and adult children, partners and any other arrangement where one person is helping another.

One of the confusing aspects of accepting the identity of a mental health carer is that the roles and tasks involved can vary considerably over time, it can involve a wide range of activities. The public perception of a 'carer' tends to be those often (but not always) wonderful people who call in to your home, make you a sandwich, pass you your pills, take you to the toilet and then, with a cheerful wave, say goodbye until a few hours later. They also get paid. The family, partner, friend or child may find themselves helping with any or all of the following for free:

- Shopping
- The whole prescription palaver from start to finish

- Trying to make sure people take the right meds at the right time, every single day
- Trying to make sure they eat properly
- Trying to persuade them to wash/change their clothes/ let the bed be changed
- Cleaning their flat
- Managing their bills or claiming their benefits
- Trying to persuade them not to get into debt
- Getting their food/cider/grass/heroin/cigs/chocolate for them
- Facing up to people who have insulted them
- Listening to them on the phone up to fifty times a day
- Listening to them on your sofa/their sofa up to fifty times a day
- Listening to them at 3 am
- Trying to get them to talk
- Trying to get them to talk to a professional
- Trying to get them to appointments that they don't want to go to
- Trying to look after their physical health
- Cleaning up after a crisis – this could be a variety of bodily fluids or a mess of broken objects

I am sure you get the picture and if you recognise more than half a dozen of these roles then you're probably a carer. It's more difficult to define when the person who needs assistance is younger and could quite well be needing similar support anyway at that age, but it is usually clear if there is that bit more help required.

Some carers' duties are quite light, some are overwhelming. The thing about mental health is that it is usually a variable condition, particularly in the early stages, which means it is an unpredictable roller coaster. Hopefully the carer role will be a temporary one and no one will need to take on this 'carer' identity long-term. It depends on a wide range of variables that are not always apparent from the early days.

The main reason for grudgingly accepting the title of 'carer' is that it is a term used in local policy and national law, so if there is anything going that can be taken advantage of then it's good to know. Within mental health services it may save time and effort to make sure that the carer(s) are clearly identified early on, because they are entitled to get information that other friends and relatives may not be offered. The confidentiality rules are complicated, especially in the NHS, and having an identified carer will help get through those complications more smoothly. (See 'confidentiality' section.)

It also may help to realise that this situation is more than the usual family /friend support and that it is recognised as such in law – recognised but not greatly rewarded.

Carers often have no training and no back up. They can usually access professional help on a quite random basis, a few are recognised as being under considerable stress and are offered support, but this may be only at the point of collapse. Often this is because they keep quiet about what they are going through.

This is all slowly changing; the role of carers is better recognised now but resources are limited. My experience has been gained in one county and I am not sure if this is representative of other areas, I suspect that there are places that are better than the one I know and some that are far worse.

Supporting someone with mental health issues is potentially more complex and stressful than other caring roles in my opinion, (inflammatory remark No 1). All carers have higher rates of mental and physical health problems than the rest of the population. But mental health conditions especially (including dementia, but for different reasons) are a real test of endurance. Why is this?

Maybe:

- The 'symptoms' constantly change, sometimes predictably, sometimes not.
- The person may be up for a chat or impossible to communicate with in any meaningful way.
- They are frequently distressed beyond anything the family have witnessed before and it feels like the carer's job to do something about it.
- Is the situation as it appears? Is this 'attention seeking'? Are they 'putting it on'?
- Is it happening because the family or partner are causing it?
- Why do they sometimes apparently reject the people who are trying to help?
- Carers might have to make what feels like crucial decisions on their own and quickly with no back up.
- Professionals apparently expect the family to take responsibility for things that they cannot or will not do themselves such as 'just make sure he takes his medication,' or 'just take her to A&E'.
- They may also be faced with situations that professional staff would only go into in pairs and after four years of training.
- It requires enduring long-term feats of amazing patience when dealing with repetitive conversations, worrying habits and poor self-care.
- There are well meaning relatives and friends who tell the carer(s) what to do, despite the fact they have far less detailed knowledge of the situation and no mental health expertise.
- There is a lot of extra practical work to do to keep the person functioning, like cleaning and shopping and taking them to appointments. They tend not to be grateful and occasionally appear quite capable of doing it themselves.
- Professionals' planning the treatment don't always include the carer in discussions, except for occasional meetings

where they are invited to say what they think; then nothing apparently changes.

- There are major emotional issues of guilt and loss to deal with, because this unwell person is someone the family care deeply about and have a lot of love invested in their wellbeing. But there is no time for this soppy indulgent stuff right now.

A lot of people that I met felt that they have gained strength and wisdom through their caring role. They have been remarkable in accepting how things are for them and the people they care about. No one is saying it is an easy option though. Universally, carers seem to feel more that they are on their own and that their situation is unique. In fact, carers in general are seven times more likely to say they are lonely than the average population. (Carers UK 2019 survey)

I hope that finding something familiar in the pages of this book might encourage the realisation that mental health carers are very much not alone. There are so many of these partners and parents out there all feeling cut off and finding it difficult to talk to others because, well, you know, it's mental health.

Things are getting better. Some may read this book with disgust at its dated attitudes. But I think there is still a long way to go. Many mental health teams and services support families well, but some need to get a move on and put the dusty 'carers' action plan' into practice now, rather than having it constantly on the 'to do' list.

I have included some personal stories that people have told me and made them as anonymous as possible. If it was you that told me these things, then I do hope you feel that you are safely unidentifiable and that the story will help others. I also hope you have long since forgotten about these situations and can remember with relief that it was a long time ago and things are much better now.

The book is about choices, particularly when faced with difficult situations. Supporting someone involves challenging decisions, the aspects that the family realistically has control over are limited. Taking time to consider options is helpful, so is monitoring what is working and what is not. There is a choice how to respond to situations, but the bottom line is always 'you cannot change another person, you can only change yourself' - and hope that this brings the right results.

UNDERSTANDING MENTAL HEALTH

The words that are used around mental health are sometimes complicated and confusing. We talk about mental wellbeing meaning being mentally healthy, but we also use the term 'mental health' to describe the presence of the opposite, as in 'he's not well, it's a mental health issue.' There have been changes regarding what words are acceptable as part of the battle against negative public opinion and stigma but sometimes this makes things less clear.

I use mental health 'issue' or 'problems', but a lot of people don't like those terms. I think it is an issue or a problem or else we wouldn't be talking about it. I wouldn't say mental 'illness' as that implies it is caused by a physical malfunction, which may be partly true – or not. I also use the word 'condition' which is not always accepted although to me it means 'the state of something', which is fairly neutral. What is annoying is when someone says, 'He's not right, he's got mental health.'

Mental health doesn't have to be perfect, it is 'good enough' if it keeps the person functioning above survival level. It is apparent that some people feel that constant happiness is possible and the inevitable failure to achieve this brings on a sense of being unwell or disadvantaged in some way. Those who access constant peace and tranquillity in their daily existence are great role models, but it should be publicly acknowledged that we are not all made that way. It's not an easy option, being mentally well; we live lives that go against our basic human programming, especially in cities. It resembles those early experiments with too many rats crammed together in a maze and all battling for food, and the unavoidable rat battles that ensued.

People, without exception, are going to have a dreadful time on more than one occasion in their lives, often because of an incident, a trauma, a bereavement or a bad social experience. Any experience from being dumped by a partner through to being involved in a serious car accident. On the whole we accept that we need to get through these excruciatingly stressful times the best way we can and 'tough it out'.

Not all of us our equipped for this though, some are more resilient than others and some have inherited flaws in their basic programming that allow cracks to appear where the rest of the population would shudder, go sit on the toilet for a while and have a little cry, then just manage to carry on like we don't care. This inability to fight on through is not always weakness, it can be innate vulnerability; it is the hand you have been dealt.

We have day-to-day vocabulary that includes many mental health terms, often used poorly or with a lack of respect. For example, I usually check my front door is locked and the iron is off at least once more than I need to, but I wouldn't call myself 'a little bit OCD'. This asks for some small sympathy for my suffering, which is wholly unjustified as I could change my behaviour with some minor effort. It doesn't make me special, just a bit lazy and a bit anxious. It is also insulting to those whose lives are controlled by obsessive behaviour and who need superhuman effort and endurance to get through each day.

We also use terms like 'bonkers', 'mad', 'schizo' and 'psycho' as a description of another person's actions, usually people that we find either hilariously entertaining or very disagreeable. Do we expect people who have a genuine mental health issue to act drunk or flirt outrageously or be mean, nasty and unpleasant? Using these words is not a problem until there is suddenly someone in the family who has a real mental health issue and a description of their condition is used as a means of insulting people.

Many people feel the need to have a public confession of a terrible trauma in their lives. There are numerous celebrities recalling times when they experienced abuse or rejection and how much it impacted on them. That is not to say that these experiences don't happen and that they shouldn't be met sympathetically or with offers of support when appropriate. It is part of the great social media debate, the current need to create an identity that makes you flawed and vulnerable – but in a good way. Some people want to be recognised as a little sad and struggling, valiantly coming to terms with past suffering. Like most of us do, most of the time, but more quietly. Those who have faced mental health challenges and overcome them should shout about it as a means to inspire others facing the same issues, not as a way to get sales or votes, or sympathy, or to excuse behaviour they actually can control perfectly well with a little effort.

This does make it confusing for families who are suddenly faced with an urgent need to understand what is going on with a person they care deeply about. Finding the way to leave the frequently misleading public view of mental health behind is crucial in order to support someone in the real world.

STARTING OUT

A lot of the tension involved in being a mental health carer is because no one says what to expect. Comparisons made with physical health care or with the media representation can lead to misunderstandings. It can easily appear that this particular situation is unique, everyone else's experience is going more smoothly and turns out differently /better. Families supporting someone often don't get chance to compare notes, opportunities to mix may be rare or too much of a challenge when there is little spare energy.

I have heard mental health professionals talking about the importance of addressing unrealistic expectations from families, but the problem is by the time they get to have that conversation the seeds of confusion, anger and perhaps desperation have already been sown.

This is a list of very random facts that are all explained in more detail later but present a good place to start addressing some possible uncertainties:

- There is a wide variety of mental health issues with quite different symptoms. Any one person will only experience a small range of these, there is no need to worry that they will go through them all.
- Not everyone with a mental health issue gets seen by a consultant psychiatrist. Depression and anxiety, particularly, are often treated at GP level. This is not a lesser service for those diagnoses, it doesn't mean they are missing out.
- Mental health issues are entirely different from learning disabilities, they do not affect someone's intelligence, whatever level they had before will stay. What may change is their ability to express themselves in words or maybe to think things through in a clear manner.
- Having a mental health diagnoses does not mean the person will become aggressive. Only a very few do, and this is usually noticeable early on. Using drugs or alcohol does greatly increase the possibility of violent behaviour, however, this is true whether there is a mental health issue or not.
- Psychiatric medication is generally not a cure, it is a means

of reducing symptoms. People with long term condition may have to stay on meds or go back on it if their symptoms return after a period of 'wellness'. Some of the medication can have unpleasant side effects but these don't affect everybody equally.

- The condition may go away on its own or it may not. It is optimistic to expect a psychiatrist to offer any information about how long it will continue or how things will turn out in the end, because they cannot tell with any certainty. This may make the situation even more stressful for the family.

- Talking therapies (conversations about past or present circumstances and thinking about how to make them less distressing) are enormously helpful to some people some of the time. In certain situations it can make things worse. If it is not being offered it may be with good reason – or it may simply be because it is not available locally.

- The mental health teams are not 'blue light' emergency services (unless there is a local arrangement for urgent crisis care teams, which usually have their own criteria as to who they will see). In most areas it is the police who are the first choice for an emergency where there is risk to the person or others.

- Social care services do not treat mental health conditions. They may well be involved in someone's care, but they are not the first people to contact if the issue is about mental health symptoms and the person needs clinical help. The GP is the first choice.

- Over four in ten carers are men. They are often caring for their partners and may experience a degree of isolation and health problems because they, and others around them, may be less likely to recognise their role than when the carer is female. Male carers may have to shout louder to be noticed.

- The mental health services will not do all that the family wants them to do. They will never have the resources to offer the constant care and attention that most families want for their cared-for person. Recognising and accepting the limitations of the mental health services and what they can offer is one of the major challenges of being a carer.

Do not expect a person with a severe mental health condition to recognise what has been done for them and be grateful. In time they may appreciate the part the family played and understand what they have been through; this happens more in the less severe conditions. The more distress and confusion the person is dealing with in their own world the more they are likely to appear totally self-absorbed. This is not their choice or a reflection on how they feel about those around them, but a form of self-preservation for them.

FROM THE BEGINNING

FIRST SIGNS

Families don't know what they don't know, this can make it difficult to ask the right questions. Information about mental health is now being taught in schools but I suspect that this is often relating to most frequently occurring conditions, which are depression and anxiety, and that little is said about the other diagnoses. Most people do not have much knowledge to fall back on and have to take on a lot of new information in a short time when it happens to a family member or close friend.

What do you do when someone close to you is 'not themselves' anymore and starts to show worrying signs of something wrong? The first response within many families seems to be to ignore it, which is completely understandable as there is always the hope that it will go away by itself. Many difficult periods in people's lives cause temporary changes and although this can be worrying there are often no long lasting implications.

They haven't come out of their room all day except at 4 am, they can be heard talking to themselves and they have the curtains drawn. Normal adolescent behaviour? Well it could be, so they will grow out of it.

They seem to be moving constantly between silent and

withdrawn to angry and shouting and back again. Normal menopausal behaviour?

Perhaps they come home from work and sit in a chair looking exhausted, not responding to enquiries as to how their day was and not eating much. They can be heard pacing about in the early hours. Just having a hard time at work maybe and they will work it out. Maybe so.

If someone is bereaved it is normal to be very distressed for a while, yet if someone in the news describes how they 'had to see a therapist' to recover from a similar situation then this suggests that grief is an abnormal reaction that needs treatment. What is a realistic expectation of how a person should be following a very distressing experience? How should someone experiencing a period of high stress react, is this a mental health problem if they are coping with it?

It's a difficult question but there seems to be a growing tendency to 'clinicalise' (*wince*) any signs of distress or anxiety even though it may be a normal response; this leads to an expectation that it should be 'treated'.

My colleague once heard a woman in a supermarket queue talking to her friend. She explained that the family's pet hamster had died recently and that her daughter was apparently terribly upset. She felt she ought to see a counsellor as a matter of urgency, this was a family crisis. My colleague joined in the conversation, uninvited I suspect, and suggested that what she ought to have was a few treats and perhaps at some stage a new hamster. I bet those suggestions were welcome. There are testing times in everybody's life that may cause perfectly normal temporary reactions.

So, it is possible to respond by either ignoring any change in behaviour or to jump to the opposite conclusion that there is something damaging and terrible going on before there is any real evidence.

Some changes are slow burners and it is tricky to decide

at what point the alarm bells should start ringing. Some come on rapidly and dramatically and the decision then is a lot more straightforward.

The behaviours listed below are those that indicate there is a need for increased attention:

- Changes in mood or in behaviour that seem extreme and out of character, such as distress, anger, agitation, withdrawal, despair or, in contrast, periods of frenzied happiness or high energy. The person may apparently not be able to control or bring themselves out of these states.
- Strange beliefs, talking about unlikely ideas as fact. This is only part of some mental health issues and isn't always present, but it is a strong indication if it is.
- These changes go on for some time, weeks or months, and the person's everyday functioning is being affected. This behaviour tends not to change with circumstances; if they are agitated with their family but always fine when their mates come round then there is less reason to worry.

What people do, how they behave, is a direct indication of how they are feeling and thinking. The difficulty is translating this to understand what is going on in their heads. What if they stay in their room for twenty-three hours a day and will not respond to appeals to come out? Is it because:

- They are excellent at sulking
- They are very anxious, unable to face people and cannot deal with the confusion in their head
- They have taken a drug which has knocked them off their feet for a while
- They cannot see a reason to come out as they have lost all interest in life

- They are physically unwell
- They are experiencing some sort of interference in the way they think and perhaps some confusing misinformation, which is too overwhelming to deal with

The family may have to turn detective, searching for clues as to what it may be. Is it a period of high tension for this person or just an ordinary time with nothing going on, as far as anyone knows? Is this the latest in a line of incidents of unusual behaviour that have all been temporary before? Are there signs of drug use?

A natural response if it doesn't go away after a while is to reason with this 'not OK' person. This takes many forms but usually comes down to one or more members of the family informing the person that something is not right, in fact they are causing lot of concern. Everyone is worried about them and just wants to help but they don't know what to do.

'Please tell us what to do. Please make changes and find a way to stop being like this and go back to your old self. We will do whatever it takes but we need a clue. Talk to us, tell us what's happening to you. Tell us why you are like this and then it will surely go away'.

The family want an explanation and a set of instructions on how to make this right again. This, however, relies on two factors:

1. The person can explain what is going on and why.
2. They know what will help and what needs to happen for them to change (back).

In a time of great distress an individual may have insight into what is going on at the time, or they may not. Many people in the middle of a period of mental agitation, anguish or hopelessness cannot stand back enough from it to be able to describe it. They are in this place and cannot see it from any perspective other than their own. Knowing something is wrong is not enough to offer a satisfactory explanation to worried family and friends, even if they have a mind clear enough to put the right words together in the right order.

Some mental health issues can be sorted out by the person making some changes themselves. No-one can make these changes for them; it must be their own battle. I think back to my experience of giving up smoking and of losing weight. Both took outside intervention at the right moment, often unintended help but it worked only when the time seemed to be right for some unfathomable reason. Those are small challenges compared with fighting one's internal demons of fear, self-doubt, or hopelessness.

Other mental health issues will not respond to a person's efforts alone, they are not within their control and may need considerable outside help. This support can take a variety of forms, but it does require that the person cooperates with the process, unless it is a dangerous situation where they must be forced to accept treatment against their will. This is always a fear for families, but the situations where this happens are rare and most mental health issues never have to go down this road.

What will help most is getting a professional involved, not just because they are more experienced at deciding what is going on but because they can then hopefully do something about it. This is not an easy decision or necessarily straightforward to arrange.

It is all about context and timing. If there is a new behaviour which is worrying, you have no explanation for it, it doesn't change over a few weeks and it is really taking over their lives, then it may be worth considering a professional opinion – scary as it is to cross that line.

WHAT CAUSES MENTAL HEALTH ISSUES?

The current explanation is very much a work in progress with a long, long way to go before anyone can be totally certain of any one answer. There is constant new research, the situation is developing all the time.

When they were first identified, mental health problems were regarded as the responsibility of the church as it was clearly all about possession and devils. Exorcism and leeches were not that successful as a treatment strategy, alternatives became available although they seem to have been based on the 'beat it out of them' school of medicine. Cold water baths and manacles don't seem to have worked either. Eventually mental health was put under the same spotlight of scientific reason as physical health and medications began to emerge. To begin with, these drugs seem to have worked primarily through powerful sedation; they had vicious side effects and were still around when I first went on a mental health unit, although many would see that as a long time ago.

This was the 'chemical cosh' medication approach, which was basically taking pills or getting an injection in the bum once a fortnight. At that time people were either kept in a psychiatric establishment or lived in the real world where they were probably as socially isolated as it was possible to be, except for those who managed to hang on to their family support of course.

Then came the 1950s and 60s, with a growing recognition of personal life-experiences in causing mental distress (think Freud and R.D. Laing). Mental ill health was therefore a direct response to unfeeling parents, abuse and a cruel society, so just chuck away the meds and talk for hours about how dreadful and unfair life has been. It did present a major leap forward in recognising how the average human being reacts when something traumatic happens to them and how this can cause serious long lasting damage.

This explanation, that personal life experiences were wholly responsible for mental health issues, has proved to be not wholly accurate either but at least more attention was paid to what and how people were thinking after the 60s, rather than merely ticking off a list of symptoms and writing a prescription for medication for life.

These two perspectives: it's a physical flaw, a system gone wrong or it's the person being traumatised by their life events (the biological and the psychological) still exist as different explanations and have not reached a suitable compromise as yet. There is a sort of midway situation which is loosely labelled 'the bio-psycho-social model'.

This is a more upmarket way of saying that there is currently a pick 'n' mix approach to how mental health issues develop, where no one explanation fits all and the various factors may or may not play a part. There are three main components (and one extra one) which, if they all come together in a certain combination which varies from person to person, increases the risk of a mental health issue developing.

BIOLOGY Genes, chemicals, neurotransmitters, proteins etc. Don't ask me for any more detail please, I just think of it as the hard wiring, the physiological components of any individual. This can be inherited or it can be affected by experience such as birth trauma. In my experience people with mental health issues could often identify a relative somewhere who went to live in the 'house on the hill' or who never got invited to family weddings and funerals. Previous generations wanted to hide the eccentrics or socially unacceptable people in their family, so this historical aspect can be hard to confirm. It gets easier as time passes and mental health is more openly acknowledged.

A family vulnerability can create a problem that appears early on in life or is triggered by a period of stress or trauma. Not everyone in the family will have this predisposition but it may appear randomly across the family tree. A sort of Russian roulette.

Another possible cause that is becoming better understood is stress levels during pregnancy. This is often hard for a mother to hear as it can be yet another reason to feel guilty. It's not clear how much stress is needed to make an impact and, personally, I am convinced that no one goes through being pregnant and giving birth without getting fairly wound up about it. Outside of normal stress levels it seems probable that more severe periods of distress would be as a result of outside influences and out of any mother's control anyway.

PSYCHOLOGY This is the new kid on the block but a very welcome one, which acknowledges that the way a person thinks about life events can affect how well they cope with them. Glass-half-full people are contrasted with glass-half-empty ones, it is widely accepted that the world can be regarded from a wide range of perspectives.

An example of thinking styles that can affect mental health is the link between ruminating a lot and anxiety-related problems. Just to clarify that this is not the ruminating that cows do but the constant thinking about what has happened, what you should have done, what is going to happen next, what will you do if it goes wrong, what did you say, what can you wear, what did people think, etc. Social media is a real pain here and makes a bad situation so much worse. People can help themselves to control this habitual overthinking and there is a lot of information and support available.

Any individual develops their attitude to life's quirks through a combination of inherited tendencies coupled with all their experience from before birth, through childhood and the early years. As we get older these ways of thinking become more deeply entrenched and harder to change. A person who is brought up to regard money as a scarce resource to be carefully managed probably won't go wild with it as a pensioner.

SOCIOLOGY This is what happens to via the outside world, possibly family, immediate community or wider issues that impact on any particular person. This could be childhood abuse or neglect, divorce or redundancy, bereavement, war or being a 'stranger in a strange land'. Immigration can result in little sense of connection with the place where you live; maybe with poor communication with those around. We are social animals and this isolation is very damaging. Perhaps online communication is a positive here rather than being all bad? It has been invaluable during the corona virus lock down for example.

The brain adjusts in line with the person's experience and those alterations can result in a long term modification. If someone has spent a long time being very afraid then their mind may be tuned very sensitively to the smallest sign of threat, perhaps to the point where they can no longer deal with everyday life.

SUBSTANCE MISUSE. It's very well documented that some drugs have a link to some mental health conditions but it's not that straightforward. It's possible that smoking a lot of skunk (strong cannabis) early on in adolescence can trigger psychosis, but if it was enough on its own why aren't thousands more people affected given the numbers who use it? Skunk isn't the only risk factor and psychosis isn't the only result. Several drugs can result in paranoid thoughts and this can increase levels of long-term anxiety but it's not the same for everyone, every time. Perhaps there still needs to be at least one more from the list as well.

These possible causes are hard to pinpoint, it is difficult to unpick any one situation. Supposing one hundred combat troops were caught up in a horrific incident, there were many casualties and they were all very much at fear for their lives. Five years later, eighty-three of them had this incident as a powerful and unpleasant memory but they lived a reasonably ordinary life, ten had occasional flare-ups that wrecked marriages or involved aggressive drinking binges and seven were more seriously affected because they experienced frequent sudden and unpredictable flashbacks, panic attacks, behaved anti-socially or lost control and became aggressive.

But why those seven? Why not all one hundred? Is it because they were the ones with the inherited genetic or chemical differences (i.e. biology)? Is it because they were unable to find a way of putting the experience to one side and close the lid on it? Could they not convince themselves that it was all justified by the cause they were fighting for (psychology)? Or was it because they witnessed the death of close friends or were not supported by their peers (sociology)? Or was it all three?

Looking at depression as another example, there are several factors that might significantly affect someone:

- The chemistry of their brain, genetics, maybe some hormonal abnormality, something triggered by an illness or getting older.
- They have experienced a trauma or a serious loss that they have not been able to 'find a way back' from.
- Perhaps they face poverty and hardship, feel very alone and cut off from support; maybe they have experienced abuse or a life changing event.

More women than men are diagnosed with depression, is this a clue about there being hormonal causes or is it because women's lives are more miserable (Valium being the housewife's friend in the 1960s.) Or is it because men are 'not allowed' to talk to GPs about feeling terrible so they just go to the pub? Please excuse the sweeping ancient stereotypes here, it is just to make a point.

This illustrates the complexity of the situation. You have possible causes, any one of which can be enough on its own. We know some diagnoses are more biological and some more sociological (bi-polar, for example, seems strongly biological) but it remains confusing. Psychological and sociological influences can lead to changes to biology; how can you tell if depression is started by a chemical change or a bereavement which then results in a chemical change? This is the area where new discoveries continue to be being made - the relationship between body chemistry and life events, with their effects on future wellbeing.

The mind-body connection is still a huge mystery. There is new research around proteins (neurotrophin-3 if you're interested) which lessens the anxiety level in rhesus macaque monkeys. Gut health is also linked to anxiety levels so digestive processes may affect mood. Or is it that anxiety affects digestive processes? Taking recreational drugs causes physical changes but the effects can continue after the drug has left the person's system. Chemistry and mood. This link between what we are thinking and what our body is doing is far from being understood.

Rationally the cause of the mental health condition should dictate the treatment, so if someone's mum develops depression after her husband dies then logically it's a sociological(bereavement) and psychological(feels overwhelmed by it) cause, so the doctor should offer a talking treatment. If she spends enough time talking through this bereavement, then her mood should improve. Bereavement counselling can be enormously helpful for some but for others less so, and sometimes medication may be the only option that works – a biological treatment for an apparently psychological problem.

There can often be a sense of frustration in the family when someone becomes overwhelmed by their mental state. If they were only less emotional, more determined, more rational, etc, then surely this wouldn't be happening. It's hard to shake off the belief that they always have the option to 'fight' it more effectively. Of course, it may be true up to a point, but surely if the person could just make it go away then they would choose to do so, rather than suffer the way they are doing? They may in fact have limited control and be unable to rectify the problem without help.

Asking the person concerned what is causing the problem is not always the answer. They may or may not know and they may or may not be right. The point of the story here is that it isn't worth spending too much time and energy trying to find out what has caused this mental health issue. The origins are never going to be 100% certain, and in the long run it may well not be that important to know. Having fixed ideas about what is causing all this upset in the family could be based on a lack of information, some misunderstandings and red herrings, and may only be partially right. Sometimes it's best to move on from the thankless search for causes and focus on the effects.

GETTING HELP

There seems to be something wrong that is serious enough to really worry about. It's been around for a while and doesn't look like it is going away any time soon. What are the options here? Not many it seems. The simple response is to 'take them to the GP' but this is a glib phrase that trips neatly off the tongue for those who don't have to do it. Whether someone is mildly affected or in a seriously unhappy state, there are two possible responses to the offer of a visit to the surgery. They can say 'Yes' or 'No'.

Of course, it is great if they say yes and the appointment is made, help is on its way. What if they say no? The minefield of patient confidentiality measures makes it largely a waste of time to go on their behalf. It could be useful to get some questions answered but they won't get offered any treatment unless they appear in person (or are at serious risk).

No one can make them go but bribery, blackmail, begging, threatening and cajoling are all options and carers have tried all these. The last resort is to leave them alone and wait for them to eventually accept that there is something not right and that they need some help. That may be the only option.

One strategy to get them to the GP is to remind them that they don't have to accept any treatment, it may just be useful to find out if they meet the criteria of having a mental health condition. However, this can backfire if they are prescribed medication and they say, 'but you told me I didn't have to take it'. And of course, they don't.

In mental health a diagnosis is made when a person is found to be suffering from a collection of specific symptoms that have been going on for some time. In order to do this, the clinician must know what the person is experiencing and how they are behaving. One of the major features of having any serious mental health issue is that it is likely that the 'patient' will be either an unwilling or inaccurate witness, so the second hurdle presents when they get to the GP appointment and the conversation goes like this:

> **GP:** So, what did you want to see me about today?
> **PERSON:** Nothing, I don't know why I'm here.
> **CARER:** Tell them about how anxious you get.
> **PERSON:** I have been a bit stressed but it's nothing I can't handle.
> **GP:** You feel you are managing all right?
> **PERSON:** Yup, no problems.

CARER: But you're up all night pacing about and talking to yourself.

PERSON: That's not true. I had a bit of a bad patch, but I'm sorted now.

CARER: And what about the crying? I have never heard you cry so much, and it's been going on for weeks.

PERSON: I think it's you that needs help. I'm not sure what you're on about. You do exaggerate; you're a real drama queen.

CARER: Me! I'm just stressed out by your crying and pacing and refusing to talk to me!

PERSON: You are just making a fuss about nothing. I really don't need any pills, Doctor. Can I go now?

GP: It seems as though there is nothing I can do at the moment but do come back if you would like to talk about this further.

No admission of symptoms equals no progress. It is possible to have sympathy for the doctor in these situations, after all it is an impossible choice, one person's word against another. They need evidence which comes from the person themselves or from other professionals. At the very heart of the problem is the person's sudden and miraculous ability to hold it all together and appear perfectly fine as soon as any NHS or social care staff hove into view. As soon as they leave, this self-control disappears, they revert to their agitated, distressed state leaving the family in a state of advanced despair.

For professionals to take 'evidence' from relatives or friends is a tricky one. Family members have struggled to be regarded as credible witnesses for a long time now. Unless and until they have proved themselves over time as being accurate, reliable and largely unflappable they may feel they are not listened to. It can be frustrating when a GP appears not to believe the relatives, this can start a tense relationship with professionals that can be hard to fix later.

The reality is that there are some families who, either deliberately or unintentionally, create distorted views of the person's behaviour because of their own agendas, perhaps to get them 'locked up', punished or to create attention for themselves. There are families who deliberately damage people and are a cause of mental health issues through abuse or neglect. No one is denying that these families exist, but they are a tiny minority.

Sometimes it does appear that a doctor or nurse has an apparent default position that any family member, particularly a distressed or angry one, is probably unreliable as a source of information. My views are probably dated in this respect because I know that there is a lot of work going on to ensure that any family's input should be respected until proven otherwise, rather than the other way around. Some areas and teams have this well in hand, some don't. The fact that there is a push to make it happen implies that it doesn't come easily, the approach of some services seems to be that the family is well intentioned but 'emotionally involved', at best and downright damaging at worst. How you don't get emotionally involved when your mother constantly threatens to kill herself I am really not sure.

The bottom line is that the GP, and indeed any other mental health professional, is not going to offer treatment based on a family member's information alone. This applies to physical health too; I can't get a prescription for my dad's piles without a doctor having examined him. In mental health this seems more frustrating as the reasons for the 'patient' not being honest or open with the GP are not necessarily good ones.

There is also the problem of the 'bad' GP. Not the ones who disagree with the family's viewpoint, I'm talking about those who have poor interpersonal skills or who resist getting too involved in mental health issues because it's not their strong point. GPs can be life savers, literally, but they can also add a layer of misery and frustration on the top of everything else. It is possible to change the person's GP but it's tricky and requires persistence when energy levels are probably low. There is usually a doctor in bigger practices who specialises in mental health, they should be identifiable and if the carer can look the receptionist firmly in the eye then an appointment may be possible, or book online if you can. It is worth making the effort as soon as there are suspicions that the usual doctor may not be helpful, it is worth the fight.

The family may have to decide whether their GP is not well informed or whether what they are offering is realistic and appropriate but just not what they expected. A tough call sometimes, so it is worth asking around. A pharmacist can give unbiased information about medication if that is part of the concern.

Those who have successful visits to helpful GPs will start on a path to treatment which may include the offer of medication, talking treatments or referral on to the consultant / mental health services level. None of these are compulsory but at least everyone is aware of the options even if they are not taken up immediately but returned to at a later date, after a period of thinking it through.

If they won't go to the GP or won't be honest about the behaviour that has been the cause of the worry, then all that happens is to wait, although this can be torture for the family. They are often left trying to contain a very distressed person who may be 'acting out' through threats, often against themselves or sometimes others. Or they may be withdrawn to the point that the family has no idea what state they are in, they have locked the bedroom door and no-one has heard any movement for several hours, and every sound is being noticed these days.

There are three possible outcomes to not getting any help

1. The problem goes away. Many mental health issues, particularly the less severe, resolve themselves as a result of family support, time passing and/or the person's own determination and energy. Or possibly just a physical adjustment.

2. The person acknowledges that there is a difficulty and that they might need help, so they change their mind about seeing the GP.

3. It gets a whole lot worse and some sort of crisis happens, where professionals get involved despite the person's reluctance to see someone.

If it feels as though the situation it is getting out of control and there are concerns about risk, then perhaps the section on 'crises' will be helpful.

THE MENTAL HEALTH SERVICES

People who are experiencing anxiety and/or depression are most probably going to be treated by their GP and perhaps try a specialist talking treatment. These are dedicated primary care services and not at in any way inferior to the mental health teams. The GP can refer on but only if it is thought that there is a more complex diagnosis, as they specialise in psychotic symptoms, bi-polar and personality disorder. Other diagnoses may be considered but there must be a high level of risk in the situation.

Secondary services vary according to locality both in name and team structure, they can restructure at regular intervals, so this is a sketchy outline that covers the most likely options. If you are in an emergency situation then skip this bit and go for the crisis information.

No one can self refer to the mental health services, except

via a GP or the Police or A&E. The last two will only step in if it is a high-risk emergency and this translates as someone being at risk of serious harm or likely to cause it to others. Otherwise the system requires going via the doctor, they are the gatekeeper and can ask for an urgent referral if the situation needs it. Usually it is a wait of a few weeks for a first appointment if it isn't an emergency. These can be long weeks!

Some areas, but certainly not all, have a walk-in centre where help can be accessed without a referral. Asking the GP or searching online should help track it down if there is one.

The first appointment with a mental health team will be at the Assessment and Treatment Service (ATS). The initial assessment gathers evidence by asking the person what is going on for them, watching how they present in the appointment, and perhaps but not definitely talking to the carer if they come too. A decision is made whether the criteria for a mental health diagnosis is met and what treatment package will be offered. It isn't unknown for someone to be referred back to their GP if the criteria for a specialist service aren't met.

Often the first offer seems to be medication; there will be a follow up appointment to check how the this is working. There could be talking therapies or a further assessment, perhaps by a psychologist. There is probably going to be a wait for these.

There may be specialist teams that will take over delivering the care package after the initial assessment:

CAMHS: The young people's service is called the Child and Adolescent Mental Health Service. There seems to be a bit of a national crisis around resources in this area with a rapidly rising rate of referral. Hopefully, this will get sorted soon as I met quite a few families who were really suffering the consequences of this lack of specialist support. The situation has been flagged up nationally so if families can keep on asking for them and campaigning on this issue then it may improve. Again, it is geographically variable.

EIS: The Early Intervention Service is for younger people (up to around 30 or 35 years) who are experiencing a first or second psychotic episode. Research has proved that more intensive interventions at this early stage make for a better long-term outcome.

OLDER PEOPLES' SERVICES: This could be specifically for people who have organic issues such as dementia or Alzheimer's or for the full range of possible mental health issues. Some older people like this divide but I have met several that dislike the presumption that they should see an age-based service.

CRHT: Crisis Resolution Home Treatment teams make more frequent contact with the person in their home (other teams usually require attendance at an outpatient appointment). This is to prevent people having to go into hospital unless they absolutely must and to get them home quicker if they are admitted. From the carer perspective, this may leave the family responsible for a very unwell person between professional visits, so it is useful to ensure that team's emergency number is on everybody's phone.

AOT: The Assertive Outreach Team, many areas have abandoned this title or amalgamated it with other teams. It specifically targets hard to engage people, not just anyone who won't turn up for appointments or take their meds but those people who would present serious risks to themselves or others if they go off the straight and narrow.

There can be another divide between Assessment and Treatment Service (ATS) teams that do the 'first bit', including assessing, prescribing, monitoring if the meds are working and arranging other treatments, and the later bits where things are relatively stable and the person needs fewer contacts and practical rather than clinical support to get back into everyday life.

Some teams will stay with a person right through their treatment, which can be a relief as there is nothing worse than changing teams just when the person has built a good relationship with a professional or is feeling a bit better. However, feeling a bit better is often a cue to be referred to a different team or back to the GP.

One thing that has changed in my working life is that people used to be 'kept on the books' for years, which meant at minimum an annual appointment to see how they were doing. Now there seems to be a practice of passing people back to the care of their GP as soon as things settle. There should be a fast track system back into the team if a relapse occurs in the first few weeks after this, but after that it's back to the GP to get a referral and to go around the system again.

Getting people back to the care of their GP as fast as possible is not all negative. Being under the care of the mental health team can undermine people's confidence, they may feel like a second-class citizen. Realistically, the mental health services cannot do that much once the person is on their optimum medication, maybe is having or has had talking treatments and is managing day-to-day life to a reasonable degree. Both the person and the family can find leaving the service difficult though, as it seems that the safety net has been pulled away. A carer may need to make their opinion clear if there is talk of referring them back to the GP but it feels too soon.

A final note, as a carer it is important to feel heard by the GP or local mental health services, to accept that the situation is being taken seriously. Inevitably, there is often a Grand Canyon of difference between a highly anxious family who hears their daughter talking about suicide and a mental health nurse who has seen seven people that day who want to end it all. The result can be a distressed and angry carer, and a defensive, less sympathetic professional. Yet again, it may have to be the carer who works on this, they always seem to be the meat in the sandwich. See 'Talking to professionals' if this topic seems relevant.

PROFESSIONAL JOB TITLES AND RESPONSIBILITIES:

PSYCHIATRIST, a specialist consultant with years of extra training whose job it is to prescribe, monitor and diagnose.

CPN (Community Psychiatric Nurse) or **CMHN** (Community Mental Health Nurse) are (Senior) nurses who work in the community. There will also be senior nurses within any inpatient unit. Specialist Practitioner Nurses can modify prescriptions within boundaries set by the psychiatrist. They monitor medication and help people with their coping skills.

HCA Health Care Assistants/ Support Workers are less highly trained than nurses (but often wonderfully experienced). They are found on inpatient units or help in the community with getting people back to an independent life. There are fewer of them than there used to be, sometimes these support staff are now available through voluntary organisations such as Mind, Rethink, Together or other local community services.

PSYCHOLOGISTS / CLINICAL PSYCHOLOGISTS / COUNSELLING PSYCHOLOGISTS assess people to see how their symptoms affect them, particularly their ability to think, reason or remember. They can recommend talking treatments such as counselling or CBT or design individual programmes to help with coping strategies and often deliver these themselves, particularly when the situation is complex.

OCCUPATIONAL THERAPISTS assess a person's skill in living an independent life and managing their symptoms. Again, they may work on these areas themselves or set out a programme for a support worker to follow.

SOCIAL WORKERS are crucial within Safeguarding

and the Mental Health Act sectioning process (although it may sometimes be another profession) but also work with individuals, usually in the community, often regarding planning care or getting services that may need funding.

PEER SUPPORT WORKERS are a growing number of people who have direct experience of mental health issues themselves and are now employed to help others. They often have a great deal of influence because they represent those who have made it through to the other side, they can empathise with the struggles and fears that others are currently facing. They can be found in the NHS services and/or in voluntary organisations.

An individual may get to see all the above over time, or just a psychiatrist, depending on the severity and complexity of their symptoms.

GOING INTO HOSPITAL

Only a very few people with mental health diagnoses ever go into a psychiatric hospital. These low numbers are down to the development of the crisis teams who see very unwell people at home, often several times a day. This work is to prevent admissions, or to speed up discharge if they do have to be admitted.

The alternative to this short stay approach is to have the old-style psychiatric establishments where people were admitted for quite minor symptoms and stayed for years and got to know the squirrels really well. Although this dated system is no longer acceptable it seems that the increased burden on the family has not always been adequately met with appropriate support and resources in the community.

There has also been a reduction in available beds in recent years. There are many that say this should be regarded as a shortage because it results in people having to wait to be admitted, or to go to hospitals many miles away. It may also put pressure on staff to send people home before they are completely ready. Getting a place in hospital can be challenging, the situation must be critical. This problem seems more acute in some areas but it makes life both worrying or expensive for the family as they may have to support the person at home while they are extremely distressed, or visit them in a unit that is miles away but has the nearest 'out of area' bed.

Bear in mind that the hospital has no magic treatments available that are not also found in the community. They may get more done in a shorter time because the services are all present in one place, but the options are much the same.

Most often, the people who go into hospital are under a Mental Health Act section, which means they haven't agreed to go but it is felt necessary for their safety and the safety of others. Most people in any acute unit are very unwell and may be 'behaviourally challenging' or noisy or socially inappropriate. That is one of the reasons why it isn't always a pleasant place to be, especially if you are feeling vulnerable and anxious. Patients should be able to get some peace and privacy in their own room, but it can still be an unsettling environment. Same sex wards improve the environment greatly, especially for female patients, but they may still not be completely tension free.

People who are admitted under the Mental Health Act can be made to accept treatment and are not allowed to leave the ward without permission. This sounds harsh but it is necessary for some people's safety. (see Mental Health Act)

The good thing about going into hospital is that there are staff and routines in place which make it as safe as possible. Patients can join in activities which can be group meetings, one-to-one sessions or creative options. If they don't want to do that then they can chat to other people or sit quietly in their rooms. There are staff to talk to, although there is inevitably feedback that they are never available when you want them. (I can't say anything here as I often hid in the staff office when I was working in centres; it can be unrewarding listening to people who are focussed on their negative feelings all day and, despite good intentions, it is easier to hide now and then). Units vary greatly and there is no hard and fast rule about how they operate.

From a family member's point of view admission into hospital can produce emotionally conflict. There is a mixture of relief that the person is now in a safer place, concern as to how they are coping, hope that they get treatment that works and possibly anticipatory anxiety about how they will be when they come home.

This could be a time to get some rest after an undoubtedly stressful period, but it may also feel that a daily visit with necessary rations/ goodies is required and that is an opportunity to catch up with all the neglected home chores while they are gone. This is all optional, especially the last bit.

A family member or friend who has been actively involved in supporting the person before they were admitted should immediately make themselves known to the ward staff who are most involved in their care. Identifying as a 'carer' rather than just a family member or friend gives a different status and entitles that person (or people) to more information and involvement. Once the key staff are known then communication should be regular, carers should be involved in discussions and have the opportunity to talk to staff. Problems may arise because staff invoke 'patient confidentiality', this is a frequent issue, there is more detail under the section of that name.

One of the features of being an inpatient is the 'ward round'. Some areas have worked to make them less of an intimidating experience. It used to be a bit like a job interview for the patient when you are judged as to whether you can go home yet. No pressure. There tends to be a sizeable gathering of professionals in the room, some will be total strangers. Carers are often invited depending on whether the person they care for gives their permission, they have the final say. It can be just as hard for family members to talk in this environment, especially as the person they support is in the room. If they want to say 'Actually I don't think she should come home yet as she has told me that as soon as she gets out she is going to go on a huge drinking binge' then it may not be an ideal environment to do this.

The other issue is that these meetings often run late, so for those taking time off work or with other caring duties it can cause great inconvenience. Some hospitals have worked hard to keep things on time and to reduce the number of people in the room. They may make other arrangements altogether and just see people independently.

Attending a meeting during the cared-for person's inpatient stay works better if the family/carer comes prepared with brief notes of their questions and concerns. Having the key points to hand ensures that they don't get lost in the professional's priorities. It is also possible to ask to talk privately before or after the meeting which could be useful if there is something best not said in front of the 'patient'.

Just as an aside, this is a good time to consider if the current situation can continue. It may be that the family feel they cannot cope with the person returning to live with them. It is perfectly possible to refuse to have them back, but this is horribly tough because:

- The family feel incredibly guilty and worried if it is the right decision
- There may be subtle or not-so-subtle pressure from staff on the unit to take them back
- There may be subtle or not-so-subtle pressure from friends and relatives either way.

The situation must be unbearable at home before most will even consider this option, but sometimes the survival of the rest of the family must take precedence. Quite possibly the person may improve after a stay in hospital and a change in medication, but it is a good time to say 'enough' if it is felt that there is no other option. There is a more detailed section called 'Can I stop being a carer?' later.

After the first admission (and hopefully the last) there is likely to be a period of worry as everyone wonders how they will adapt to home life, whatever that may be. A short admission makes this easier but if it does turn into weeks on the ward it may be a really wobbly and tense time when they first come out.

Coming home may be carefully planned and gradual or it may be sudden and unexpected, which can be very unsettling for everyone involved. Some families have had the experience of people being sent home in a taxi at odd hours because an urgent admission has been necessary; they were the 'most well' person on the unit so they had to 'make room'. The main problem with a rapid and unexpected discharge is that the person may not be as well as the family would like them to be. If there are worries that there is a real risk that is just not manageable at home, then the mental health professionals need to be told this, repeatedly if necessary. The community team should follow up quickly but sometimes there is a wait for them to pick up the referral. If it is felt that the situation is not practicable, that something is going to go horribly wrong, then the hospital team and the community team need to be informed as to the possible risks as soon as possible.

It's worth mentioning that those relatives or friends who were involved in the cared-for person's admission and were perhaps seen to be collaborating with the sectioning process may face a lot of anger and rejection. Many carers have spoken of this bad feeling which may take a long time to go, for the relationship to get back on track. General advice is not to get caught up in lengthy discussions about what part the family played in this. It may work best to adopt a simple phrase such as 'I was worried about you, you seemed to be at risk and this was the only thing I could do to keep you safe' and stick to variations on that theme.

With time and as a person's insight grows, these memories and resentment will most probably fade away. If there is some lasting damage done, which has affected the trust between family members or partners, then the challenge may be to remember why those decisions had to be made. It is an important fact that three professionals had to agree that the section was necessary, so it must have been needed.

FORENSIC PSYCHIATRIC CARE

This is a very brief summary because it affects only very few people, if these services are required then everyone involved should get a great deal of relevant information during the process.

Some people with mental health issues break the law. If they do and they are caught, then there are several possible outcomes. If the 'crime' is relatively slight the police may not press charges because of the mental health issue - or then again, they might. If it is more serious the courts have a difficult decision to make. It seems to be well-publicised that many people in the prison system experience mental health symptoms. This means that either it hasn't been brought to the attention of the court or there was a mental health medical report, but it was not enough to convince the judge that the person was not thinking rationally and were deemed to be responsible for their actions.

If the person with mental health issues is in trouble with the law then the number one priority is to make sure that any legal representation in court is well briefed about their diagnosis and that a medical report is a vital part of the evidence.

For people who have committed crimes that have serious consequences there is an alternative to prison, the forensic mental health service. The person doesn't get a criminal record and is offered treatment, rather than punishment. During the trial the decision may be made to send someone to a forensic unit for as long as they need to be there. This is not time-limited like a prison sentence would be, leaving the unit will require a clinical decision to be made that the person no longer presents a risk to society.

There are various levels of security just as there are in prisons and people may move from one to another according to their state of mind. There are many high-profile offenders who live out their lives in these units, but not everyone goes to the famous places such as Broadmoor; there are often smaller local units that are low or medium security. Families can usually visit; one positive aspect is that staffing levels are generally high as there is extra money in this system to ensure a safe outcome for each individual. There is a very intense after care system as well, to keep life on track back in the community.

My experience of families who have a cared-for person in a forensic unit is that they have many extra factors to deal with, even more so than a straightforward mental health diagnosis:

- The stigma of a mental health diagnosis and the stigma of having committed a crime.
- Possibly the difficulty of knowing that someone has been hurt or even killed because of this crime.
- Not knowing how long the person will be in the unit and how they will cope when they are discharged.
- Having a public/ media aspect to the incident where families who experience a straightforward Mental Health Act section can probably keep it relatively private.
- The normal carer 'is this all my fault' guilt, is even stronger.

Although the person with the mental health problem will not be in the immediate care of their family, there can still be a devastating effect on the people who are emotionally involved with them. There can particularly be a real struggle to understand and to accept what caused the incident and how it happened. It may well be even more important to seek opportunities to talk things through, perhaps with a counsellor or a carer support worker / group.

VOLUNTARY ORGANISATIONS

I have to say a bit about these as I think they are often misunderstood and seen as second best, which is currently far from the truth. These services are funded by local authorities, possibly by NHS grants or by money from other sources such as charities. They are independent of the statutory services but must meet exacting standards and are monitored regularly. They are not a group of well-meaning volunteers with a lot of good intentions and little expertise. They are increasingly subject to contracts which set strict standards, funding can be withdrawn if these are not met, which doesn't happen with the NHS or local authority.

Often staff are paid less than other services, which is why they may be increasingly a major part of any mental health provision.

Mind, Together and Rethink are big national organisations who each run a large range of services. I have worked for two out of these three and would say they are always worth researching. There is also an assortment of other local independent organisations, some of which specialise in tenancy or benefit advice. There may be wonderful projects in other activities such as pottery, bike repair or gardening – hopefully there is still funding going to these.

There seem to be two different ways of finding out about what is around. One is to do-it-yourself because no one seems to be passing this information on. The local mental health trust or social care website may list organisations, searching through the internet can be fruitful, so can finding one service and asking them about others that could be around locally.

The other route seems to be leaflets. Carers get given leaflets all the time it seems, one carer told me she was tempted to wallpaper the downstairs loo with them. It is easy to ignore these because they require time and energy that may just not be available at this moment. Sticking them in a pile somewhere, rather than binning them, means that when the situation is calmer there can be an energy efficient search to find anywhere that looks like it might be helpful. If the service accepts self-referrals it is easier, but if a professional referral is required this may just take a phone call.

The most important voluntary organisation may be the local Carers' Centre. This will have all kinds of information across all conditions. They may have a specialist mental health section or not, but they will be able to inform about all things carer-related, such as rights at work, benefits, organisations that might help, as well as having groups for different interests. They may also have carer support workers who can offer one to one support if required. I believe that each area has got a Carers Centre as there is usually funding for this one service for carers, as a minimum.

The upside of a voluntary organisation, also called a third sector or community organisation, is that they can be a bit less intimidating than seeing a nurse or a social worker. They are less formal and more flexible. That means that a person with the mental health issue may feel able to walk through the door of a service that has no psychiatrist around and therefore a reduced threat level, in their view.

There was a time when a gaping abyss stood between the NHS and these smaller voluntary concerns, but these days cross referrals flow more freely. The shrinking funding means all the services in any area need to be put to maximum use and sharing the workload and the funding makes for more mutual respect.

If the mental health services refer on to a voluntary agency don't feel it is less of a service. My experience is, after over twenty-five years of working in them, that they have staff and services that are as good (and as flawed) as any found elsewhere. But inevitably I am biased.

PEER SUPPORT WORKERS

These workers are all people who have experienced mental health issues themselves. This means they have a first-hand understanding of how it feels and that they are excellent role models of people who have made it through the worst. They may work for the NHS or for voluntary organisations or frequently run their own specialist services.

The benefit to involving these workers is that they talk the same language, the formality of an appointment with a professional is not there. This may work better with some people who find the relaxed attitude helps them to relate. Developing self-management techniques or discussing medication may work better if the worker has experienced these themselves. Peer workers started off as a small movement with just a few volunteers, but this is now embedded as an important component in many NHS mental health services.

TALKING TO PROFESSIONALS

In some areas, family carers seem to have an automatically healthy and happy relationship with any professional they meet from the mental health services. In other areas, it seems quite the opposite.

Professionals are busy people, usually very overstretched. They do get to go home at the end of the day but that doesn't mean that they are not occasionally tired, fed up, unhelpful and unsympathetic. It is far from being an easy job.

So saying, they should be polite, respectful and reasonably reliable, turning up if they say they are going to or not always cancelling at the last moment. If there is a problem then they should let the family know. They should take the carer seriously, even though they are not a professional and may be emotionally involved and therefore expecting far more than can be realistically offered. That doesn't seem too much to ask.

This next bit is just a short series of ideas that may help this relationship, but they are just suggestions; it can be a tricky judgement. Some families really are unrealistic, demanding, rude and even abusive to staff, which makes life more difficult for the rest. Each carer wants to come to be regarded as a useful and reliable member of the team supporting this distressed person – this is the aim. The communication that comes from the family can either help or hinder this process.

- Prepare before prearranged meetings or conversations. Decide what points need to be included in the discussion from the family's point of view and write them down, another opportunity may not come for a while. Remembering to take this list to the meeting also helps!
- If they are promising to call back later, keep that bit of paper to hand so there is no chance of being caught without it. It can be a challenge to remember everything that needs to be said when the phone suddenly rings, trying to rearrange yet another call could just be too complicated.
- Focussing on key topics means that the carer can make their

input shorter and to the point. Less is definitely more. This isn't because what they have to say is not important but because busy people often have short attention windows as they are under pressure of time. A long ramble might camouflage the important bits that the family really feel should be considered.

- Carers getting angry or upset is always a possibility. These circumstances could only be described as 'stressful' but trying not to insult professionals directly can make it simpler to keep communication channels open. Commenting on the actions that have been taken is effective rather than personal insults and it keeps tempers more in check. So 'I really am not happy about how this situation has been handled' is preferable to 'I think you are a totally incompetent waste of space.' The word 'try' is crucial here, it can be a very emotional situation.

Keeping a diary of how the person with the mental health condition is behaving can be helpful. This sounds a bit like spying but for things like spotting side effects, shifts in mood or the beginning of a relapse, when symptoms may be returning, it can provide useful evidence. Concrete information is good, opinion less so. Straightforward is good, woolly less so.

EXAMPLE 1

'My mother is getting worse, she is driving me crazy, I don't know what has happened, but she just goes on all the time about weird stuff. She frightens me with her stupid ideas and when I try to help her, she gets nasty.'

EXAMPLE 2

'My mother has got really agitated since last Sunday, she can't seem to stop talking, mostly about how the police are watching her and trying to arrest her. I have tried to talk to her about this, but she gets angry with me and has pushed me away quite roughly a couple of times.'

The difference is in the amount of facts in the statement, describing the actions that happened and what was said.

It may vary a lot from service to service and from person to person, but it appears rare for a carer to be offered a great deal of time or emotional support on a personal level from a mental health professional. There are lovely staff who offer a lot of time to listen to family members, but carers frequently report that exchanges tend to be quite brief and mostly focussed on the cared-for person. Some teams have carer-only appointments or run their own carer groups; this can be a valuable source of support. Alternatively, there may be a referral to another organisation outside of the NHS, perhaps a carer support group. These are helpful particularly as they are 'neutral' territory, (it is possible to swear about the psychiatrist or nurse).

Finally, it is valuable if the family can acknowledge the limits of what the professional sitting in front of them can realistically offer. It helps to recognize their effort and make an appreciative remark – but it's a fine line between being sensitive to how they may be feeling and false sounding flattery.

If things get bad and the local services are apparently not doing their job, then a complaint is an option. These take a long time to be processed and will not result in an immediate change. Details of how to make a formal complaint should be on the website of the organisation in question or phone the local team for contact details.

A more direct approach could be to request to see the local manager of the team or to email them personally. Email is a valuable tool, copying in the GP and any other people who are potentially involved can act as a reminder that there are others in the situation too. This is more likely to get a swift response than a form being fired off to HQ, but again go in prepared with facts, dates, conversations etc. Calm, factual and assertive speaking may be more listened to than a wild rant. Some situations are undoubtedly not wild rant-proof though, and the best plans may be abandoned in the heat of the moment.

A lot of carers I have met seem reluctant to make a complaint because they fear being labelled a troublemaker and they also fear that the service their cared-for person receives will be affected. This may be true, as people, even mental health professionals, are human.

It seems obvious to me that these professionals won't ever be able to help as much as families would like them to. Everyone wants an instant cure and/or twenty-four-hour availability, this isn't going to happen. This mismatch between reality and expectation is a major source of carer / professional tension, possibly more honesty, even negative facts, might help with this. Professionals are aware that the rate of change for someone with a mental health issue is often extremely slow. It would be better if they explained that to the family though, rather than leaving them frustrated and occasionally angry.

A lot of families have a good experience, they feel heard and included and get the information they need. My cynicism comes from the fact that carers who were wonderfully happy with the service they received tended not to seek support from organisations such as the one I worked for, so this may appear an unnecessarily gloomy picture, but it is as well to be prepared.

If a carer feels particularly furious it may be worth a moment to check who or what really deserves this anger.

The professionals that they have been in contact with.

The current incomplete information about mental health issues and how to fix them.

An underfunded system.

The unfairness of anybody getting such an unpleasant set of symptoms to live with.

Or all of the above.

There is a very high chance that the person with mental health issues will be able to move towards a much better quality of life, even if it takes a long time (as it will with the more severe diagnoses), and even if they don't get back completely to the way they were. The family's job is to weather the storms and survive the buffeting. Getting on reasonably well with the professionals can only make life a little easier, so it is worth some effort.

DIAGNOSES

HOW TO GET A DIAGNOSIS

It appears that people attach great importance to the labelling of health conditions both in the physical and mental health worlds. Maybe it is because there is a confidence that if the problem is identified then a solution will soon follow. In the realm of physical health it is certainly more straightforward, there is usually an identification of the problem, an explanation as to what is involved, an offer of treatment and some fairly fixed odds as to whether it is going to work, or there is a shake of the head and a 'sorry'. The picture is clearer, and everyone knows where they stand and usually quite quickly.

In mental health there is a lot more guesswork in diagnosing and predicting what is going to happen next. The range of physical 'hard fact' tests are limited here. What is central to the process is information that isn't always easy to get.

What the GP or psychiatrist needs is an accurate description of the person's behaviour, mood and cognitive functioning. Are they racing around and unable to stop talking? Are they lying on their bed for days at a time? Can they think straight? Are they having delusional ideas?

The first source of this information is the person themselves, who may well have an agenda that doesn't encourage honesty in an appointment with a psychiatrist. They may be petrified of being found 'mad' and then locked up or they may be convinced that everything is just as it should be, it is the world around them that is irrational.

The best evidence is the person themselves showing symptoms in front of the relevant professional. This relies on them not being able to disguise their behaviour or mood at the important time. However, it is remarkable and not at all uncommon for a highly distressed person to stay 'fine' for the time it takes to see a health professional.

The next source of information is the family, but this too has its hazards. Most carers are of course both honest and reliable witnesses, but how do you prove that? Some families have their own reasons for misrepresenting or exaggerating. Some will be in a hurry to hide what is happening because they are involved – and not as a positive influence. Can the psychiatrist always just take things at face value?

Making a diagnosis is not a quick decision, it tends to take a long time and create tension. The family may believe that because no official label has been given then the person cannot be successfully treated, but this is not the case. Medication is about the reduction of symptoms, so if an individual appears highly anxious then a useful prescription can be issued, regardless of whether it is rooted in OCD, PTSD, a phobia or a personality disorder. Of course, it really helps if more detail is available immediately, but information may just emerge slowly for many reasons.

There is also a question of whether labelling people is particularly helpful. It may reassure the person, and the people around them, that there is something 'real' happening, but it might also make them think differently about themselves. Being told that you have depression could make anyone feel even more hopeless. A psychotic condition, once labelled, may create feelings of being excluded from the rest of society and increase distress. Diagnosing is a double-edged sword; it gives a sense of confidence that someone knows what is going on but also can cause upheaval in the person's view of themselves. It places them in the world of mental health, this is not always helpful. Many psychiatrists and GPs are slow to offer a firm diagnosis and many even try to avoid it. This may partly be because of the uncertainty in the early days but also because it can massively effect someone's self-esteem.

It is highly probable that as new information emerges over time and as different medications are tried and either succeed or don't, then a new diagnosis is substituted or an additional one added. Some people end up with several labels. This is more complexity for the family to deal with and adds to the sense that the first one(s) were 'wrong' and they are 'just guessing'.

We seem to have been left in a tricky place; there are definitions of a variety of mental health diagnoses, these have been constructed by fallible human experts. They were not always in possession of all the facts at the time of writing and some labels are well passed their use by date. Looking at the historical attitude to homosexuality, defining it not so long ago as a mental health issue demonstrates that public opinion and expert research can change the 'boxes' that are used to classify people.

There is enough invested in the system by those working in it and little enough invested financially to do a wholesale remake of the rules and definitions that are in place. Change is happening but slowly and, in most cases, the current system seems to work and often very well. A different system would save some confusion but not necessarily change the success rate of treatments, it seems.

This labelling of people is, in my view, necessary even though there are many voices which are appalled by the lack of humanity in this 'tick box' process. Professionals need a shorthand way to refer to aspects of people's mental conditions in the same way as we label physical health. No one wants to write a paragraph where a sentence will do (no comments about this book please). Labels like 'personality disorder' or 'bi-polar affective disorder' are shorthand for a particular cluster of symptoms.

There are two mighty tomes which form the practitioners' bibles. One is the *International Statistical Classification of Diseases and Related Health Problems* (ICD) which is on revision number ten and the other is the *American Diagnostic and Statistical Manual of Mental Disorders* (DSM) on version five but being updated.

Crucially there are criteria in these books (anyone can look, they are on the internet) that outline which symptoms must be present, also how long they must continue, in order to justify a diagnosis of a mental health problem. These criteria must be met to get an offer of treatment. This makes sense if you think that many people experience temporary reactions to their circumstances, which may last a short time and then start to lessen by themselves; they do not need mental health medication, they only need time and a little support to recover so the time factor is important.

The person getting the diagnosis and their family should have accurate information as to what any label means, there is still a lot of misunderstanding. A good place for more detail is the Royal College of Psychiatrists website (patients' section), which has some sensitively written leaflets that can be shared with the person with the mental health issue, if that might help.

MAIN CATEGORIES IN MENTAL HEALTH

This is a brief description of two ways of classifying diagnoses into different categories.

ORGANIC

These have roots in biological functioning, there is a fault in the hard wiring either from conception or before or during birth. They may also develop later because of injury or deterioration due to old age (or not so old sometimes).

They are not what this book is about.

These conditions include dementia, Alzheimer's, ASD (autism spectrum disorder), ADD (attention deficit disorder) and ADHD (attention deficit hyperactivity disorder). Apologies again this book disappoints in not covering these, but they really are such complex issues in themselves with specialised approaches that would take pages and pages to explain.

It doesn't mean that some of the principles and responses in this book may not be useful though, hopefully they are.

FUNCTIONAL

These are the conditions that this book is about. They can be caused by biological issues and/or the way the person thinks and/or what has happened to them or all three. The line between is not always clear but the major categories are anxiety, depression, bi-polar, schizophrenia and personality disorder.

The research into the causes of all these conditions may also make the organic/functional divide redundant at some stage soon but mental health services may have separate specialist teams based on this categorisation.

MILD TO MODERATE

The majority of people who go to see their GP with mental health issues fall in this category, they have some form of depression and /or anxiety issues. Treatment can include medication but in the last few years there has a been a major effort to make talking treatments, usually Cognitive Behavioural Therapy (CBT) or similar models, easily available. This avoids putting people on medication unless it is necessary and allows them to learn tools that will be useful for the rest of their lives. A lot of people get a lot better – despite some areas having waiting lists and scant resources. Treatment is usually managed by the GP and the specialist talking treatments, the IAPT services (Improved Access to Psychological Therapies).

Just because it is called 'Mild to Moderate' doesn't mean that people don't go through devastating experiences, it is not a title that is meant to imply that it does not involve major challenges both for the individual and their family.

MODERATE TO SEVERE

These are the other functional diagnoses such as bi-polar, psychotic conditions (schizophrenia), the most disabling forms of depression, personality disorders etc. The people experiencing these will probably be referred to secondary care and see a psychiatrist, equivalent to seeing a physical health consultant in outpatients.

Moderate to severe conditions do not always result in a person being admitted to hospital, in fact only a minority of people ever use this third level (tertiary care) service as it is reserved for people who are high risk. One of the misunderstandings that often occurs with family members is that people should go into hospital to get 'cured' as they would with a physical condition. Although people do get treatment in hospital it is primarily a place of safety where they can be kept under supervision and observed, so staff can find out more about what is going on and target medication and therapy with more accuracy.

Most people are seen at outpatient appointments although home visits do happen but only when necessary.

These more complex diagnoses are often treated by medication. Establishing the optimum treatment programme, which may also include talking treatments and support with restoring independent living skills, requires the specialist knowledge of the mental health teams.

DIFFERENT DIAGNOSES

DEPRESSION

A confusing term because of its many meanings in everyday language. Some days people feel sad, desperately alone or lacking in energy. Everyone experiences times when the world seems a horrible place and there are doubts that it is possible to ever be happy again. True clinical depression is a whole different level from this day-to-day down time. Although it may be a matter of degree it seems impossible to imagine what it is like to be completely overwhelmed by mental darkness for a considerable period without personal experience of it.

It can appear as a withdrawal into the self, a shrinking away from contact with others and being less able to think things through. For some people this can mean spending every day in bed and not eating. For others it could mean being glued to daytime TV, eating vast amounts of anything in the fridge, drinking too much alcohol and not washing. It may mean going completely off the usual pastimes of pub, sex, sport or conversation; a total inability to function for hours or days at a time. At its worst it is like the fuse box where every fuse has blown, the mind/brain has shut down and taken a lot of the body systems with it. Everything seems hopeless, the future is a concept that has no meaning. This gloomy and sometimes agitated state needs to continue for a few weeks to be considered a mental health issue.

Women are diagnosed in higher numbers than men, but men have a higher suicide rate. There are all kinds of social reasons that may be influencing this, there is a strong cultural expectation that men should not be susceptible to mental health issues, fortunately there are many current media campaigns attempting to change that myth.

Depression can lead to the overuse of drink and drugs, and self-harm. It can also include some psychotic symptoms which definitely need professional help. If there are suicidal ideas then again help is needed, starting with a GP or the police if it is an emergency. If there are any risks to their physical health through not eating or self-harming, it will need a GP's attention sooner rather than later. At its most severe, depression requires urgent and specialist treatment.

If a person has a traumatic experience, maybe a bereavement or redundancy, their ability to cope with everyday life can be reduced. The impact is an emotional one, thinking or even talking things through rationally may not be enough on its own to make the negative feelings go away. For example, independent adults who have functioned alone for many years can still be highly affected by the death of a parent, even though they haven't really relied on this person for support for a long time. Logically there are reasons why this loss should be small and manageable, but the death represents so many other things. There are feelings of being exposed and alone; perhaps there was no opportunity to say goodbye or to tell them how much they were loved. There are a lot of belongings to deal with that bring back many memories. There are thoughts of the nature of life and mortality. These emotions trigger the dramatic change in mood and sometimes brings on depression.

Depression doesn't have to be about anything, it can just appear apparently randomly for some people with no specific trigger events. It may be rooted in a chemical or other physical change or an inherited tendency and not at all related to what the world has thrown at them.

Women seem to be particularly vulnerable to this condition soon after they have given birth. This would suggest that it has a physical cause that is somehow linked to the birthing process. However recent research has found that men can have a 'postnatal' depression, which indicates that this life changing event may affect new dads too. That is less likely to be hormonal!

Having a baby is undoubtedly a moment of great joy for nearly everybody, but it requires participating in an intense and sometimes petrifying process, viewed either from the mum's or the dad's perspective. Then this virtual baby is made wonderfully and life changingly real, and needs parenting skills that are, as they say, a steep learning curve. Some have suggested that post-traumatic stress could result after giving birth, again for either parent, but depression can also feature.

One of the difficulties for a family is deciding if medical intervention is required. There are periods in everyone's lives when they may experience symptoms of depression, particularly in adolescence and old age. Why not? Life can be pretty grim, too many hormones, an extremely critical peer group and a developing quest for an identity can be as challenging as facing the loss of one's teeth, functioning knees and eyesight. It could be part of a normal process of adapting to difficult circumstance, especially if that individual is more genetically vulnerable.

Being diagnosed with depression usually takes the form of getting a prescription or the offer of talking therapy, which implies that the person meets the criteria for depression. This can happen with quite mild or very severe symptoms depending on when the individual chooses to see the GP.

If the person can't or won't go to the doctor, then the depression could lessen and eventually disappear, or it could stay for years.

Anti-depressants can be effective but they don't work for everyone; they can make the world a much better place, but some people struggle to tolerate them. I took one once and was worried by how unnaturally good I felt, I can understand why they are popular with many. Withdrawal from this medication is potentially difficult because of physical and psychological effects so it is always preferable to have a gradual, planned strategy monitored by a health professional. Sudden stopping can be very unpleasant.

Depression gets a bad press, it is sometimes regarded as a means to avoid the tedium of everyday life with a get-out clause for anything at all challenging, such as work. Some people do exaggerate and depression is one of those 'hard to prove' diagnoses. Nevertheless, there are many thousands who have horrendous symptoms and whose lives are totally wrecked by this condition, there is clearly no choice involved for them.

For family members this ambiguity can create a strange mix of confusing thoughts:

'Poor soul, how awful it must be to feel so low and unhappy'.

and,

'Is this really something they can't do anything about? Surely if they just tried a bit harder? I would never let it take over me the way they have'.

This uncertainty can create tensions within a family circle with people disagreeing about how to approach the issue.

As a carer, trying to persuade the depressed person to join in and do some activities probably won't work during the worst bits. It is good to offer but preferably without putting on too much pressure. If a positive response happens then keep offering, if not then back off for a while and then have another go. People have said, after they recover from the worst, that they appreciate the family's efforts even if they don't immediately take up the opportunities. The problem is that they appreciate them afterwards, when the worst has past, so those offering support need to have a little faith and keep trying.

Cheering people up is not an option either, so it is best to let go of it as a goal. Trying to reach a person who is very withdrawn is frequently unappreciated, which could easily produce frustration for the carer - which can easily turn to anger. It seems clear that if they would just come out of their dark and rather smelly room and sit in the garden with a cup of tea, they would undoubtedly feel better. This is the carer's apparently sensible logic, but it may be completed rejected with no good reason given. Enough to make anyone irritable.

It is important that the family don't go into this depressed state with the person and keep on living their other lives in order to keep a clearer perspective on this situation.

Many carers take anti-depressants, this is not a sign of a failure to cope but an acknowledgement that life is currently extremely stressful; a sensible person considers all available means of help. The goal would be to use them for a short-term 'time out' when the issues in life seem completely overwhelming. This use of medication can prevent the situation from becoming critical, I have met many carers who use anti-depressants and anyone else who met them would find them far from weak or needy, as I did.

Family members may be the target of the depressed person's despair and be subjected to verbal abuse. This is not uncommon, it's human nature to get angry when you can't make things right in your life and you feel you should be able to fix it. Those closest are often first in line for that anger. As a carer, your goal is to not take it personally. Hang on to the very strong likelihood that when this hysterical person who is calling their carer terrible names does actually start to feel better, and there is a high chance of this happening, then they will really appreciate how they stood by them. Honestly, it's true.

ANXIETY

This word covers a wide range of experiences. Like the myth that Eskimos have forty words for snow where this country has one (two counting 'slush' I suppose), forty words are needed for anxiety, at least.

When our bodies react to perceived threats the feeling is one of anxiety, which is the sense of fear. This is a very physical presentation with rapid heartbeat, fast shallow breathing, feeling sick, butterflies, whirling brain and being 'twitchy'. Fear allows our bodies to function in a focussed and fast way, fight or flight, which uses a lot of energy. What was a useful response when facing the Stone Age bully boys from the next tribe fast becomes a real disadvantage in the queue at the supermarket. Helpful fear causes people to slew the car round and miss the cyclist without their brains having consciously made the decision to do that. There is also unhelpful fear and that is when it becomes a mental health issue. It often occurs alongside depression.

Watching a horror movie leaves most people in a state of heightened awareness. When the film finishes, probably with a blood thirsty finale, it can take a while to settle back to normal. In the meantime, they are left jumping at every noise and being strangely unwilling to walk into another room and definitely not look behind the shower curtain. These feelings of threat are not under their immediate control, it isn't a question of talking themselves out of it. It fades slowly as the reality of dealing with everyday objects and situations starts to return. These sensations are a short and small illustration of the much greater long-term anxiety that people can experience. The brain is focused on a nightmarish outcome which is just about to happen; even when it doesn't there is no relief as it just moves on to the next worrying scenario. There is no returning to 'normal.'

Raised adrenaline creates that energy to run or to fight, although I was told recently that there are two other possible reactions to being very afraid. One is to close down, like the rabbit in the headlights, to freeze. After all, if the rabbits got 'flight' and ran really fast there would be far less roadkill. Some people do seem to become unresponsive and 'blank', but their minds remain agitated.

The other is to obey the natural law that says if the end of the world is near the priority is to produce new humans, I don't get this at all. An interest in sex may not be the most obvious result of being petrified, perhaps only the hotels near Alton Towers can provide statistics on this.

So, there is fight, flight, freeze or... make babies.

Some people have a naturally anxious view of the world it seems. Whether this is inherited, the result of a frightening experience or being repeatedly told as a child that the world is a dangerous place, well who knows, it is not possible to always have a firm answer. Some people are better equipped to do battle with their own fears, they develop tools and techniques which keep their own anxiety levels low. Some are more easily overwhelmed and as a result lead lives that are far less than they could be.

Anxiety can lead to several different mental health issues which may stand alone or overlap.

PANIC ATTACKS

When a fear response rises past a certain level, the brain seems to cut out all hope of control and gives up coordinating any response. The adrenalin takes over and there are palpitations, nausea, sweating and rapid breathing. This is accompanied by a lack of activity in the brain, except the frenzied focus on the feelings of imminent threat and dread. It is a highly unpleasant experience that is particularly terrifying because, until the sensation is identified, it feels like a heart attack and death seems inevitable. Numbness in the arms and legs can add to this sensation.

The terminology is confusing, some people claim periods of everyday intense worry to be panic attacks rather than an inevitable jump in anxiety that comes before situations such as job interviews. A genuine panic attack is unmistakable, I know – I had one once. I was on a pedalo in about a metre of water. My husband was half asleep and gazing out to sea and my kids were leaping off the back into the water like little fishes. I can't swim and I suddenly became convinced that one of them would drown. I stood up in the tiny pedalo and started shouting to get back to the shore. I had no control over it whatsoever and yes, it was very embarrassing for the rest of the family and very unnecessary given the depth of water. Panic attacks are not rational.

If a panic attack happens at the checkout at the supermarket, which seems to be a popular place, the repercussions can be far reaching. There is a dilemma:

- The person can stick it out and try to cope with paying and packing, although their eyes won't focus, their hands are shaking and they look like a sweaty bloodless zombie.
- Or they can dump their trolley full of shopping, push past people and run. It's hard to avoid attracting attention and people will stare and mutter.

These incidents can be far harder to recover from than merely embarrassing the family at a noisy, cheap seaside resort amongst total strangers. There can be a fear of having been recognised, that this embarrassing scene was witnessed by people who know you.

The panic attack in itself is a traumatic experience, it is incredibly challenging to go back into the same situation again. Extreme efforts may be made to avoid any similar circumstances and the fear of a repeat can become a constant dread - which could increase the chances of another. If the panic attack was in a lift, then they take the stairs. If it was at a party, then they stay home Friday nights. This can radically change an individual's confidence level, this avoidance behaviour may become a phobia.

PHOBIAS

This is not a 'I have a phobia of spiders, if one runs towards me I'll scream' phobia. It is the 'I am not going in any room under any circumstances until someone I trust has gone in and checked for spiders, with a torch and all the way under the sofa' sort of phobia.

Most people have a fear of something: mice, lifts, spiders, snakes, wasps, the list of common nasties are well known. The state of fear can vary between a small flutter of apprehension to a major meltdown.

Some objects of fear appear to be inherited or part of a communal belief system. Not many people seem to like heights or spiders. Why a dread of snakes persists when there are so few about, at least in the UK, seems a bit of a mystery; surely it should have faded by now.

Phobias often originate in personal experience. One person I met had a serious phobia of moths (mottephobia, if you must know) that prevented her going out at dusk, spoiling many a romantic encounter. She remembered as a small child seeing a large death's head hawkmoth, which had really frightened her and her mother, and caused her to have nightmares. She knew what triggered her fears but still it limited her life to some degree. Someone with a fear of dogs may well have been scared by one, often as a young child, and may well have forgotten the incident.

It is possible to learn to be anxious from other people. Parents who become frantic at the sight of a wasp may well find that their children grow up to do the same.

Having a moderate fear of certain objects usually causes little inconvenience. A phobia, however, means that an individual is drastically re-arranging their lives so that they never have to encounter the focus of their terror.

Agoraphobia is widespread, this is the fear of being in a situation where there is no apparent escape route. A person could be a bit agitated while they are in a lift and relieved to get out. An agoraphobic will not get in one, even if their friend lives on the eleventh floor. This can also be a problem in large shops where the exit is frequently invisible or in crowds when there is a sense of being blocked in.

People can have fears about the most unthreatening objects. I remember a man who was a frequent visitor to one of the services I worked in. He was constantly referring to men in shorts, he would limit his activities particularly in the summer for fear of seeing one. This caused some amusement, as you might imagine, as men in shorts can be a source of a lot of bad jokes (sometimes for good reason). Staff are not immune to treating some people's symptoms with humour, hopefully behind firmly closed doors, everyone needs to survive somehow. However, on one occasion, another member of staff who had known this man for a long time informed us that he had been sexually attacked by a man in shorts when he was a boy. It is always worth considering where these fears may come from.

Researching all the phobias that have occurred often enough to warrant naming, such as a fear of beards, clowns, buttons, etc. is entertaining, but for genuine phobia sufferers it is not a passing whim. It has the potential to ruin someone's life.

One of the brain's major functions is to keep that person away from danger, so when a threat is identified it creates a strong fear reaction, and the feared object is moved away from at speed. If the same situation, or one that apparently resembles it, happens again then the brain sends out a warning by creating a fear reaction. Sensible it seems.

Some people seem to have overactive protection systems

though, like a badly adjusted car alarm that goes off with every puff of wind. Some are tough nuts and it can be difficult for them to understand how these people can be petrified to the point of hysteria at the sight of a small pet rat and to accept that this is not, in most cases, a contrived response. What is frustrating to the outsider is that everyone knows that domesticated rats are harmless, at least their bites are small, but the person who is highly afraid of them will never take the chance to come close enough to find out how cuddly they can be, there is just the indescribable terror of any encounter.

Help and support can undo this 'programming' if the person is desperate enough to seek it out. This may include learning coping skills such as relaxation and then gradually being exposed to the feared situation (not to be tried at home especially if the person is not giving their full permission). Hypnosis is also useful for some.

SOCIAL PHOBIA

There seems to be a high incidence of this phobia, it has dramatic effects and may result in becoming housebound or only going out only when there is no option. The root of this issue is that some people see themselves as different from others, as having flaws that cannot be hidden. They are immediately identifiable as somehow inferior; they feel unable to face other peoples' reactions so any social situation could end in unbearable humiliation. The phobic reaction is towards other people, especially unfamiliar ones.

This means that, in any social situation the person is experiencing a high level of anxiety and is constantly on edge. This could particularly apply when there is an authority figure involved (like a doctor).

Some people are bullied by their peers or their parents and have their confidence undermined on a daily basis. Some appear to be born anxious and interpret situations in a negative way from an early age.

Adolescents particularly can experience this dread of being recognisably different and somehow lacking. Most recover but for some that feeling never goes away, nor does the sense that others are always sitting in judgement on them for their weight, their nose, their accent, the colour of their skin, their inability to find someone to love them, their stupidity, their wicked thoughts or their terrible character flaws.

When was I working on a mental health helpline, I remember having a conversation with a woman who was housebound and completely dependent on her husband and children for support. Her story was that she had gone shopping and bought a large quantity of fruit and had eaten a large portion on the way home on the bus. Walking down her street she was suddenly overtaken by very violent diarrhoea and didn't make it back home in time. This awful embarrassment, potentially in front of her neighbours, led to her withdrawing into her home and when I spoke to her, she hadn't been out for eleven years. It is possible that she was a highly anxious person already, with a raised level of concern about what other people thought about her, but the consequences were appalling for both her and her family.

OBSESSIVE COMPULSIVE DISORDER (OCD)

This diagnosis currently has a high profile and lots of people identify with its symptoms which can vary from inconvenient to completely disabling. The phrase 'a little bit OCD' should be banned though, it is normal behaviour to double check things or set up small rituals, like wearing your lucky pants to an interview or putting shoes in a line in pairs. Normal behaviour is what the majority of people do, so if 51% of the population must check the iron is off at least twice then that is not OCD, not even a little bit.

Worry is part of the human condition, but most people

believe that it is under their control or at least they talk as if they do. It is perfectly acceptable to constantly tell others, and ourselves, to 'stop worrying' although in reality, worry is not easily managed. Usually, when faced with a threatening situation a loop of thought is created, replaying over and over the terrifying scene that is surely about to happen. Focus is on the worst aspects of the situation and how unbearable it will be - rather than planning what can realistically be done to cope. No-one can just stop themselves worrying, the most successful people have had to practice, using certain techniques that do not always come easily. Yet the impossible phrase 'don't worry' is seen as helpful and reassuring.

People who experience OCD seem to have a thought loop inside their head which is one of death, destruction and suffering, or even just something nameless but nightmarish. Some people with OCD can trace fears back to events in their lives when they felt threatened, some to feeling constantly unworthy and inferior, and some seem to have 'intrusive thoughts' – not the same as voices. They berate the sufferer with threats and unspeakable terrors if they fail to follow the required actions. Some people just seem to have a constantly raised level of general anxiety and this is how they cope with it.

Control of this anxiety is through frequent repetitions of physical or mental actions such as washing, counting, touching things, organising, or checking. Completion of these repetitions may allow that person to leave the house and go to work / school – or not.

Fear of contagion is a theme that seems to occur regularly, thoughts of contaminating the people around, both family and the wider population. Woe betide the person who tries to wash his hands only ninety-nine times when it should be one hundred. The rest of the day is spent in a state of dread or they are obliged to start again from wash number one.

This is really being stuck between a rock and a hard place; either these rituals are completed satisfactorily and this person can keep their mental state at less than total panic level, or there is a failure or a refusal to do this, which will potentially bring a great deal of distress.

OCD at its worst can create a house full of tension. When the family home has been 'taken over' by these rituals then visitors can be regarded as possible plague bearers or disruptive intruders. The whole family can become socially isolated. In addition, the person may require that the rest of the household obeys their rules. The consequences of not complying are so distressing, causing agitation and even aggression at times, that the family can end up joining in the imposed routines. This is all exhausting and increases the level of anger and frustration all round, it may well feel impossible to challenge.

I met a carer whose son was clearly very unwell; part of his anxiety was shown through the restrictions he placed on the household. He had taken over the main room and no one else was permitted to enter without following a lengthy ritual. He hadn't washed in a few weeks and was very smelly and wore few clothes. He demanded that his meals were brought to him on a tray but only one member of the family could enter the room and they had to perform several rituals such as turning around three times and touching certain things before they could come in or leave. In addition, he had a firm grip on the family dog and would only let it leave his grasp for a few minutes at a time.

This is an extreme situation, which fortunately ended when he was taken into hospital, but it created an unbearable strain on the family for a while. One parent felt they should cooperate less with their son's rules and one felt they had no option, bearing in mind the extreme rage that resulted from breaching them. These situations can test even the strongest relationships.

It is impossible to set clear guidelines in these situations, but personally I would attempt to do as little of the required rituals as possible right from the early days. It just seems easier not to start than to try and stop after a time. This is easy to say but hard to stick to.

Carers can be valuable in supporting any individual who does decide to fight it, say cutting down from checking the door thirty-three times to thirty-two, and helping them to cope with the panicky feelings through distraction or doing relaxation breathing with them. Any change must come from that individual though, if anyone else tries to force this alteration in routine then the distress levels are going to rocket; the effect is likely to be the opposite of the one intended.

Getting frustrated with people with OCD who are apparently not making any attempt to stop their rituals is inevitable. It is worth thinking about how easy it is to give up smoking, drinking alcohol or coffee, or looking at a phone. Changing deeply ingrained behaviour is not straightforward, even if the original reason for doing it is now lost.

Professionals can be extraordinarily successful and help to break even the strongest patterns given time. They have the advantage of knowing how to approach the situation and their professional distance can mean that the person is more able to take on the challenge, where family may just be too close to make major changes despite their best efforts. They can support and encourage but really are waiting for the person themselves to decide to take a stand.

POST-TRAUMATIC STRESS DISORDER (PTSD)

People who develop this condition have been through a personal trauma which may have been some form of violence, an accident or witnessing other people experiencing harm, often it is a matter of life or death. Classically we think of those who have been in a war zone, but it could equally be a car accident or incident(s) of abuse.

PTSD originates in the way memory works. The brain stores the factual contact of events alongside the emotional responses at the time of the incident. There is little need to remember the boring stuff from day to day, such as what was eaten for dinner last Wednesday. The strongest memories make an emotional impact. I don't like to listen to 'Fix You' by Coldplay because it was included in a short play my daughter and her friends put on at school. I was proud but also shocked by their maturity and depressing view of the world (hence early Coldplay). Most people have similar poignant memories. Over time these emotional responses fade and we can recall the moment without feeling teary every time.

There is a process of recovery from even the most devastating moments. In a normal bereavement, for example, there is a period of overwhelming emotion where the bereaved person could cry unpredictably or feel overwhelmingly sad and unable to get on with life. Their focus is often on the last moments they spent closest to the point of death or to the circumstances at the time. This gradually fades so that in time they can remember the person with a manageable emotional reaction and recall happier memories of their life.

With PTSD this fading of impact doesn't seem to happen. The vivid memory comes back often unexpectedly (flashbacks) and the merest trigger will set off the full emotional response. Hence the cliché of the war veteran diving behind the sofa when a car backfires, the adrenalin kicking in completely inappropriately.

Whatever the cause of PTSD there is one factor that is worth noting. If a thousand people go to war or a thousand people are in awful accidents, why do only a small percentage of these go on to develop this condition? The answer may lie in the biological or the psychological structure of that individual. On average about 15% of people get mental health repercussions following a life-threatening event and this can be depression or PTSD. It may not be just the experience but a trigger that has activated some physical change that this person cannot simply turn off again.

They may turn to drink or drugs or blame someone else for their feelings of anxiety. Families who live with people with PTSD report social withdrawal and aggressive defensiveness. There are specialist services for those returning from war zones although it can take years before armed forces personnel feel ready to ask for support, it seems to go against the culture of being trained to fight. (They can develop a variety of mental health issues; it isn't only PTSD. Some just find it incredibly challenging to fit in back into ordinary life after such extreme experiences.)

Identifying triggers, things that set off an episode, can make a difference but this is not always easy. Some situations are difficult to avoid such as loud noises or crowds. Reassuring the person may not have an immediate effect either, but hopefully will help over time. Medication may reduce the anxiety, but you can't medicate away a memory.

Some talking treatments are used but I understand that there is currently advice not to talk over the traumatic experience in any detail because this just strengthens the memory and makes it more vivid. This flies in the face of the general belief that if you talk about an unhappy memory it will inevitably improve. Cognitive Behavioural Therapy is widely used but a more recent alternative is Eye Movement Desensitisation and Reprocessing (EMDR). Weird as it may seem, it works without the person having to recall the unbearable memories in any detail and through eye movement and other strange distractions allows the emotional intensity attached to that memory to be reduced to a manageable level. It is provided on the NHS in some areas, there are also private practitioners.

ANXIETY: HELPING

When a person has highly anxious ideas it can be easy to slip into a 'yes it is', 'no it isn't' pantomime routine. They are convinced that the supermarket is a frightening place but the rest of the family pop in and out without a second thought. It is easy to become judgemental and even annoyed, losing sight of their perspective. Staying supportive, positive and encouraging is hard but it is the best help.

If it is possible then using the carer or other family members as an on-call support system might make them feel braver to meet new challenges. This is not always possible but it can be set up while they try new situations at least? If the person who answers the call encourages them to manage their breathing, or distracts them, or reminds them of what they have achieved already, all these things can be useful.

Don't raise the topic unless they mention it. People can be highly suggestible and when a topic that causes a rise in adrenaline is mentioned it may make a negative reaction more likely. So highly unhelpful things to say would include

- 'OK, lets go to the shops. Don't worry you probably won't have a panic attack'.
- 'I think we should go and see Uncle George. I know you hate lifts but he is only on the eighth floor, it will be quick'.

All anxiety-related conditions have common features which involve an increase in agitation and distress. The family can help by encouraging anything that helps the person relax (except alcohol or street drugs). Anxiety responds well to things like yoga and meditation, not necessarily a complex routine for either but maybe a few quiet minutes learnt off YouTube if classes are out of the question, or a guided meditation available online. It's about having a routine that distracts and calms.

Agitation makes the breathing speed up so more oxygen is taken in, which fuels the anxiety further. Reducing the oxygen intake will slow the body down a bit and help restore calm. Slowing the breathing rate is a skill to be practiced with anyone who will cooperate, don't wait until the panic is escalating. This can be done by counting; breathe in to the count of four and out to seven. It is fine to adapt the numbers if that isn't comfortable, but the key is that the outbreath is longer than the inbreath.

Singing is great, pick a favourite cheery song (so not Leonard Cohen, or Adele) and sing it together, this will regulate breathing too. It used to be that advice was to breathe into a paper bag, so the air is recycled, with less oxygen breathed back in. Having a paper bag to hand is not always easy though, but a plastic carrier bag is not a good substitute.

Anxiety in all its forms can be very contagious and unsettling for others, this makes it even more important that the family has a life outside of the house and this fearful person's world. It can be exhausting supporting someone who seems relentlessly agitated or prone to episodes of panic or aggression that are hard to really understand or apparently help. Self-preservation becomes a real priority.

DEPRESSION WITH ANXIETY

'Depression is when you really don't care about anything at all and anxiety is when you care too much about everything' – someone must have made this insightful observation but its origins are lost in the pages of the internet. It's a good quote though. Anxiety and depression often occur at the same time, they are commonly diagnosed together. So, there is no motivation to get out of bed or to do anything but lie there, but then there is just a sense of blind panic about what should be being done or what other people are thinking about the situation.

In some ways it seems contradictory. With depression there is that absence of light, of happiness, of motivation. Nothing seems to matter. Anxiety is the opposite in the sense that life becomes dominated by 'important' topics that become constant and threatening. Having depression and anxiety means the chances are that the person is hammering at themselves relentlessly even if they appear to be unresponsive. They may fluctuate between agitation and inertia.

Common denominators include that sometimes poorly understood concept of self-esteem. For most people this is at its lowest during adolescence, this constant insecurity gets forgotten as time passes and life gets more outwardly focussed. People are often quite critical of themselves, particularly the (my) older generation. Younger people seem more able to say, 'Actually I am excellent at this and pretty brilliant at that' without even a hint of self-doubt. There appears to be a cultural and age-related expectation about how a person should describe themselves publicly, although what they are actually thinking might be a different thing altogether. There is a further section on 'self-esteem' later.

As with all other mental health issues there is an optimum time to work on these issues, this is likely to be when the person themselves feels strong and motivated enough. This opportunity cannot be forced, it relies on factors that may be outside anyone's immediate control. While the family are waiting for small chinks of light to appear here is a selection of suggestions:

• Notice any positive changes that are happening and use them to keep everyone going. It is sometimes easy to overlook small improvements and new behaviours, but they are signs that change is possible.

- There may be a level of anger, frustration and insults that are aimed at those around them. It's not personal, it's part of the package. It is possible to let them know that what they are saying is hurtful, but the challenge is not to get into a fight about it. This will probably make a bad situation worse.
- They are most probably doing as much as they can to cope and to control their mood unless there is clear evidence to the contrary. The family can demonstrate that they recognise this is a struggle for them by avoiding passing judgement on their behaviour.
- Presuming that because they managed something yesterday they will be able to do it again today will lead to disappointment, which is better not expressed.
- Making hopeful comments such as 'Won't it be great when you can…' or 'I am looking forward to the time when we can…' lets the person know that the family are thinking positively, but puts little time pressure on them.
- The family need to keep reminding themselves that there is an extremely high chance that this is a temporary state, although the person may remain a bit vulnerable for a while there is a strong possibility that they will be in a much better place at some point in the future.

This may appear vague but there is little direct action that a family can offer other than general support. Medication can tackle both issues and can bring much needed relief. Talking therapies are wonderfully helpful too and fortunately are far more widely available than they used to be. Close friends and family members are crucial as they provide the means to keep going from day to day until either the situation improves, or the treatment works.

EATING DISORDERS

This is a complex issue that I have never worked with

directly, but it is an important category to include. It is more complicated than just not eating, there are a variety of disorders involving different attitudes and behaviours around food. The most frequently occurring one is when people won't eat at all or will only eat the smallest range and amount of food (Anorexia Nervosa). It also includes those who eat a lot in one sitting, , and who may then purge by self-induced vomiting or taking quantities of laxatives (Bulimia). There are also people who focus on eating only 'healthy' food to the point of effectively starving themselves. There are many reasons why these problems begin, they can affect anyone at any time, regardless of age or gender.

The most popular explanation of the roots of an eating disorder is that of control. It does seem to occur often in adolescents within family settings, inevitably this is when control issues seem to be at their most critical. This could be about family attitudes, school, bullying, work or social pressures. Controlling food intake is a possible response to feeling a lack of power in other situations.

There is also the issue of self-image, people making comparisons with peers and celebs. It can be a real struggle for older people to really understand just how completely central this is in some younger people's lives, although it is not limited to the latest batch of teenagers. Social media just piles it on and most reassuring positive messages about 'loving yourself for who you are' seem often to come from physically perfect, unnaturally thin famous faces.

There are other factors in the eating disorder mix though. There can be a phobia of vomiting. This is not uncommon; it can lead to refusing to travel or go to public eating or drinking venues. Taken to the extreme if you don't eat then you can't vomit.

In addition, there is an upside to feeling hungry, there is a certain energy and satisfying feeling when the stomach is empty. After eating there can be feelings of nausea or bloating.

If anxious people fixate on these sensations, they can become heightened out of all proportion.

Being a carer for someone with an eating disorder is one of the more frightening situations within mental health because there is a greater possibility of physical damage. Whatever the cause, and no one may ever know for certain, it can result in a relentless daily battle with deeply ingrained behaviours. There is no respite until the person is taking in something close to enough nutrition.

Eating is logically under someone's control as they can choose whether to put something in their mouth, chew and swallow, they should be able to do this simple thing. It must surely create helplessness and anger at this person's apparent stubbornness and refusal to accept the risks they are running, especially if time passes and nothing changes. It is tough to accept that the control this person has over their behaviour is limited. It is as if they are fighting an addiction, in the sense that it is a deeply entrenched habit that involves body chemistry as well as cognitive processes.

There are some recommendations about how a family can cope. Mealtimes are often the source of great tension, it seems to work better if they are planned in advance together with the person who has food issues, and there are no surprises or pressures. If agreement can be reached as to what will be served, how it is cooked and how big the portion will be this seems to help keep the tension down.

Food should not be the focus of attention, maybe some distraction such as conversation or the radio could be helpful. Keeping up the distraction after the meal might prevent purging.

It helps that the panic that the carer feels doesn't show too much, that the person doesn't pick up on the desperation to make them eat (sensibly). This requires a monumental feat of willpower on the part of all the family members, to remain calm and non-judgemental while watching this person become thinner and thinner, or bingeing and purging. Attempts to coerce them will add to the anxieties around food and mealtimes; it is the difference between pressure and support. If shouting and pleading worked then the NHS would use it more, and the bottom line is that no one can make a person eat against their will without using the Mental Health Act to enforce physical interventions.

Staying calm and empathic requires practice, probably gained through losing it occasionally and seeing how a flare of anger affects the situation. It must be reassuring when a professional steps in, although this may not happen soon enough for the family's peace of mind. There is still the pressure of coping between clinical appointments, but it helps if the situation feels monitored.

There are eating disorder specialist services which might include a period as an inpatient in a unit where diet is highly controlled. These admissions tend to be offered only when a person's weight loss has become critical. The staff may put more pressure on the person than a carer would dare to, but there are a team of them, they are experienced, and they can physically measure what is happening. This doesn't mean that this service is cruel, a mix of being kind and sensitive but assertive and firm is required. Easier for them than for the family. They also have the optimum incentive that 'you don't go home until you weigh X'. There will also hopefully be follow up support to keep things on track after the person leaves the unit.

Because of the implications for physical wellbeing, and at its very worst, survival, the family carers are more vulnerable to becoming unwell themselves. Crucially they need to find a place to take all this unbearable tension, and either run marathons, talk too fast, dance wildly, exercise frantically, paint giant murals, write stories or scream into a pillow for a while. Seeing a counsellor may also be a useful source of support.

There is a charity called 'beat' which gives a lot more valuable detail online than I possibly could and has some helplines. Finding another carer going through a similar nightmare could be an important survival technique too.

BI-POLAR AFFECTIVE DISORDER (MANIC DEPRESSION)

There have been several high-profile celebrity revelations recently regarding bi-polar, this is both positive and negative. If these people really have suffered this frightening illness, and undoubtedly some of them have had the real experience, then it can inspire those who are also diagnosed to feel that there is hope of a good life in spite of it. A person can have this condition and be popular, talented and able to cope with life.

The downside is that these people on screen look so healthy and undamaged that the public can get the impression that it is a simple battle to win. Everyone should be able to get back to normality or a good quality of life judging by these examples, but it's not always that easy. People who claim to be 'a little bit bi-polar' need to spend time experiencing the real thing. Everyone is capable of different moods and of contrasting levels of energy without self-diagnosing a mental health issue for effect.

Bi-polar is a game of two halves as the name 'bi' implies. There are periods of time being low and withdrawn, with varying degrees of desperation and depression. Some people are almost imperceptibly affected and some completely disabled; some for only a short space of time and some for longer. There can be withdrawal from social contact, and often a poor sense of self-worth. It has the features of clinical depression; more can be found in that section.

The other bit is the high, the 'mania' period, which is a

hazardous time for many, although it may seem comical to those who do not have to witness it in someone they care for. There is a burning energy that will not be stopped, this channels itself into behaviour that often involves risk, sometimes to life and limb. The person can feel powerful, a super-hero with a mission. This may translate into bold plans and reckless actions. They may talk without apparently drawing breath but have lost the ability to listen or to stop.

Choosing to ride down a busy street on a powerful motorbike with no jacket and no helmet is a risky decision. Going as fast as possible in the middle of the road to show the traffic who is boss, then that takes it up a notch. If this ride involves taking your young daughter on the pillion then the risk suddenly jumps to another level altogether.

People often spend a great deal of money as part of this high, sometimes on boats, planes, cars or clothes and sometimes on drugs and alcohol. There is no sense of danger so there are no rules, so sexual or drug taking activity is not restricted to the safer variety. Sleep? That's a waste of time.

One carer told me about his wife, who was invited to the birthday party next door, so she enthusiastically entered the house by climbing across from her bedroom window to theirs, not a safe route, and appearing at the party suddenly – without clothes. The neighbours were very understanding, but it's not so funny if it's your partner.

There are two levels of severity here. Hypomania is a bit more controlled; people may be able to carry on doing what they usually do including going to work. It may only last a few days. The more severe version of mania can last a bit longer, the mood is more extreme and there may be psychotic symptoms. It is unlikely that the individual could continue to control this enough to manage their normal routine.

Depending on the individual, this high can be a brief period or a long one but, whatever it is, it will be frightening for family and friends. It can cost them a fortune if their money is not protected and lose them friends if it is socially inappropriate. Police may get involved if behaviour has become conspicuous or criminal. What if the person is your partner and has sex with other people during this time? Is that their choice or the illness; what about sexually transmitted diseases? How can a carer approach this topic when the person is less manic but is now depressed and guilty, already seeing themselves as dreadful people?

There is another possible variation which is a 'mixed episode' which, strangely enough, is experiencing the low depression and the high mania at the same time. This might be simultaneously or rapidly changing from one to the other. This is particularly exhausting and confusing for both the person with the mental health issue and the people round them.

Bi-polar is one of the conditions where there is a higher risk of suicide than the national average. Maybe this is because of the aftermath of extreme behaviour during the high period or perhaps there is more insight into what is happening, especially when a depressive phase is about to start. This doesn't apply to everyone with this diagnosis by a long way but the section on suicide has more details if this would be useful information.

Medication, although not an easy option by any means, often puts a life back on track. In my career I met a couple of people who have abandoned medication after years of taking it and who survive well, but they do it by total stress avoidance. No drink, no late nights, a strict routine, meditation and yoga, and a contingency plan of medication if they feel themselves starting to slide. Many people can end up on the lowest dose of medication if they manage their lifestyle successfully, but it needs constant dedication.

An obstacle to accepting treatment is that being high just

feels too good sometimes. I have vague memories of adolescent nights when I felt the world was mine and everything was just going to be fine. This may well have been after the second drink and before the fourth one. But if a person could feel that good and much, much more, why would they want to take medication that turned them into an unfeeling zombie by comparison, slowing them down and dulling their fizzing brain? For a bi-polar sufferer to accept that they need to take medication can be a long and exhausting fight for both them and their family, it could take several years. There tends to be an ongoing circular pattern of missing being high, coming off it, getting unwell, going back on it, missing being high, etc.

People with bi-polar can be charismatic and attractive; their racy, excessive lifestyles are often paired with great creativity. I have met a lot of partners who paired up with this wild and exciting person who had great ideas and loads of energy but realised after a time that it was too damaging to live with. Maybe it is because, unlike most other mental health issues, the person appears on the surface to be having a great time, with no regard for the others in their life.

A family supporting someone who has bi-polar has minimal control in the situation. I have memories of trying to have conversations with a man who was high, talking without pause about his wholly unrealistic plans for a new project. My efforts to ask about how he was going to afford it had no effect at all, he just couldn't hear me. Shutting up was probably the best option, but I felt I had to try. Carers who find they also have no power to change anything maybe forced to adopt 'self-protection' mode. Here is a list of the steps that carers have told me they have taken:

- Hiding any available alcohol or similar substances.
- Hiding the car keys.

- Making sure that any bank account they have access to has limited funds. Talking to the bank, some are very understanding and can be helpful in setting limits.
- Trying the impossible task of preventing other sources of credit.
- Using protection during sex.
- Explaining to family, friends and employers what is going on.
- Taking away their front door key.
- Protecting younger children by minimising contact during the very worst times.
- Talking to the police about the situation and setting up an alert so that any call about highly risky behaviour is responded to without too much explanation.

Family members need to bear in mind that this is an unpleasant diagnosis to have despite the apparently enjoyable times. If there is verbal abuse or disregard of the effect their behaviour is having on the family it is not under their control, there is no element of choice here. If they appear to be having a great time it will all come crashing down when the high ends or when they recover enough to recall how they have behaved.

Support from relatives and friends can help this individual to maintain as much control as they are able and gives them some safety when they are at their most vulnerable. Getting to the point where the person is accepting treatment can be a long road but usually successful in the end.

PSYCHOSIS – HALLUCINATIONS AND DELUSIONS

These are symptoms, not a diagnosis in itself. Often schizophrenia, which has psychosis as a major feature, is now called a 'psychotic condition'. This is because it has often been misrepresented and misunderstood by the public, so some services avoid using the word. There is a bit more on this diagnosis later, which includes other symptoms that can often be overlooked.

Psychosis is sometimes found as part of the presentation in bi-polar, severe clinical depression, borderline personality disorder and some other diagnoses as well as being central to schizophrenia.

If someone experiences hallucinations, then they are getting information which appears to be real but most other people would consider as imagined. The most recognised hallucination is hearing voices, but there could also be unreal visions, smells, taste or a sense of touch.

Some people hear pleasant voices or have visions that can be a source of help or comfort. They will probably not come to the attention of the mental health services at all. Why would they report this? There is someone nice to talk to who is good company. Many people live with manageable psychosis and cope with it in their own way. A sizeable proportion of the population say that they hear occasional voices, often just someone calling their name, some a little more than that.

The people who are supported by the mental health services tend not to have a manageable situation to live with. Visions are often alarming and smells and tastes very unpleasant. People with hallucinatory touch sensations may feel they are being attacked or raped. Voices are often threatening or critical.

I spent a lot of time with a man who used to bury his trousers in his garden when his symptoms were at their worst. He could smell 'bad eggs and shit' on them and this wouldn't go away. His poor mother must have spent a fortune on new trousers for him. I also knew a young man who struggled with visions of the room closing in on him when he lay in bed at night. He said the walls would ripple and the ceiling suddenly zoom down. There have been many who feel their food is poisoned because it tastes rotten. This frequently leads to suspicious thoughts about the other people in the house being part of a plot to poison them. I also met one woman who would regularly report being sexually attacked at night in her bed, she seemed quite matter of fact about it. She could not describe her attacker or understand how he got into her flat, but she knew it was real. A GP check reported that she had no physical signs of being injured.

There is false information being processed as real in the brain. The person has no reason to doubt it is anything other than it appears to be, that it is genuine. A psychotic experience is powerful, maybe like taking hallucinatory drugs. As a teenager in the 1970s I'm keeping quiet here, but I do wonder if there are chemically any similarities in what is going on. I'm sure someone will tell me.

The cause of this symptom is currently unclear. It could be that it is a physical malfunction which causes the brain to interpret information incorrectly, a fault in the cognitive processing. Alternatively, it could be that it is what the brain does in response to being 'overloaded', a reaction to a traumatic situation that caused extreme distress. This creates a distortion that somehow interprets the unbearable information or offers a representation that makes it tolerable. Certainly, there seem to be a considerable percentage of people who experience psychosis who have also been through a major trauma, but then again there are many who have relatives with the same condition. So, is the cause genetic or from their life experience? Or both?

Whatever the cause, there is no dispute that the sights, sounds, smells, tastes and touch are very real to the person and it is only through time and experience that they can learn to distinguish the difference between hallucinations and what is loosely called reality. What would it take to convince the average person that when they are hearing people talking there isn't anyone there? How long would it take for the anyone to believe that this sandwich doesn't actually smell of rotten eggs, it's their brain that is getting it wrong?

The other piece of the puzzle is that of delusions, holding an idea or belief that does not fit with the apparent facts of situation. Some appear to have their roots in the individual's hallucinations and arise because of the unreal information that the person is receiving at a time when they are extremely vulnerable.

Delusional beliefs can include feelings of great power, being capable of changing the world or having control over the weather, wars or natural disasters or who wins the lottery. This isn't as enjoyable as it sounds because if you can cause an earthquake then there may be consequences and for some this power feels a heavy responsibility.

Frequently the delusion brings a strong sense of paranoia. Raised levels of anxiety create a feeling of being in danger and this leads to a conviction that 'beings with special powers' are meaning them harm. These beings will vary according to the local culture; it could be associated with religion, aliens or any well-known espionage/intelligence agency. In the UK there often seem to be men in black cars for some reason. If a person hears voices then a frequent explanation is that 'someone' is controlling electrical devices or beaming signals, so they must be powerful beings.

A man I knew well had unimaginable struggles with his psychotic symptoms. He was brought up in a strictly religious household where good and evil ruled. He used to attend one of the centres where I worked and would cycle home down a busy city road. On a bad day he 'knew' that the Devil was just behind him reaching out his talons to grab him off his bike and take him to hell. This Devil was very big and had all the features that a good Devil should, with burning eyes and a flaming mouth. The man would cycle far faster than was really safe. Logically he could have stopped and looked behind him, but I felt for him when he said he just couldn't take that risk because he would have had to slow down and might have got caught. He would have this waking nightmare for twenty minutes of hectic cycling until he reached home.

Another frequent delusion involves neighbours, (there is always the chance that these stories could be true though, neighbours can be difficult!) Often these awful people are doing dreadful things to deliberately persecute the person with the mental health issue. They are making terrible amounts of noise or smells or are sneezing deliberately to wake them up every morning. One person told me that the people next door were pumping gas into his bedroom every night to knock him out. I asked him why he thought this, he said that every night when he lay on his bed he felt a bit dizzy and very tired, so it must be gas coming through his air vent. The neighbours were the obvious suspects.

One of the trickiest delusional beliefs I ever encountered is one that I believe is increasing in frequency. If a person feels that he (usually this is a man) is a wicked and terrible person it used to be that the obvious explanation was that they were the Devil, or at least one of his close relatives. Contemporary society is not so aware of devils as we used to be, so the current manifestation of the worst possible social evil is the paedophile. I met a young man who believed he was one and his shame was ruining his life. He confessed he had never actually done anything, but he knew that he 'looked lustfully' at schoolgirls and he didn't know how old they were, so he must be a paedophile. I would suggest that only a minority of men (or women) didn't 'look lustfully' at schoolgirls or boys at some point, but this reassurance didn't make these devastating beliefs go away. He had a deep seated conviction that he was wicked and dirty; this delusion gave him an explanation for those feelings.

If a family are coping with someone's unreal beliefs, either with or without hallucinations, then it is useful to discuss how everyone is going to respond to this. It helps to be consistent and predictable but there are lots of ways of approaching these issues. One option is to collude with them and say, 'yes dear, whatever you say'. Another is to challenge them with 'that's all rubbish'. Often the favoured approach is to say something like 'I know this is real to you, but I don't see it that way' and perhaps to add 'I think it is because you have a mental health issue that is causing your brain to make some mistakes at the moment'. Many carers and professionals use this last one, the acknowledgement that the person is telling 'their truth' but that it isn't reality for the rest of us.

I always thought that the complication with this approach is that the underlying message, either implicitly or explicitly, is, 'this is because your mind is not working properly'. The person with the mental health issue may not accept this observation calmly. The average person would react strongly if they were on the receiving end of these comments, particularly from a close relative that they depended on. It is the equivalent of saying, 'The reason why you believe in God / love football/ play Fortnite/ think you can sing is because your brain isn't working properly'.

Colluding, just agreeing with whatever is said may result in a quiet life in the short term but it is not helpful over time. The carer may be one of the main sources in learning to tell the difference between what is real and what is not. Joining in with the delusion is not necessarily reassuring; if they are frightened then agreeing that there are people out to get them is not going to offer much comfort.

Neither is it that helpful to challenge people, certainly in the early days. This can quickly become a confrontation in which there is little chance of winning. Their logic is real to them and borne out by personal evidence that has great emotional importance. It is their reality, and as such it is as pointless as attempting to convince a teenager that they really can manage without TikTok, or to convince regular drinker that life would continue if they went dry. Stating that their beliefs are flawed just creates a divide that reduces the chances of useful communication.

The middle way for the carer is to acknowledge the feelings that arise as the result of these beliefs and to help them to cope with these by planning together. Please note the word 'together'; coming up with a cunning plan on their behalf stands a real chance of not working, despite good intentions. Their plan may include strategies such as putting foil over the windows, having curtains permanently drawn or never having the TV on when they are around.

I always remember a young girl who was a frequent caller to a helpline that I worked on. She had terrible hallucinations of rats running all over the floor in her flat. She would be close to hysteria at times but had started to phone the helpline when she wasn't coping. We learnt to help her by asking if she could see a way to make it to her bedroom, and this always seemed possible somehow. She would take the phone with her and you could hear her panicky voice as she ran through the rats and into the next room. We would suggest that she got into bed and under the duvet. For some reason this was her safe place. Once there we could just reassure her for a few minutes that she had made it safely, then talk about the weather or something on TV for a while. She would say, 'I'm all right now,' thank us, and hang up.

We got to this point because one of the volunteers had the insight to ask her if there was anywhere that she felt safe. Once we all knew that under the duvet worked for her we could offer some genuine support without challenging the existence of the rats, just by supporting her to go somewhere that allowed her to relax and let the fear fade away. Helping someone to see a way through a frightening situation, and possibly talking them through it if they are overwhelmed, might be the most effective help that can be offered.

When all this is new, families often prefer to stay on safe ground and not get into any confrontations about these beliefs and experiences and this seems wise. As time passes, if there is a good relationship then some gentle challenging might help to sow the seeds of making these experiences less powerful. Challenging sounds like a strong word here but I can't think of another one. Avoiding a 'yes it is', 'no it isn't' pantomime showdown is important, so it is worth some planning. If the delusional idea isn't shifting but the person is usually fairly controlled and calm, only then might a 'doubting' question be a possibility.

Suppose they think they are responsible for a great catastrophe such as an earthquake on the other side of the world, which is not an unusual belief. It would be easy to say, 'How could you be, you're miles away?' or 'Don't be daft, how could you be strong enough?' This immediately demonstrates that they are not believed. Suggesting possible alternative explanations such as 'earthquakes have been around a long time. There were a lot of them before there were any people on the earth, weren't there?' perhaps may sow a seed of doubt. It isn't about a long argument but more asking them to think about what they are claiming as truth.

Trying it a couple of times will probably give feedback as to whether it is worth 'challenging' or not. They may avoid questioning their ideas under any circumstances, any forced conversation will soon become 'you just don't understand'. There are professionals who are trained to work with these delusions, but they would only focus on issues that caused the individual substantial distress and would mostly try just to lessen the impact rather than to remove the idea.

If the person with the mental health issue hears voices, then it should be established reasonably early on that this topic is not up for discussion. People have reported many times that talking about their voices makes them worse, sometimes far, far worse. There may be a bit more flexibility after a time, or if they are on helpful medication. It is not a good idea to bring up this subject, the timing of any conversation needs to be controlled by the person who is hearing them. Even professionals are extremely cautious if someone is experiencing great distress because of voice hearing.

I learnt the lesson (slowly) around challenging a long time ago when I was working with people who had psychotic symptoms. One man used to become very agitated at times, bordering on aggressive. He had spent much of his youth being a runner for a local criminal gang, a very minor role. He now believed that this gang was after him because of what he knew. He believed they could monitor where he was at every minute, to the point that he was sure they would be coming to get him at any time. This was before mobile phones so I asked him how they could do this? He told me that they had placed a 'platinum implant' in his anus (he didn't use that term) and they could see it on their radar.

I immediately set out on a mission to persuade his psychiatrist to order an X-ray of this part of his anatomy to convince him that the platinum implant didn't exist. It took me a long time, I thought the psychiatrist was being unhelpful, but actually he was just experienced.

Eventually the X-ray was taken and the psychiatrist revealed the results to this man; there was, of course, no implant. His response was, 'It's a special sort of platinum that doesn't show up on X-rays.' Challenging may not work at all or it may work very slowly, so don't expect quick results. You can only sow the seeds and hope.

It would be safer to ask if they are feeling frightened then to suggest a selection of activities that may distract or calm things down. This could be music, playing cards, going for a walk or whatever that individual responds to, the list will grow according to experience. Changing the subject takes some skill, it is tough to do that subtly.

Delusions can also be very persistent. If the person is not doing a great deal all day then they may not have much else to think about. Talking about their ideas and beliefs can become their comfort zone, especially if they feel confused or overwhelmed by other day to day experiences.

'Dad, those men are outside again.'

'No, they aren't, remember you looked five minutes ago? Try to think about something else.'

'I can't think about something else, they are waiting for me to go out.'

'I realise that you are really worried about this but you are safe in here right now.'

'You don't care that they are trying to get me.'

'You know I care, if I thought you were in any danger I would help you, you know that.'

'You're not listening to me.'

'I am listening to you, you tell me this every few minutes.'

'That's 'cos it's true and you don't care. You're a useless father.'

'I do care, I just can't see any danger right now. You have told me about these men every day for the last month and several times a day. I'm not sure what more I can say?'

Dad is starting to get a bit edgy and probably not for the first time. The conversation is getting stuck and his daughter is fixed in her anxiety. Dad can't do anything practical to help, if he marches out into the street and accosts some passing motorist she will not be reassured – and neither will the motorist. Her fears would undoubtedly be transferred to something else if this idea disappeared and the men outside went away.

Dad is stuck with hearing a very repetitive story and his daughter is stuck in telling it many times a day.

What are the options? Firstly, he could consider if this is a possible boundary setting situation. He is being driven round the bend here, but what about his daughter's perspective? He is saying all the right things in trying to reassure her, not belittling her, confronting or mocking her but she seems to be stuck. Would it help her to try to limit this topic of conversation? Would it help change the subject and try together to come up with new ideas to talk about?

It could be worth trying to limit the time that they spend on this subject while acknowledging that it is necessary to take her ideas seriously.

'I know you are very worried about men in a car outside, but it seems to be all we talk about. I would like to be able to talk to you about other things and not just focus on this all the time, so I am going to suggest a rule that we should follow.

I will look outside and check what is going on every hour. I will let you know if I am at all worried about anything. You can come with me and look too if you like. But after that, for the rest of the hour I won't talk to you any more about this car or these men. I will talk to you about anything else you might like. Maybe we could look at a film together or do some cooking or something like that. But for the rest of the hour, no car talk.'

Then of course dad has to stick to this, even in the face of possible opposition, as long as she doesn't become very distressed or agitated by it. Hopefully if he can keep cool and persevere then they can both move forward a bit and have some more varied conversations. Notice that he is not asking her to be quiet or to go away, just to talk about other things so his attention will still be there, she will just be encouraged to broaden the conversation.

None of this is easy, the person with the mental health issues is convinced of their viewpoint, probably frightened and anxious and they want to be believed. The family wants to show support but doesn't want these ideas to dominate the household. Setting this sort of boundary takes planning and having a strategy in mind (see 'encouraging change' for more ideas). If possible, check out any idea with a mental health professional, if there is one available.

Hallucinations and delusions are usually more emotionally powerful in the early days and this is when the family must tread most carefully. As time passes they may be regarded in a more matter of fact sort of way and cause far less upheaval from day to day.

Medication can greatly reduce the impact of these experiences but doesn't always completely remove them for everybody, some people are treatment resistant. These medications can make the person feel quite subdued and anaesthetised. The choice may be between this rather restricted, flat feeling or the unpleasant hallucinations. The side effects vary considerably, although weight gain can be a common feature, but a lot of people accept in time that they prefer life with the medication.

Talking treatments, specialist approaches, can also be useful in helping to interpret these confusing experiences and to cope better with the effects of them, but this must be timed right. The person needs to be open to discussing the situation and brave enough to attempt a change.

SCHIZOPHRENIA

Schizophrenia is one of the most familiar mental health diagnoses, maybe because it is seen primarily as hearing voices. This gets more press coverage than other symptoms, perhaps because on the rare occasion someone who is experiencing this commits a crime, they may say it was because the voices told them to do it. But this is a tiny minority, but they cast a long shadow.

Sometimes people believe schizophrenia is a 'split personality' and I can only say as loud as possible 'No! It's got nothing to do with that' – let's leave that idea completely behind please. It appals me that this mistaken belief is still used to make jokes on panel shows.

The term schizophrenia is often replaced with 'a psychotic condition' because it has so many negative connotations but calling it just 'psychosis' can lead to overlooking the other aspects of this diagnosis.

Additional symptoms occur because the brain may not be able to process information or problem solve to the same degree that it used to. Many intelligent people experience schizophrenia, there have been films and books about the more famous of them. It can be hard to remember that this person has an accountancy qualification and has worked for one of the big banks, as one man I knew, and is now furious every day because people slam their car doors when he goes past. They wait for him to walk down the street and synchronise the door slamming for his benefit.

Reason and logic can be a struggle to maintain although intelligence is not directly affected, it is just that they may be unable to process information and have difficulty in communicating and thinking in the way that they used to.

Some believe that they can read other people's thoughts. This leads to a level of distrust and despair as, in their view, other people are usually thinking negative things about them or planning to cause them harm. They might pass someone in the street and then declare that this innocent passer-by was trying to control their brain. This can be hard for families as they may become distressed or even abusive.

Some feel that their own thoughts are being broadcast. Personally, I am relieved that no one else knows what I am thinking most of the time, it tends not to be publicly acceptable. It must be worse for those who have critical views about themselves or are constantly in fear. In many situations a person may say they 'just knew' what the other person was thinking or 'just knew' that others could read their mind. Others may feel that there are rays or special powers that are passing between them and others.

There is also a strong sense of anxiety a lot of the time. Being rational people there needs to be an explanation behind those feelings of fear and with possible hallucinations and a lack of cognitive clarity it is not hard to put together one that fits. The delusional beliefs or the ideas that people construct to explain what they are feeling often contain a sense of menace or paranoia, which infiltrates the person's whole life.

There may also be an apparent lack of motivation which does not work in that person's favour. Having a lack of any drive to change anything, as well as taking medication that can also reduce energy levels, may lead to an overwhelming inertia. Change is likely to be slow and hard fought. This is often misunderstood by family to be reluctance or deliberate refusal, whereas it might be because the process of changing requires more processing power than the person can manage at this moment.

Another possible symptom of schizophrenia is an inability to filter incoming data. At any moment vast quantities of information are being assessed by the brain and usually this does a wonderful job of filtering out what is not needed. It selects the bits that are necessary and pays no attention to the rest. When crossing the road special consideration is paid specifically to traffic that is nearby and coming towards you and the general confusion of people and shops in the background is lost. But this filter fails in some psychotic conditions, information comes into the brain uncensored as an overpowering flood.

It isn't surprising that people with this way of experiencing the world often seem to prefer a quieter life and shy away from noise or crowds. There is no means to protect themselves and they are hyper-sensitive to any form of chaos or hectic environment, and easily distressed. I always thought it was a bit like being in a TV shop with all the sets on full volume and tuned to different channels.

Schizophrenic symptoms apparently come and go in waves. It can just present in one episode - sometimes this can be triggered by drug use. However, the drug use may stop and the psychosis continue. It can come for two or three episodes and then go, but for some people it becomes a chronic recurring condition. They may be prone to relapse in periods of high stress or if they stop their medication. Even in periods of calm they may be reluctant to abandon any delusional beliefs, they may know that it is a feature of their psychosis but still, at one level, believe it to be true. These things are difficult to leave behind as they are such powerful experiences.

So, in summary, schizophrenia consists of seemingly real information which isn't, overwhelming masses of data coming in which is not effectively filtered, a frequent state of terror and/ or of mind blowing super powers alongside a lack of motivation and an inability to put these experiences into some kind of manageable framework. It is not surprising that it is a challenge for the family to understand what is happening and to adapt to coping, particularly in the early stages.

The previous section on psychosis has more detail, there are also hints and tips that may be helpful both in the 'crises and relapses' and 'everyday challenges' sections.

SCHIZO-AFFECTIVE DISORDER

This is evidence that we have an imperfect diagnostic system as some psychiatrists use this label and some don't. Briefly it describes a situation where there are symptoms that fulfil the criteria for schizophrenia but there are also mood changes, highs and lows as found in bi-polar disorder. It is not that commonly diagnosed and may take some time to identify. Often there is a diagnosis of schizophrenia or bi-polar that gets amended as new information comes to light.

PERSONALITY DISORDERS (PD)

This diagnosis is particularly hard to understand if you have not come across it before. It implies that someone's personality is 'wrong', which is not immensely helpful. Different terminology is being introduced as more mental health professionals find this label inappropriate and are reluctant to use it. They prefer to see the individual as having certain needs and behaviours, rather than using such a potentially demoralising description.

Often PD seems to appear after other diagnoses have been tried and seemed not to fit. Symptoms can often be observed from an early age, unlike many other mental health issues which have a later onset.

Personality disorder is often associated by the public with criminal acts, particularly violent ones. The common view is that people will lack empathy and will be capable of harming others without conscience. This is only partly true and refers to an extremely small minority with a very particular form of PD. Looking at the each individual and how they behave is the best clue as to whether this is going to be applicable.

There was a time when this label meant being excluded

from any help, as the mental health services were only obliged to take on people who they could potentially treat effectively. Personality disorders were considered outside of this range because they didn't respond to medication. (Of course, there was always a suspicion, especially among the families involved, that the more challenging people would end up with this diagnosis as a reason to discharge them from mental health services).

Treatments for PD are available now, they can be remarkably successful and there is no reason not to accept people as 'patients'. Medication is still not a cure in itself; it can only reduce symptoms such as anxiety. Drugs cannot make someone change the way they see things, or how they interpret what is going on in their lives. Treatments for PD tend to be more of the talking variety with some medication as appropriate.

Everyone has a view of the world that influences how they behave and how they respond to other people. In PD this view is unhelpful and usually results in the person not managing their life well. It develops through sociological and psychological factors; what happens to the person and how they deal with it. Although this is always under review as medical science progresses, now there is increasing mention of genetic factors also being involved, which makes sense.

People begin life with a reasonably blank canvas and learn to interpret what goes on around them. There may be an influence from the inherited 'hard wiring' - perhaps being born naturally anxious or prone to aggression. Soon after birth, or even before, the information that is taken in and processed by the brain is used to construct a sense of how things work in the world and how they fit together. This bank of information carries on growing through childhood and adolescence and is divided up into chunks of information called 'schema'.

As an example, a baby boy was left in a cot in a dirty nappy all day and when he cried for food or comfort no one came;

abuse by neglect. One of that child's schema might be that no one cared about him and his needs, both physical and emotional, and therefore he could never rely on other people. Help and support are not available so why on earth should he feel compassion for these other people who have no compassion for him? Why should he feel OK about himself when no one else cares? This is not a rational argument but more an emotional response to experiences before a person is old enough to understand and consider all the factors involved. He does not know what it is to feel safe or to feel emotionally attached to a caregiver.

Once the schema are formed people tend to pay attention to information that fits with them and ignore things that contradict them. If someone thinks cricket is boring and they are forced to sit through a match, they are likely to sigh and tut all through it rather than suddenly seeing it as fascinating, whereas their friend the cricket fan who made them come, might see it as the most exciting event ever. This is a normal way of processing new information, it is a kind of cognitive short cut. Minds have been made up and things that are observed are made to 'fit'.

PD is mostly (but probably not completely) down to a child's world being shaken by one or a series of events which could take many diverse forms, abuse being one of them. An early life trauma could be anything that is overwhelmingly distressing to that child – it is down to their perception of the event at the time. As an example, suppose a child is involved in an accident, there is injury to them or to other important people in their life. Their sense of being safe and protected by their family may be damaged and they may have to cope with the adults around them being distracted and distressed themselves. A schema may develop which interprets life as being dangerous and full of risk.

I would like to stress that the vast majority of the families I have met who have an adult child with this diagnosis do not seem the type to treat their child with great cruelty and I have met too many for them all to be well disguised child abusers. The sense of having experienced a trauma could lie in a wide variety of other events, maybe frequently moving to a new house or school, or the loss of an adult they were close to, these may be beyond anyone's control. It's not all down to abuse. Sometimes families can struggle to find an explanation, I have had no problem in believing many of them when they say, 'I can't remember anything that I would call a trauma happening to him/her.'

There are ten main types of PD, here is an extremely summary of the main aspects of each type:

CLUSTER A: SUSPICIOUS.
1. Paranoid: Unable to trust anyone, suspicious, people are always plotting against them.
2. Schizoid: Doesn't form close relationships with anyone, prefers to live without other people interfering. Can be 'cold'.
3. Schizotypal: Think, talk and behave in unusual, eccentric ways. May believe they can read other's minds and are psychic. They feel uneasy if others don't agree with them and paranoid in social situations. Relationships are tricky.
4. Antisocial: Includes now largely redundant term 'psychopath'. Only used over eighteen years old. Takes risks without thinking or considering others, often dangerous or illegal acts. Puts own needs first even when this means harm to others, with no sense of guilt. Gets bored, acts on impulse. Believes it necessary to be ruthless to survive/succeed.

CLUSTER B: EMOTIONAL AND IMPULSIVE
1. Borderline (BPD) otherwise known as emotionally unstable personality disorder (EUPD): Very intense emotions that can change rapidly at any time. Frequently anger or fear / paranoia. Petrified of being abandoned. Poor sense of

self, changes to fit with what is happening from moment to moment. Impulsive and sometimes harmful behaviour, often self-harm and suicide threats. Feels 'empty' or numb. Could have psychotic experiences.

2. Histrionic: Wants to be centre of attention - 'everyone look at me'. Needing the approval of others. Constantly 'entertaining' or flirting. Dramatic, easily influenced and emotional.

3. Narcissistic: Sees self as special and better than others. Looking for others to validate their 'specialness', distressed if this doesn't happen. Comes across as selfish, everyone should put their needs first, and resentful if others do well.

4. Avoidant or anxious: Avoids other people, anticipates criticism, worried about being found out or made fun of. Relationships or new situations difficult as they fear being rejected. Extremely sensitive.

CLUSTER C: ANXIOUS

5. Dependent: Constantly needs support, takes no responsibility for self. Submissively will go along with anything rather than be left to cope alone. Low confidence, other people are 'better'. Passive.

6. Obsessive compulsive personality disorder (OCPD): This is a personality type (but obsessive- compulsive disorder is a type of behaviour). Everything needs to be kept to high standards and under control. Sets very exacting standards for self and others - 'my way is the only way'. Fears mistakes being made, exaggerates outcome of any failure. Spending money and throwing things away are both challenging.

Often several of these can develop together, frequently from the same category.

Everyone can see a bit of themselves in these descriptions,

undoubtedly it is the easiest diagnosis to have an immediate sense of identifying with, both in the self and others. However amateur attempts at labelling a person's behaviour are usually wildly incorrect and potentially damaging; despite the temptation it is best avoided.

There are even more details online about subcategories and the different American classifications. It's hard not to dismiss them as meaningless because they apparently refer to so many natural human feelings. 'Oppositional defiance disorder' (ODD) means that there is 'persistent and excessive rebellion against authority figures'. Like anyone who is 14 years old? The difference is, of course, one of degree and how much it disables the person from living as most people live (avoiding the word normal here).

Anti-social PD is the form most likely to lead to law-breaking or acts of cruelty. There are no forgone conclusions though, it is vital that the individual is regarded only within the range of his or her own behaviour and not pre-judged until concrete evidence starts to appear.

EUPD (emotionally unstable PD) or BPD (borderline PD) is the most frequently diagnosed and can be devastating for a family to live with. It often involves self-harm and / or suicide attempts that regularly create a high level of stress. There is a separate section on EUPD following this one.

There is one additional PD condition which is 'dissociative identity disorder' (DID) which used to be called multiple personality disorder or split personality (please note that this is not a symptom of, or any way related to, schizophrenia despite the media and jokes). There is more on this topic in the section on 'disassociation'.

Some people with PD presentations can be particularly good at getting their own way. They have excellent abilities with what some would call 'manipulation' and others would call 'people skills'. That is why many rise to the top in the world of politics and big business, as an ambitious, clever and ruthless person can go far.

This persuasiveness can be a constant challenge for families. Threats of self-harm or suicide can become a means to an end, how do relatives risk taking a stand against these? People can get money for drugs, drink or other things that a family really don't want to subsidise, but don't know how to stop. These threats can also control a family's behaviour. The 'suicide' section and the 'encouraging change' section could be useful.

I had a very enlightening experience with the first person I met with PD. He told me he was a member of the S.A.S and that he was suffering from PTSD. He told me he had killed someone while on tour in Ireland and couldn't get over the experience. He told me he was desperate for help and that I (a gullible girl in my early twenties) was the only one who understood him and really listened. Then he stole my purse.

PD creates unhappy and isolated lives for those who have no option but to live with such disturbed ways of seeing the world, with damaged and unhelpful schema. It is incredibly difficult for the carer to keep in mind that this is not a deliberate choice, something has become unbalanced in the way their interpretation of events has been put together and the usual comfort of feeling safe and supported, at least some of the time, is just not available.

The treatment for PD (the Steppes programme) focusses on individual or group work that requires each person to review and test out their own schema and consider whether they are accurate. Perhaps they describe their mother as mean, cruel and out to punish them. Does this fit with the evidence that she drives them everywhere they want to go, gives them spending money and cooks their favourite meals? This work is challenging for the professionals and unsettling for the person, it addresses the very core of their personality. People need to be 'in the right place' to accept this therapy, to cooperate and to benefit from it.

A quick summary of useful points picked up from families with experience:

- Remember it's not personal, no matter what they say or do it is not a reflection on the carer. Neither are they choosing to behave this way or feel this way, they have no ability to 'turn it off'.

- If the family realise they are being persuaded to do things they are not happy with, that the person is going back on their word or 'telling stories' that turn out not to be true again and again, then this pattern should be identified. It could be that everyone involved needs to adopt a way of responding to these situations that lets the person know that this strategy is not going to be effective. (see 'encouraging change' section).

- Set boundaries. This means saying 'No' firmly and consistently to unacceptable behaviour or requests and being unchanging in the face of the angry or distressed reaction. If there is more than one person involved in the situation then they must all stick to the agreed boundaries in the face of any persuasion or attempts to 'divide and rule'. (See 'boundaries')

- Getting hung up on what caused it is not going to help. There is little that can be done even if there is an awareness of what might have been the trigger event(s), talking about it is probably not going to help to change this person's perspective. Ask professionals for advice here if that is a possibility.

- Identifying situations that may increase distress is useful although this can be like trying to hold back the sea but, at a minimum, if a potentially upsetting situation is identified early enough there can be an attempt to avoid it, or at least feel a bit more prepared.

- It is important to use whatever help is available, even if the

person is upset by the carer talking to other people. If their behaviour is worrying in any way, then someone needs to know because these situations can be exceptionally difficult to handle alone. If they are at all threatening then involve the police. (see 'crises and relapses')
- Have a safety plan if it looks like it might be necessary, one for them and one for the family.

This list sounds harsh and punitive, as though the person experiencing personality disorder traits is mean and unscrupulous. They are making poor decisions because they do not have the capacity to see the wider picture, they have desires that are not in their own best interest. Sometimes it sounds as though the family need to prepare to defend themselves, but it isn't just about this. Firm guidelines help the person who may be frequently highly distressed to be protected from their own lack of control.

EMOTIONALLY UNSTABLE PERSONALITY DISORDER (EUPD) OR BORDERLINE PERSONALITY DISORDER (BPD)

This is the most frequently diagnosed personality disorder; it potentially causes a great deal of distress to all concerned.

It was called 'borderline' PD because it used to be considered on the line between the conditions such as anxiety and depression and those that include psychosis. People may experience voices or visions. It can also involve strong feelings of dissociation, of not being connected to any sense of a 'self', instead there is a feeling of being detached and observing from a distance. (See 'psychosis' and 'disassociation' sections.)

It is now more frequently called 'emotionally unstable personality disorder' as that seems a more meaningful term.

Often, (but not always?), individuals have had experience of periods of abuse, trauma, neglect or prolonged isolation. These events have caused considerable damage, but the person may be reluctant to identify or talk about them directly.

They may have EUPD alongside several other diagnoses such as anxiety, depression, addictions, bi-polar, etc. It may be difficult to define what symptom fits where.

Some characteristics can be noticeable from an early age. Mood changes are rapid, with frequent periods of depression, anxiety and often extreme anger. These shifts are not under the person's control, at least not until they have had some help with this. Their behaviour is unpredictable, impulsive and can be very unusual. They are acting out the extreme emotions that they are experiencing.

They usually have low self-esteem and think of themselves in completely negative terms.

Any relationship with someone who has this diagnosis is likely to be full of extremes: overwhelming affection followed rapidly by anger and insult. The intensity of the affection or hatred is felt far more strongly than most people experience. They may have periods of doubt that their affection is returned and can 'turn off' and reject the person closest to them, apparently to test the other person's feelings, to see if they really mean what they say. People are regarded as either all good or all bad, there is no compromise. Their anger can be overwhelming and apparently without any sense of control or consequences. This constant and rapid fluctuation can be hard for others to follow, to understand and to tolerate.

Fear that they will be abandoned may result in dramatic gestures. This dread of being left alone is fuelled by a sense of emptiness; nothing means anything, nothing allows them to feel satisfied or complete. This sense of desolation can result in impulsive and reckless behaviour, perhaps self-harm, or suicide attempts. A lot of people with this diagnosis may use alcohol or street drugs to reduce this frightening sensation of not having a proper identity. They may also engage in uncontrolled spending sprees or reckless, unprotected sex. The person may not have any sense of why they are feeling and behaving this way.

Self-harm can take many forms and I shall always remember talking to the mother of a young girl in her early twenties who had EUPD; she was at her wits' end. Her daughter would go out two or three nights a week and hang around in places like underground car parks where she would have sex for money or drugs. There was no one else around and sometimes her 'customers' would beat her up or use sexual violence and often they wouldn't pay. She would stagger home in the early hours, it would be her mother who would clean her up, wash the blood and other bodily fluids off her and put her to bed. She would accept no treatment from mental health services and her mother knew that even if she were taken into hospital again, she would simply go back to this self-punishing lifestyle as soon as she came out. I find it hard to imagine how her mum kept going. This extreme behaviour is rare even with EUPD, but it illustrates how careless people can be with their own wellbeing, which then impacts on those around them too.

It is crucial that the family recognise that the person has little control, their emotional 'dysregulation' and impulsive risk taking is not through choice. They may well be doing their best to fight their own reactions.

This is an attempt to describe some of the ways that people with EUPD might see their world:

Other people are either wonderful and perfect, or wicked and bad. No middle ground.

The way I feel is the result of what is happening around me, it is not my responsibility because I am helpless – my behaviour is the fault of others. If people are not kind and don't appreciate me then I will reject them.

I must be surrounded by approval and affection all the time. I need a perfect person who will always be there to give me constant selfless love and care. Without them I am conscious of how flawed and imperfect I am so when this person doesn't help, I get angry, upset and try desperate things to make these feeling go away.

I try extremely hard to get people to love me, I try to prove how much I need them. Somehow, they never give me as much love as I give them, they always leave me in the end.

If people do love me and care about me then there must be something wrong with them.

Being alone is unbearable, I cannot just be 'myself' by myself.

Medication can lessen the effect of the extreme anxiety, but it doesn't change beliefs. There are talking therapies that can help a great deal, but they rely on the person being willing to cooperate with the process. A lot of people find the prospect of these therapies absolutely petrifying but those who bravely take this on can achieve wonderfully positive results in time.

Some recommendations from families with hands on experience:

- Remain calm (within realistic expectations). This is particularly challenging when someone is angry and hurling verbal abuse. Somehow it is about holding on to the knowledge that this is not personal, it is an expression of their own needs and frustrations.
- Stand back a bit, observe any patterns or triggers and monitor how the family responses affect the day-to-day events. This requires a rather 'clinical' detachment, watching rather than reacting too strongly, but this may help reduce the emotional temperature in the house.
- Set clear boundaries that everyone sticks to consistently, this might be about giving time, money or supporting them to

do something that is inappropriate or damaging. This means that it is OK to say 'No' and actually more helpful in the long run than being persuaded to give in. The key word here is 'consistently'.

- The carer needs to weigh the process of standing firm in the face of anger and any resulting risky behaviour. What happens if this behaviour continues, what are the long-term implications? If a person is likely to make a high-risk gesture such as a suicide attempt because their demand is refused, then it is a fine balancing act. Professional advice is useful. The 'suicide' section has more on this.

- This diagnosis can give the family a real emotional 'battering' and so it is in everyone's interest to keep as mentally and physically well as possible. This self-care supports people to hold things together for longer when there is a dramatically charged situation to cope with on a regular basis.

- The GP and mental health team must be made aware of whatever is happening and shouting for help is a wise reaction if the situation deteriorates - regardless of what the person concerned wants kept quiet.

This description is portraying this condition at its worst, for many it is not so extreme and more manageable. EUPD is never easy to understand or to live with though, even if the dramas are not so intense. Many people with this condition report how much they appreciate the patience and support of their families even if they are not able to show this in a consistent and controlled way.

DIAGNOSES SUMMARY

There are other less common categories of mental health issues other than those listed here. Useful resources for more details are available in the patients' section of the Royal College of Psychiatrists' website or if you want the full information then use the *ICD 10 (UK)* or *DSM 5 (USA)* (psychiatrist's main textbooks.) Just searching online can be useful but be aware of the individual blogs and posts. They can add more detail to understanding a condition better, but also can be highly personal and be coloured by the writer's own agenda.

USEFUL TERMS

These are some key features that may appear as part of many mental health diagnoses – or they may not. It can be helpful to have a bit more detail as to what they mean when they are mentioned by professionals, as there may not be the opportunity to ask many questions.

The topics are

- Stress
- Addiction
- Disassociation
- Self-harm
- Self-esteem
- Nervous breakdown

STRESS

This is a useful catch-all sort of term, which has come in recent years to mean many things to many people. It isn't a mental health diagnosis in itself, but it can be a factor that contributes to one developing. Increasingly it is part of people's everyday lives and some will cope with it well and some won't.

If an individual believes that the world they live in is expecting more of them than they can offer, then it becomes a stressful situation. Experiencing feelings of apprehension and dread about how they are going to cope with what is happening to them (next) and their lack of control over these events raises the level of anxiety, sometimes substantially.

Normal worry is not a threat to health. People should expect to feel stressed about their exams, a job interview, proposing, retiring, attending a funeral of a loved one or crossing the road in busy traffic. In all these situations a little anxiousness raises awareness of what is going on and may well improve how well it is coped with. A life without any worry is going to have to be one which involves a lot of sedatives.

Stress becomes a problem when it is severe, long-term or threatens to overwhelm the person. The level at which any individual becomes affected will vary with their resilience and coping skills. The threat may be an emotional one but the brain will react as though there is a physical danger and increase certain functions in the body, generally the ones that speed people up both physically and mentally - but prevent them from performing efficiently. If these reactions are frequent or present for long periods of time, then they are much harder to turn off and relax. This means that a person can be racing away on full speed most of the time.

Someone who is expected to 'deliver' at work but finds that they have insufficient time or don't know how to tackle a specific problem may become stressed if the pressure doesn't lessen. A new parent may feel incapable of caring for their baby in the way they feel they should, and there is no escaping the demands. A young person might see university as being a challenge that they cannot cope with, either academically or because it means leaving home, but they are stuck there unless they admit defeat, go home and maybe live to regret that decision.

Or it may be that someone is in the process of acknowledging that a person they care for very much has developed a mental health issue and there is no certainty about what will happen or how to cope.

Signs that stress is having an impact on people include:

- Feeling low and miserable, always looking on the negative side
- Feeling agitated or jittery, unable to settle, pacing around
- Feeling irritable or snappy
- Feeling overwhelmed
- Feeing alone or cut off from others, withdrawing
- Feeling the mind is whizzing or unable to focus, unable to concentrate or make decisions
- Feeling unable to remember reliably
- Sleeping or eating more or less than usual
- Sex? No chance
- Neglecting jobs and responsibilities
- Increasing nervous habits such as hair twiddling, nail biting
- Increase in using drugs including nicotine and alcohol
- Increase in minor ailments/aches and pains
- Feeling sick or changes in bowel habits
- Faster or stronger heartbeat, maybe some pain or tightness in the chest

This is unfair wear and tear which, if it continues for long enough, will result in mental and physical health issues. These may include blood pressure, ulcers, some skin conditions or digestive issues as well as increased anxiety, exhaustion and depression.

Stress in the face of an unchangeable problem is like revving a car at a red traffic light. The body and mind are racing but no-one is going anywhere, the result is a knackered engine. It is a kind of warning signal that things are getting out of control and if it isn't addressed the consequences can become more serious and harder to reverse. If there is a noticeable change and a person, (even a carer!) appears to be having trouble coping then perhaps some attention needs to be paid to this issue.

It may not always be possible to take away the 'stressor' – the cause of the stress. Learning coping skills such as relaxation, mindfulness or distraction can be useful. For example, if a person can identify when their tension levels are rising and take deep breaths for a while it can restore a level of self-control and stop things getting too out of hand.

Coping skills may include assertiveness, discussing the problem with confidence so that it is open to negotiation and not a secret worry. This is more difficult when the problem is a mental health issue.

It is not a weakness to take medication as a short-term solution that provides some respite and at least allows the body to rest a bit. Of course, it doesn't take the problems away but may allow a new energy to tackle them once the adrenalin levels are a bit lower.

The trick is to spot stress signs in the self or others; it can be a major feature of the caring role especially in the beginning when there are more unknowns and less help around. This may require a pause every now and then and check in with yourself, preferably at least once a day. Maybe reluctantly look at the 'self-preservation tactics' section too.

ADDICTION

Addictive behaviour is unfortunately often found alongside many peoples' mental health issues. Research indicates that some people have a predisposition to addiction, it is a sort of built in, hardwired tendency. For others it is an unintentional development started through using drugs or alcohol occasionally to feel better or to have fun. It is important to remember that this is not just the choice of people with mental health issues, it occurs widely across the population.

Addiction is a vicious task master which some people find impossible to beat. Helping someone with these problems is both frustrating and distressing as results are not likely to be immediate. It can appear that the family's support is apparently making no impact at all on the person, but the fact that someone is continuing to be involved and is caring about what happens to them can be worth a great deal, it can change the outcome. No matter how hopeless the situation appears it is worth persevering for as long as possible because people do make it through, however there is little benefit in the carer sacrificing their own health and wellbeing endlessly without any results. At some point a decision will have to be made.

The person knows that their habit is harmful, when someone tells them this it probably won't help because they are firmly convinced that they can't manage without this substance. There are not many people who smoke who don't know about lung cancer. They will give it up when they are ready and they feel like it, or so they believe. Those who have given up smoking or other deeply addictive habits, or failed to give them up, may understand better how this behaviour takes a hold.

Admitting to having an addiction is a useful place to start but that requires overcoming several psychological barriers such as:

- They are fine right now and see no reason to change.
- They do not want to admit their dependence on these drugs to anyone – or to themselves.
- They may not want to risk people finding out.
- They will not talk to a professional, this is admitting that it is a problem that is out of control.
- The drugs may mask another issue, such as mental health problems, which they feel unable to face.

- The carer's focus is the long-term outcome, but the goal of the person is the short-term relief of symptoms, including those of withdrawal. They can always stop it tomorrow.

It doesn't seem necessary to go into enormous detail about different types of drugs here, better to look for information just on the bit that is relevant. So just a few points and apologies if it seems to be stating the obvious. Although most people have a fair knowledge of drug use – and may indeed indulge – it becomes a different and even more complex when there is a mental health issue involved.

There is the conundrum as to whether drug use causes mental health issues or vice versa, the chicken and egg puzzle. The figures that are often mentioned say that about half of the people who misuse various substances will have a diagnosed mental health issue. So half haven't.

There is some proof that there is a direct causal link, a high likelihood that there is a connection with some drugs causing some symptoms (note 'some drugs and some symptoms'). There was a lot of media coverage a while ago about the stronger versions of cannabis and their part in triggering psychosis. But if a large group of people all took identical drugs (as many younger people do use skunk) only a minority would develop a long-term mental health condition. Other factors could be genetic, or maybe it's about stress levels and how well they are coping with life. Drug use often starts in adolescence, which is a highly testing time, so it may play a part but perhaps not be the whole picture.

The phrase 'self-medicating' is often used, perhaps with negative connotations. It may be more complicated than it seems. There is an established link between nicotine and schizophrenia, in that it helps a bit. Cannabis can really calm an anxious person and give a 'time out' from a working life of high stress – but can also apparently bring on paranoia and long-term psychosis. Stronger substances can induce periods of experiencing pleasant and even blissful peace. Very tempting when life is not how you want it to be.

There is also the rise of the 'legal highs' which seem to be a very lucrative market even though they are now illegal. These are not healthier versions of the old school basics; they are dangerous and do devastating harm. Most of us have heard of 'Spice', which seems to knock people out while they are still standing up. This, like many other substances, can be ordered for door to door service via the internet. That's what they tell me. My days of a sneaky bit of puff listening to Zappa are long gone.

So illegal drugs could in fact make the person feel better or remove them to a painless world more efficiently than the NHS can do. This avoids not only general depression about lifestyle or failure to succeed, it will also counteract mental health symptoms. The disadvantages are financial and long-term health damage, both of which are easily ignored if the next few hours can be managed.

A 'side effect' of buying street drugs is that vulnerable people may be introduced to the world of dealing. Tempted by the money or by a regular supply, this creates another level of challenges on top of everything else. Dealing also means social contact with people who can come across as friends to begin with, another temptation for an isolated person with mental health issues.

One situation to look out for particularly is 'cuckooing', which I have seen happen myself many years ago, it's nothing new. If a vulnerable person lives alone, they may be befriended and introduced to drugs by the local bad boys (sorry gender stereotype here), who can be persuasive and kind, then aggressive and threatening. Their home then gets taken over as a base for dealing and the tenant is gradually pushed out until the police hopefully spot what's going on. The person I saw this happen to was over sixty years old, had got a first-class honours degree from Cambridge University, schizophrenia and was a light user of cannabis until they got to him. He ended up spending nights on the street to avoid going home.

Alcohol is also a big topic in mental health. It can magnify feelings of depression, make anxiety worse and increase agitation and aggression. Like other (illegal) drugs, long-term use can result in poverty, poor nutrition and ill health, which greatly outweigh the short-term benefits. Alcohol is easily accessible and very importantly can bring a group of 'friends' at least for an evening. It seems that a lot of the population use alcohol in order to cope with life, sometimes this use gets out of control. Perhaps having a racing mind, frightening thoughts or just a fear of being socially outcast are greater reasons why that over-use might start.

Mental health teams can be very reluctant to take on someone whose addictions make them impossible to diagnose clearly or to form a working relationship with. They do have a duty to work with someone whose mental health issues are 'primary', their drug or alcohol habits are secondary, which can be a tricky distinction to make. Carers may need to be assertive in getting help, especially if there is a period of being 'clean' or sober when a proper mental health assessment can be made.

Trying to support someone who uses any drug, from nicotine to Class 'A's, there may be times when there are difficult decisions to make about how to react. Here are some suggestions that may be worth considering.

- Let them know that their drinking/ drug taking has been noticed and that the family is worried and upset by it; do this as soon as it is identified as a problem. Pretending not to notice means they have nothing to worry about and can carry on regardless.

- Never give them money or get them drugs, no matter how much they beg or threaten. This is easy to say but most of the carers I met who were supporting someone with a serious regular habit end up being 'tapped' for money. Saying 'yes' once means they will ask again, and again. It seems to be worth taking a stand from day one, or as soon as it is possible, and sticking to it. Watching them in a state of extreme desperation is hard to resist, it takes resolve and a conviction that this is the right thing to do.

- If they have no food then give them a loaf and some cheese rather than a tenner. If they are able to steal from the family, and this looks as though it is happening, then restrict their access as far as is possible to purses, wallets and goods that could be sold.

- In the worst situations it may be necessary to restrict access to the family home, perhaps only when another adult is present. This may mean negotiating the handover of the front door keys.

This is the famous 'tough love' approach, which holds no guarantees but as a long-term strategy has been considered better than supporting and prolonging their habit. It's not without risks, however, because if they feel the family are not supportive they may end up distancing themselves and therefore become even more vulnerable. In addition, they may resort to illegal means to get money and risk a police record. Not an easy decision to make.

Most people find a serious drug habit devastatingly expensive in the end, it is only the rich who can sustain one without financial hardship. If the family become the main source of money for an addiction it is to be expected that their lifestyle will be seriously damaged too.

If the person become threatening then involving the police

is always a possibility, even if it feels like the ultimate betrayal. It is likely that any aggressive behaviour driven by taking a drug will be viewed as a criminal offence rather than a mental health problem so legal proceedings may follow. Not calling for help means that the situation and the risks can continue unchecked.

An alternative is the 'safeguarding' option which can be worth investigating (anonymously if preferred). This applies where a vulnerable adult (elderly, disabled or a carer) is being threatened or pressured into parting with money or bullied into something they don't want to do. If Social Care is informed then a social worker will investigate. The police won't be involved unless there is a criminal act, this process works by mediation and getting the people involved to agree to resolve the problem, although this can be tough with an addiction. Getting someone else involved, particularly a professional, might help to control the situation as it is no longer totally under the person's control and their 'secret'.

If the person with the mental health issue gets a criminal record, then surely that is secondary to their wellbeing and safety. This is about balancing the carer and family's wellbeing and that of the person with the 'habit'.

There is no magic solution to stop people being addicts. If coming off the drugs or alcohol means that they experience mental health symptoms more strongly or they will lose their only group of 'friends' then it must be even harder to make that break. Professional support is there for people who are willing to accept it, but carers may have to wait a long time for them to get to that point where they ask for help, and sometimes then to get an appointment.

Pressurising people into treatment reduces the chances of it working. So what does the family do while they are waiting for the right moment? The answer seems to be mostly 'worry', so there follows some ideas about various situations that may come up and how other carers have said they approached them.

Keeping channels of communication open is easier if the family avoid confrontations. As with so many other situations, listening without judging or telling them what to do increases the chance of keeping a reasonable relationship going, and where the carer can be of some influence. Telling them what to do feels like an attempt at control, which will probably be resented, especially if they are aware that they are not actually in control themselves. A tense relationship with frequent flare ups will not be regarded as supportive, this doesn't mean that the carer can't be honest, but it could be safer to stick to talking from the 'I' perspective. So rather than 'you should' statements, maybe:

> 'It makes me very unhappy when I see you stoned/ high/drunk. I worry about you and wonder how I can help. I think of the time passing and how you seem stuck at the moment. I really hope you soon find the strength to get yourself out of it.'

It can be positive to talk about how their life could be better if this addiction stopped. They may fear this because there is nothing to fill the gap where their addiction has been. This is a tough one for people who have a long-term mental health issue as their 'things to look forward to' list may be quite short, but there is usually some new skill, an ambition or old activity they may be interested in. Talk about how things would be different – maybe more money or less hangovers. They could probably get a proper assessment of their mental health and therefore more effective treatment, whereas right now their symptoms are masked by their drug habits. Maybe there are old friends who would come back or new ones that would not be so unpleasant or unpredictable as their drug/drinking buddies.

It's the potential positives that could motivate, rather than the threat of negatives. The more they are criticized and judged the harder it is for them to try to come back to the other world. If they lose hope in themselves then this could reduce the motivation to recover.

They may blame the family for their addictive behaviour. This is part of not wanting to take responsibility for it, but it is worth listening in case there is any issue within that anger that can be addressed. It goes without saying that it is not constructive to join in an argument about who is responsible, but that is easier said than done.

If the carer or other family members also drink a lot or take other drugs then it is not a strong position to judge their actions, this will reduce effectiveness.

It is a challenge not to protect the person from the consequences of their actions. If they steal money or hit someone then, even with a mental health issue, there should be some penalties. There is no reason for them to change if nothing bad happens. Any reaction will hopefully consider the mental health aspect, but it should still be a negative consequence.

They will probably lie to the people that care for them the most. It isn't personal in that sense, it is a means to an end, their goal is always to feed their addiction. The family should let them know that they are aware of this lie, otherwise again it seems that there are no negative outcomes. The person needs to be told that they have made people upset and unhappy but that everyone still wants things to work out.

> 'I am really upset that you lied to me. I realise you are desperate sometimes, but it makes me feel I can't trust you. I would like to feel we could trust each other.'

Where can the carer get some support? If there are other family members who are directly involved, then can they share decisions? It is important that everyone involved has a consistent and shared attitude. If the carer is alone with this, then it is particularly valuable to search around locally for any organisation that might help. If there is a local service to support people in withdrawal then maybe they have a families' group. Carers may be able to go even if the person they support doesn't use the service. Is there a local 'Adfam' group, their website could also be helpful?

I have known families who have cut off contact, with the hope the person with the addiction makes it through and appear at the door again one day in a much better place. This is a horrendous judgement to make. Tough love at its most extreme. If there is damage being done to other people, then the decision will probably involve a stark choice between those others and carrying on supporting the person with the addiction. Usually this point is reached only after every effort and sacrifice has been made, and the family's influence has been greatly reduced because the addiction has taken an unshakeable hold. One of the few comforts for carers who face this situation is that they are far from being alone.

I have known people who seemed beyond help finally making changes and coming to live a safer life, so it's always worth carrying on hoping.

DISASSOCIATION

We occasionally use the term 'disassociate' when people separate themselves from a social group or a political party. In mental health there is a symptom called 'disassociation' which means that the person is cut off from other aspects of themselves and/or from the world around them.

The effect may be physical, the person may be unable to feel or move, there may be a temporary paralysis. There is a possibility of seizures in a small minority, it can be confused with epilepsy. It seems that the brain is unable to register what is happening in parts of the body for a short time, but no physical cause can be found. There is an apparent absence of any response, sensation or movement is blocked.

Alternatively, the loss may be in retrieving memories, this is 'dissociative amnesia'. This can lead to the horrible experience of finding yourself somewhere and having no idea how you got there. I used to know a young man who would sometimes find himself in places he didn't recognise but what could be worse was being in a social situation when he would blank out and then come back having missed everything. No one knew he experienced this, he would try to appear as though nothing had happened, but he struggled with anxiety and he frequently chose to remain alone.

People may also forget a skill that they once used regularly. Again, it appears that a part of the communication system in the brain just refuses to function, but no physical cause can be found.

Currently the theory is that the brain 'overloads' when there is too much fear and distress and cuts off as a means of protecting the self. It often begins after a traumatic experience such as abuse or an accident. The cutting off reaction can be a short-term response to this trauma or recur for some time, for years in the more serious cases. The episodes can be for seconds, days or, rarely, much longer. In effect the brain has partly shut down as a means of coping with extreme trauma but is repeating this action at intervals even though the threat is no longer present. There may also be other physical causes as yet undiscovered.

Disassociation is also a frequently mentioned feature of some personality disorders. This feeling of being outside or absent from the self must be frightening to say the least. People experiencing EUPD describe having no sense of identity, of being empty inside.

ARE YOU OK IN THERE?

The most extreme version of this symptom is in 'dissociative identity disorder' (DID). This used to be known as multiple personality disorder or split personality a while ago. It played a major role in some mental health mythology – but has nothing to do with schizophrenia (despite the jokes that are still told).

It is an extremely unpleasant diagnosis where the genuine sufferers are not able to identify with just one identity, they sense at least one other personality within themselves, sometimes several. They have a real challenge with the process of getting control of these separate characters who are distinct from each other and have traits of their own. The individual can move in and out of these identities, probably not in a controlled way at least to begin with. Each personality is distinctly different; this would include age, gender and abilities as well as characteristics.

This 'split personality' label is open to misuse when people self-diagnose, misinterpreting when they have different moods or see themselves as having different personalities in different situations. Why it surprises some people that they behave/feel differently on a hot date than they do when they are at work on Monday morning beats me. Personally, I don't buy into a 'real me' model, I think we all respond to where we are in place and time and how we feel and behave can differ greatly. Even so each person's memory stays intact in each scenario, they have no problem in thinking about what has happened to them a few hours ago. People with DID may not carry information across identities reliably, at least not until they manage to gain some control.

The people I have spoken to who experience this condition (and there are very, very few) talk of being in chaos, having gaps in memory, feeling unable to find a 'central self' and unable to function comfortably in a social situation. Increasingly as they may become aware of their personalities, there can be a growing ability to organise the self(s) so life is more manageable.

Sometimes a negotiation can take place between the identities or an agreement to share time 'at the front' or help each other out. Sometimes they will support each other if there is a negative character to cope with or a young child to care for within the personality 'group'.

DID has its origins in extreme and often prolonged trauma, possibly it is a result of the brain reacting by distancing itself from the present situation and creating an alternative reality in order to survive.

For someone who has not experienced DID no description will make it real, it is just so far from everyday life. The couple of people I spoke to who had apparently genuinely got this diagnosis were certainly living as well as they could. They had to be careful not to take on anything too complex or be extravagantly sociable, but they had found a means of having a peaceful coexistence with these various facets of themselves. This progress had taken a great deal of help and personal determination.

Just to repeat that despite the myths (like the one that schizophrenia is a split personality) this condition is real but extremely rare. The chances are heavily in your favour that whatever you are going to have to deal with, this ain't it.

SELF-HARM

This is not a mental health problem in itself; it is a symptom that appears when something is seriously out of balance. It's a complex topic because people practice it for varying reasons, I can only give my point of view based on people I've talked to.

Those who don't have much contact with the world of mental health may find this an alien and scary subject. What would cause anyone to cut themselves, even one small cut, it seems to be an action that has no possible explanation. It is worth trying to understand this behaviour, the fact that so many people do it implies that it is something we humans find helpful in some way, for whatever reason.

I think it is difficult to trust statistics because self-reporting is bound to be inaccurate and how do you define deliberate self-harm? Is drinking too much alcohol? Is repeatedly picking scabs or biting nails down to the quick? Is having relationships only with violent partners?

For most of us self-harm means cutting, usually the arms, but legs and stomach may also be chosen especially when the person wants to keep it hidden. Some people prefer burning, some swallow bleach, some fill their shoes with small stones, pull their hair out and some scrape themselves against walls until they bleed. People can be endlessly inventive.

Self-harm is not the same as a suicide attempt; on the contrary it is often very much a means to survive. The crucial question is if it's not a conscious attempt to die then what is it? Why hurt yourself? Self-harm is just that, it is causing yourself pain. For some people this can just be a small amount, such as one small cut or burn. It can be occasional or regular and often people have routines that they follow. Occasionally the pain and injury that is inflicted is severe, the chances of this happening increase if they are drinking or in a mental health crisis.

The damage done can be life-threatening but usually this is an unintended consequence rather than a deliberate strategy, though it can be very risky behaviour. There are people who walk a fine line between controlled actions and playing a sort of Russian roulette where they take far too many pills or jump off high bridges just to see if they will survive or not. Sometimes people who have a long history of self-harming have a great deal of knowledge as to where the safety line lies and may either choose to stay inside it or to risk crossing it to add to the experience. Nevertheless, despite knowing the risk and sometimes taking chances it doesn't appear to be a straightforward desire to die.

Pain is a warning to the body that something is wrong and loads of reactions set in to create a temporary numbness. It has been suggested that these reactions work on an area of the brain that also registers emotional distress so it may be that the healing process soothes both the mental and the physical. That doesn't seem to be enough of an explanation because when I hurt myself I definitely feel the pain, maybe there is a numb pause, but this doesn't last that long.

People who self-harm often experience low self-esteem. This is not a term to be taken likely, perhaps saying self-hate or self-loathing would be more accurate. So maybe the causing of pain is a sort of punishment. This cannot be the whole story because so many people describe it as a coping strategy, a means to survive.

It seems to be a distraction from great emotional distress, a useful disruption in that moment, a new focus. When thoughts are racing, loud, overwhelming and demanding, this act of cutting can create a pause and a temporary calm.

People have also said that they can feel emotionless, they feel nothing. Pain is proof that they are still alive.

So maybe it is to punish, or to distract, or to feel something, or even to reward as some people clearly regard it as a 'treat'. I used to have regular helpline conversations with a woman who had used self-harm as a coping technique for many years. She had come to manage it by allowing herself to do it only on a Friday evening. Her ritual was to draw an oblong on her upper arm that would measure an exact size. She then allowed herself to fill that space with cigarette burns but had to restrict herself to that area. Listening to her I realised that she looked forward to this time, it was a means of keeping herself safe. If she is still out there somewhere, I do hope she is still managing as well now as she was then.

Self-harm can be very private, in fact it is often someone's guilty secret that they would go to great lengths to hide. Some people, though, seem to parade their scars like trophies and use them to make a public declaration. In my experience, the people who are really out and proud about this have been harming a long time and have many, many scars. Often there are no fresh wounds and that indicates that these people are in a better place now and are getting by without new cuts, but they perhaps don't want either themselves or others to forget their history. It is attention seeking but that is completely understandable. We all like attention now and then, these people have undoubtedly been through stuff that most of us cannot imagine.

There are online sites where you can post pictures of even your private wounds completely anonymously. This is potentially dangerous as any peer group can offer either support or pressure. Some sites become competitive, encouraging people to greater injury. There have been cases that illustrate how dangerous these influences are, and not just for young people.

Finding that someone in the family is hurting themselves deliberately can be tough to come to terms with. It can feel as though they have not been supported enough, that the carer has failed in some way. The first reaction is often one of horror and an immediate desire to stop this behaviour. This can lead to highly emotional scenes which may be a natural reaction but make the situation more volatile and increase the distress, which in turn can lead to more need to self-harm.

Strong attempts to persuade people to stop also create anxiety, which contributes to needing to do it more. One tactic sometimes suggested is to make them promise not to cut or burn in any given period, i.e. 'I am going out until 5 pm, will you promise me not to cut yourself while I am out.' They may well agree but the promise makes them focus on this topic. A regular drinker, dependent on alcohol, if asked not to drink for a few hours would probably spend the next couple of hours panicking, focussing on having a drink and then rush out and have a huge binge. Self-harm can create a similar reaction.

Why not hide all the knives and razors? Because they will use a bit of broken cup or a shattered CD.

Offering rewards or punishments seems an obvious tactic but their need may well be far bigger than anything that can be offered right now.

It is worth suggesting that when they are feeling as though they might self-harm to ask for some time to talk, to see if this will reduce their tension. If the carer can keep that talk to 80% listening and trying to understand, rather than repetitious lectures as to why they should feel good about themselves and how it's all going to be OK this could help. This takes much practice. This may sound harsh, but I know myself that I start these supportive sessions with good intentions and end up giving the same old ineffective sermon.

If it happens and their injuries look in any way serious then they need to go to hospital. No messing about. A useful tip is to bind the wound with cling film to keep it clean before it gets treated. Calling an ambulance means faster treatment but this is only necessary if it looks serious. These days ambulances may not be readily available so it could be faster to go by car.

The positive side to this is that the experience of A&E is usually unpleasant so it may well act as a bit of a deterrent. The wait can be long and treatment uncomfortable. Some nursing staff used to be noticeably negative and make comments about time wasting and attention seeking. Rumour has it that the occasional nurse even refused to give an anaesthetic for stitches as the person must 'like pain'. Hopefully, those staff are retiring now, but it must be wearing for busy nurses to see the same person repeatedly for a self-inflicted injury.

If they don't need to go to hospital the wound needs

cleaning, antiseptic cream and a clean dressing as infection is often more dangerous than the cut itself. Burns should be run under tepid, not cold water and anything that might stick to it moved away. Get information on how to treat the wound or call 111 for advice.

The carer may want to dress the injury and they probably will the first few times. If the self-harm continues then it is preferable that the person starts to look after themselves and take care of the wound. This sounds unfeeling but the feedback is that it helps the situation stay calmer, there is no outside attention, the person must cope with the consequences but may find that they want to do this. This 'care of the self' routine can also be part of increasing self-reliance, which is very much a positive outcome.

It can be hard for a family to avoid going into spy/surveillance mode and constantly monitoring where this person is and what they are doing. Worrying about them means that the carer(s) become hypervigilant like meerkats on sentry duty, but this is exhausting. The result might be not going out, staying awake all night, set up shifts with other family members, etc. This is not sustainable, nor does it achieve much and in the end a compromise is inevitable.

One brave option is to create a self-harm kit for them that they can access at any time. This may seem like encouragement but in reality no one is going to stop this behaviour, but it can be made as safe as possible. This kit may include a sterile blade, dressings, steri-strips and antiseptic cream. The carer or the person with the mental health issue can maintain it, but it must be easily accessible without having to ask for it. Knowing it's there can be reassuring, which may in turn lead to using it less often and eventually not at all. This is a highly likely ending to the story but it's a long-term goal that has no 'fast forward' button to press.

Focussing on reducing the levels of distress that they are

experiencing is the most effective approach, tackling the cause rather than the symptom.

SELF-ESTEEM

The usual definition is 'confidence in one's own worth or abilities; self-respect.'

This term often arises in discussions about someone who has a mental health diagnosis and can take on a kind of magical quality as a catch-all reason why they are feeling so bad and are not able to help themselves more.

Talking to families it occasionally appears that this term is used in inverted commas with an air of distrust about it. Isn't it just an excuse? Is it just a sign of weakness? Why, when they have a reasonable home and the same life as their siblings or friends should they 'feel bad about themselves'. Everyone has a poor opinion about some aspect of themselves, those that say they feel they are completely competent and confident in every situation are probably in trouble and don't get to go to many parties.

There appears to be a combination of things going on under the self-esteem label. One factor is that a lot of mental health issues include a high level of anxiety, so the default mindset is 'it's all gone wrong, it will all go wrong, it will always go wrong, it must be my fault'. This is accompanied by feelings of dread and foreboding, especially where there is paranoia in the mix. If they are coming to get you then maybe you deserve it, you have been singled out for this.

Our self-image is constructed from an early age and is shaped both by our own psychological processes and the people around us. Having a mental health problem is going to interfere with the ability to be strong in the face of life events. It also possible that this person has been a bit different at school or at work and has not felt accepted or fitted in well. They may even have been bullied. Once someone is sensitive to funny looks or snide remarks they are easily imagined, even if they are not really happening. This is called 'selective perception': people see what they expect to see. Many who have mental health issues and some who don't believe that others are always talking about them negatively or thinking critical thoughts. Many live with the constant concern 'what will the neighbours think'.

I have had the experience of walking into a room and instantly suspecting that either people have been talking about me or they are ignoring me. This can be based on a couple of pieces of very slight evidence, like failed eye contact or someone looking at me in a particular way, or a natural pause in the conversation and the rest is filled in by my sense of inadequacy – and I am classified officially as 'normal'. I am sure I'm not alone, so how much worse must it be if you have long standing serious doubts about your own worth and how other people judge you. Self-fulfilling prophecy, as they say.

Example: I was sitting outside a café with a woman who has a long-term serious mental health condition and who often seemed sullen and uncommunicative. She suddenly said, 'See they are talking about me again.' I asked who and she explained that the crowd of young people next to us had called her 'Monster'. I hadn't heard anything but noticed that they were all drinking 'Monster' high energy drinks. This seemed to be a clear case of her expectations feeding into her conviction that she was a target for abuse. However, she also said that in the school holidays the local kids would follow her across the green to the shops shouting 'Nutter' and 'Mad Cow Disease' and similar taunts. That I was inclined to accept as realistic.

In addition, a lot of people hear either voices or intrusive thoughts. These are loops that replay *ad nauseam* and are frequently abusive and critical. There may be a running commentary that preoccupies the person for most of their waking hours, maybe something like this:

> 'Look at you, you're so ugly. You know you are ugly, and that people will see. Listen to that laughing, they are laughing at you. You look like a nutter. Everyone knows. You are a nutter, and everyone can see it. That man over there, he just looked at you and now he's crossed the road so he doesn't have to go near you. You are ugly and mad. You should be locked up. If people knew what you are really like they would lock you up and throw away the key.'

Not everyone gets these thoughts, voices or commentaries but for those that do, they understandably colour their whole world.

A family can really help here by being supportive although everything that is said may apparently be rejected. This may need to walk a fine line by offering realistic comments, so not just pretending that things don't matter or that they are not important. It isn't that helpful to say, 'You can be anything you want to be', because people can't. They can try though, and encouragement is valuable even if they never succeed.

If a carer says, 'It doesn't matter that you didn't go to college this week' then the person will probably understand that actually that is not true, or they may think that no one cares that they 'failed.' Finding a way to acknowledge that it didn't work out but not being critical of the situation may be more helpful. Perhaps something like:

> 'I'm sorry you didn't make it to college today. You probably feel that is a bit of a knock back. I'm sure you struggled a lot before you decided not to go, it must have been a hard decision. Is there anything you can think of that will help you go next time?'

Phrasing things non-judgementally comes naturally after some practise and could help hang on to a relationship with this fragile person who is being harsh enough on themselves without any external criticism.

Self-esteem issues may make communication difficult; it can be easy to get into a pantomime routine:

'You're a kind and helpful person.'
'No, I'm not.'
'Yes, you are. I think you are.'
'You don't know me.'
'But I know how you behave and you're always kind and considerate.'
'No, I'm not.'
'Really, I think you are very nice'
'You're only saying that because you have to.'

A family may feel despair in the face of persistent negativity or periods of self-criticism, but it is crucial to try to remain supportive. See it as sowing seeds; they may take a while to grow but they can only help.

NERVOUS BREAKDOWN

This term is used frequently as a description of someone's state of mind when they can no longer maintain their usual routine and the apparent reason for this is their mental health. Things become too much, the individual is overwhelmed and simply can no longer function. This can be a short interlude or a prolonged inability to hold it together. Sometimes it is also applied to a situation when a person 'loses it' and has a hysterical or abusive outburst that is out of character. I knew a man who worked for a long time as a support worker but suddenly, in a time of uncertainty about his job, started shouting racist and sexist abuse in his office and wouldn't stop for some time. This was also described as a nervous breakdown.

This isn't an official diagnosis; it is more a description of a major change in behaviour and the cause is not specified. The most likely reasons are underlying anxiety, depression or another mental health diagnosis, it could be brought on by a period of increased stress. It may be a useful term in general conversation to describe someone being unable to function for a time, but it is not specific about the cause.

The general public seem to accept this as description of a mental health 'incident' and as such it could be a useful way of letting people know what is going on without offering too much personal detail.

TREATMENTS

The first step to getting treatment is to be assessed by a mental health practitioner, usually a psychiatrist or a senior nurse who will decide if this individual meets the criteria for having a mental health diagnosis. If so, then a treatment package would be offered.

If the professional doing the assessment feels that this person should be under a different team, either someone more specialist or less specialist than themselves, then it can mean another referral and another assessment.

The GP, the mental health teams and the hospital units all have the same range of treatments to offer although the mental health (secondary) services have more specialist options for the more complex diagnoses.

A divide comes between 'mild to moderate' conditions, which include depression and anxiety with associated issues which are usually managed within primary care, at GP level. Then there are the 'moderate to severe' diagnoses – most commonly bi-polar, schizophrenia, very severe depression, personality disorders and other diagnoses that are more complex or that involve a degree of risk. This risk could be something like suicide attempts, behaviour that potentially puts their life in danger or could cause harm to others. It is worth noting that the definition of what is a substantial risk will always vary, a professional can seemingly be unmoved by circumstances that the family find completely traumatic, because they have more experience of these issues and are not emotionally involved.

All services potentially have three categories of treatment available:

- Medication and other 'physical' interventions
- Talking treatments
- Coping skills for staying well and increased independence

MEDICATION

I am not a clinician, I guess that is probably apparent, but that means that this bit is very much from a layperson's perspective. I am relieved (as are probably many others) that I never had the responsibility of prescribing medication, it seems an extraordinarily complex job at the best of times and even more so with mental health diagnoses. My experience comes from many conversations on the subject with both professionals and the people who take it.

It appears that some of the mental health medications were found by accident while trying to treat something else and no one really knows how they work. That doesn't sound very reassuring, and frequently there are cruel side effects to be endured, but despite that it is this medication that keeps many people alive, takes them out of extreme distress and gives them back a life.

Meds are also not a 'cure'. This is a tough one to deal with both for the individual concerned and their family. They treat the symptoms by lessening the anxiety, lifting the mood, maybe damping down the voices if that is an issue. The cause of these symptoms could be a wide variety of things that cannot yet be directly medicated away. If they stop taking their medication the initial symptoms may return. This is particularly problematic as an individual may be very keen to stop taking it, especially as they feel fine now. When the symptoms reappear there is great disappointment, but often this circle needs to be gone round quite a few times before the realisation that this is a long-term thing.

There is no list here of all the possible drugs and their side effects, details are easy to find but it is a long job to look at every possible anti-depressant or anti-psychotic and until the medication is prescribed there is little point. Once it is selected there are several options to get more information:

- Look at the leaflet in the packet. Of course, this is only available after the prescription has been filled but it is the most comprehensive and reliable source of information.
- Sources on the internet. NHS websites are often helpful because these include the complete leaflet that would be found in the packet (if someone hadn't put it in the bin). All that is needed is the name of the drug. Some mental health trusts have a section on their websites with medication information and so do the Royal College of Psychiatrists (patients' information section).
- Ask a pharmacist; they are particularly helpful if there are worries about combining drugs, especially when some may have been prescribed for a physical health problem and there is poor communication between the involved doctors, as is sometimes the case.

Looking at the side effects is scary stuff so it can be a difficult decision for both the individual and the family to consider medication. If the mental health issue is a relatively minor one, medication may be an optional, temporary fix to give some time out, a little respite, until normal coping strategies can be restored. If it is a severe problem, medication presents the only choice which works reasonably quickly and reduces distress and potential risks. Other treatments can be enormously helpful but currently these medications are the best thing available when someone is really suffering. Finding one that suits, that has manageable side-effects, and which reduces the symptoms successfully, this is the key to accessing a whole new quality of life.

Many carers take anti-depressants to cope with their situation, often as a means of surviving a tense time while having to continue to function. Some use them long-term. Strikes me as sensible when you are under pressure and in a situation where many people would either walk away or lock themselves in their bedrooms for a month or two.

Despite being the quickest response some medications take weeks to really work, it is useful to know about this. Side effects are usually worse in the first few weeks and this stop many people from persevering to the point where they can really assess the full benefit. This can be a huge blow to family who have carefully and painfully cajoled the person into asking for help only to have them reject it because the medication makes them feel anaesthetised or 'zombified' and doesn't seem to be helping much.

It is worth bearing in mind that not all side effects happen for everyone, some people get mild reactions and some stronger. If the reaction is unpleasant then the decision is either to stop the medication, change it and try something else, or tolerate the adverse reactions. Some side effects can be reduced by taking another drug which will counteract them.

One off-putting effect of some of the most popular anti-psychotics is weight gain. This doesn't happen to everybody but does seem to be common. This is hard on people's self-esteem, as are side effects such as impotence in young men.

Some medication can cause long-term unfair wear and tear on the system and have worrying implications for future, but the overall consideration is the 'big rock v. hard place' question. The family now know what this person is like without medication. Is this the best option for them right now? What is the probable outcome for them if they don't take it? How will they and the family cope if things carry on as they were?

Talking to the psychiatrist or a senior nurse is often possible and helps to make a family based decision whether the medication is or isn't the best option. If there is a consensus of opinion this can help the person with the mental health issues to think through their choices, but whatever the rest of the family agree on it is their decision alone in the end. People cannot be made to take medication unless they are under a Mental Health Act section.

Some medication is available via injection (a depot) which has both a positive and a negative aspect. It means that they definitely get the right amount and don't have to worry about it for two to four weeks, or sometimes longer, as the effect lasts that long. People have told me that the effect does fluctuate a bit though, with a strong impact after the injection but lessening over time, so the few days before the next jab can be a bit wobbly.

The type of medication prescribed first may not work as well as it should, so this means a return visit to the psychiatrist - this may be a different person - who may suggest a change. This requires the unpleasant process of withdrawing from Meds 1 with the impact of that, then starting Meds 2 with a different set of side effects. Many people with mental health issues end up on a cocktail of several different pills; this is not because of mistakes but may be necessary to counteract different symptoms or to reduce side effects.

If they are on variety of pills that need to be taken several times a day and require a complicated timetable and careful management, it may help to make this as simple as possible. 'Dosette' boxes can be useful as they can be loaded up with the daily pill regime a week in advance, this may save the carer from having to be so hands on, it is also easier to check if they have been taken. Taking a double dose by mistake can be very unpleasant so a Dosette box avoids many problems.

Managing someone's meds for them is one of those tricky carer dilemmas. There may be times when asking them to manage this is too hazardous, and they need a regular dose to stay well. However, in the long term it is important that having responsibility for their own medication regime is a vital part of independence and should always be a goal. There can be a middle phase where the carer reminds and monitors, but this can be a cause of some tension, it can feel like nagging. Sometimes the carer must play the long game of allowing the person they support to feel the effects of not getting the appropriate medication and to accept the importance of taking it as prescribed.

Don't think that there isn't research going on to improve the situation, there are millions being invested in new medication. Mental health is an expensive problem with a devastating effect on the country's workforce and care bills. When I first started out as a naïve young thing in the mental health system, the medication for psychosis was cruel and the side effects totally disabling. Men would produce breast milk and be impotent and women grew hairy chins. These old drugs basically made people walking zombies a lot of the time. There would be muscular twitches, shuffling and a lolling tongue often accompanied by drooling which all made the person fairly conspicuous. It's a lot better now, honestly, a whole lot better. I cannot say this more strongly, it is greatly improved although still far from easy to take and far from perfect.

Many families say they find their relatives over-medicated

particularly when they are in-patients. It's true that during a hospital stay the doses are often increased and the sedative effect can be very worrying. Usually it is reduced slowly after going back home. If this is not happening or not happening fast enough then it is worth asking why, but sometimes it is caution about avoiding another flare-up of symptoms. Again, a pharmacist can give advice, but it is the psychiatrist that makes the decision.

These days there are civilised conversations between psychiatrists and people with mental health diagnoses, at least I have heard many. Options are discussed and side effects openly talked about. The person's opinion and their preferences are considered. I can remember when the psychiatrist's mantra was, 'Go home, take meds, ask no questions. Oh and P.S. don't expect much of a life.' The medical model appears to still be strong but there is a much greater recognition of the importance of the individual's opinion and attitude. People with mental health issues are expected to be involved in decisions about their treatment and making it work. This sense of control and choice encourages a positive attitude towards taking medication which can be central to long term stability.

EMDR (EYE MOVEMENT DESENSITIZATION AND REPROCESSING)

This is not a talking therapy but one that acts directly on the cognitive processes, particularly around memory. It reduces the emotional impact of traumatic images by performing some odd distractions such as eye movements at certain times while focussing on these distressing topics. The actual trauma does not have to be explored out loud, it can be represented with a 'safe' symbol. For people who have experienced a devastating ordeal it can help to facilitate a much less distressed life by reducing the emotional impact that these events can hold, even long after they occurred.

Unlikely as it sounds it has been sufficiently verified by research that it is now available on the NHS, although practitioners can be a scarce resource. There are private options for treatment, but it would make sense to get a definite diagnosis and check with a psychiatrist before investing a lot of money, it will take some sessions to work. It would make sense to be certain that it stood a good chance of being effective.

ECT (ELECTRO CONVULSIVE THERAPY)

This is offered only in extreme circumstances where the person remains seriously distressed despite other treatments having been tried. ECT sounds primitive and frightening but if it is offered it is for a good reason; it has a chance of working when medication is not proving effective and there is a serious level of risk because of the person's mental health. Maybe they won't eat or are repeatedly attempting suicide.

This treatment must be approved by the patient, who is encouraged to talk to a family member or an advocate about this decision. They are offered information on the procedure and the side effects. If they do not have the capacity or understanding to decide whether they want to try a course of ECT or not, then there must be a second opinion from another psychiatrist before any treatment can proceed.

No one seems to quite know how it works. An electric current is passed across the head, which causes a short spike in brain activity which seems to 'reset' it. This feels crude but it is far less intimidating these days, it is not the grim procedure once portrayed in films. Many people feel some benefit and for some it literally saves their life – but there are possible side effects such as some memory loss.

If there is any concern about being forced to have ECT

then it is worth reminding people that there is no chance that they will go to the GP in the morning and find themselves strapped down for ECT the same afternoon. GPs cannot prescribe it; it must be authorized by a psychiatrist. It is a gradual process of eliminating other options, the patient has the final say if they are able to understand the risks and it is only used where there is a serious threat to that individual's health or safety. And often it works.

TALKING TREATMENTS

Sessions with a therapist are structured according a specific model, there are several to choose from and each follows certain guidelines according to the preferred approach. Therapists are not there to give advice but to offer a chance to consider options and encourage the person to approach the problems in specific ways. The choice of which model to use will vary with the diagnosis and how the person is affected, as some models work better in different circumstances.

These talking sessions are highly personal and most carers I met felt it wasn't their job to enquire too closely what goes on in them unless the person chose to talk about it. The drive home afterwards seemed to include a conversation a bit like this:

'So how was it?'

'How was what?'

'Your session today with the therapist/psychologist/insert name here'

'Oh, OK.'

'You found it useful?'

'Hmmm.'

'Do you think it's going to be helpful?'

'Maybe.'

'Will you go next week, do you think?'
'I'll see. Can we get a coffee now?'

Not everyone is so reluctant to talk about it but don't be surprised if this is the reaction.

Families should recognise that these sessions can also be a tough option and make people feel pressured, emotional or just plain tired; it may be a touchy and sensitive time.

There is a general myth that all mental health issues will magically disappear if the person just 'talks about it'. The right sort of talking can be extraordinarily effective with some people some of the time, but it is important to realise that not all talking treatments are suitable or effective and can increase tension and distress if mistimed. One negative outcome is when there has been a build-up of anticipation before the sessions begin, perhaps with a long wait for an appointment, but then the person with the mental health issue does not feel able to continue for whatever reason and drops out. This can be a big disappointment especially if there are few options left to try. However, many people do find the process helpful, it can literally be life changing.

Generally, the more severe the symptoms the more time and specialist knowledge would be needed to bring about change, and talking alone may not be enough, especially when things are at their worst.

THERAPY MODELS

Psychotherapy has been adopted as the generic term for talking treatments across the board, it seems. This used to describe what is now called psychodynamic therapy. This is proper old school, as they say. It's been around a long time and is associated with couches and men with little round glasses and beards. Ignoring the stereotypes, it is an effective approach for some people and involves a lengthy exploration of a person's past and present by looking at events and feelings in detail. The purpose of this self-exploration is to examine what might be causing the current unhelpful issues.

This can take a year or more and relies heavily on that individual's insight and awareness. In my experience it is prescribed infrequently on the NHS, but that may be because it is hard to research results so there are not many practitioners around, the lengthy treatment is expensive. Privately there are many options.

Counselling is also dependent on the person's own insight, but it tends to be a much shorter process. The conversation is led, to a large degree, by the client who is free to explore their key issues in a safe and confidential place. The counsellor will ask questions and make observations to guide them but does not give advice or control what is discussed. A counsellor's approach is based on the belief that everyone can find their own solutions given the right space to think about it. Again this requires a degree of self-awareness and willingness to get to the root of what is going on, which can be hugely effective with depression or anxiety issues, possibly not with those symptoms that make it harder to think clearly or reason rationally.

Some carers are offered free or low-cost counselling, it is worth considering seriously. I have met many carers who really appreciated the 'me' time. It does not mean there is a mental health issue but there is little doubt that it is a stressful situation to cope with. Counselling will not include advice on how to be a carer but will include time to talk through the effects of this experience and to 'come to terms' with what has happened. There are many emotional issues for carers that can be usefully thought through with a stranger who is uninvolved and who knows how to listen.

The approach that is used most frequently in mental health

these days is cognitive behavioural therapy (CBT). This is a relatively recent development and it has proved its value in research, which means that it is funded well and widely available particularly to people with depression and anxiety. GPs have services that they can refer to directly which could go under a variety of names, but the umbrella term is an 'improved access to psychological therapies' (IAPT) service. This could be as well as, or instead of, writing a prescription. CBT could be offered on a one-to-one or group basis.

This model explores how people are thinking, feeling and behaving as this can create disabling 'circles' in their lives. The therapist is more directive and will focus on specific topics and set 'homework'. An example: suppose a young man is not leaving his flat because he believes that he looks socially conspicuous and that anyone who sees him will know immediately that he is inferior in some way, that he is different from other people. This difference would mostly be based on self-esteem issues, a sense of being unworthy.

He may explore this feeling with the therapist, they may identify that there is a circle that keeps this self-imposed isolation in place.

THE BELIEF – I am inferior to others and people can see this as soon as they look at me.

THE FEELING – I feel frightened and anxious at the thought of going out because of what people will be thinking about me or what they might say.

THE ACTION – I don't go out. As a result, I never know if my theory that I will attract negative attention is true or not.

The therapist would work to create rapport and a sense of safety and trust. Then they would try to test the client's theory that they stood out as being different by talking about why the person thought this was true. This would not include any judgement on their beliefs. Then they would gradually encourage them to test their theory by trying small steps into the outside world.

We all seem to be fooled into believing that what we think is true, but often what we mistake for fact is just an opinion. We often believe we know what other people are thinking, for example, but in reality we have no idea. Maybe just as well.

CBT is a skilled and sensitive negotiation; it is an attempt to dismantle unhelpful beliefs and put more effective coping strategies in their place. Carers I have met seldom feel confident in the role of therapist, maybe a professional finds it easier to stay neutral and not give advice or pass judgement. It's all too easy for carers to slip into the 'what you need to do' speech or second guess what people are going to say because they know them well.

There can be a wait to see a CBT practitioner, they can be an oversubscribed service, but there are several online resources to start a bit of preliminary work that can help particularly with anxiety and depression. It may be worth searching and even pay a small fee if it means there is a mental health practitioner monitoring the site and responding now and then. Anything that helps the individual gain some relaxation skills is good groundwork; guided meditations are popular it seems.

The more complex conditions, even those with hallucinations and delusions, can also be helped using CBT but the therapist would need specialist training. This work would not be focussed on challenging any unusual ideas but joining forces with the person to make their beliefs less disabling and distressing. The classic example is about people who have a sense that they are being pursued by powerful beings who are out to harm them. These beings may have special equipment that can read that person's mind, many feel that their thoughts are being interfered with. Some of these people feel far safer with aluminium foil in their hats as it will reduce this activity.

This may seem weird to the rest of us (who may have a lucky mug or feel jumpy on Friday 13th) but the therapist has found a way to make that person's life better. They don't challenge but neither do they collude; they just support the person to suggest strategies that will help them cope better and be less distressed.

SKILLS FOR INDEPENDENCE

The final category of treatments is the 'anything else' section. Most of my career has been in centres where people had the opportunity to:

Work on how they would like to improve their day-to-day life
Work on reducing the impact of their symptoms
Talk to staff if they were struggling – and be monitored when they were in a tricky patch
(Re)learn social skills by talking to each other
Reduce social isolation
Access creative opportunities such as art or crafts, which are lifelines for some people
Get support to access other opportunities such as classes, voluntary work, environmental projects, etc.
Attend training sessions on a wide variety of topics
Get support to sort out tenancies and benefits
Have a laugh

These general support facilities are now much reduced, but they are still around. They are usually run by voluntary organisations and are worth exploring if the person with the mental health issue will go. The GP, mental health team or Carers' Centre will probably be happy to give any carer a pile of leaflets or they can be researched online, the local authority's website probably lists the ones they fund.

These services are not for everyone, bringing individuals together just because they all have mental health issues does not guarantee that they will get on well or that they will feel better for this contact. It's a bit like putting a load of people in a room and expecting them to be the best of friends just because they are all over eighty or Chinese. I have known several people who have come to look at a centre and never come back because they don't want to spend time with 'mental patients', (that is a quote). My own feeling is that these centres are wonderful for some and no appeal at all for others.

The focus these days is much more on one-to-one work to improve access to life in the community. Better to go to the local college than a mental health facility. Although that is undoubtedly true there are some people who need an interim step before facing this, after all this concept of community is mostly made up of:

- Classes and coffee mornings, usually in a local college or community centre
- Church
- Pub
- Library
- Voluntary work

These can all be either intimidating, unhealthy or unwelcoming. I shan't specify which is which. However, they can provide wonderful encouragement and support for people who find the right niche for themselves and give them a sense of purpose, which is an excellent place to start. The alcohol free ones are probably preferable.

Other useful mental health services are focussed on specific activities such as gardening, bike repair, creative arts, environmental work and others. These offer the possibility of being part of a team and having a meaningful goal to work towards. With a bit of luck there are still some of these being funded across the country.

THE RECOVERY MODEL

Sometime in the 1980s there was a slow but exciting change in the philosophy behind treatment for mental health conditions. Previously it had been pretty much based on giving people medication and trying to find them some 'meaningful occupation' or forcing them together and feeding them tea and cake. Options that were offered regularly involved painting pictures, gardening and charity shop work. These were frequently dictated by what was available or what other people felt would be useful for the 'patient' to do.

I was astounded in my first contact with an occupational therapy session for the longer-term residents in an old school psychiatric hospital where the main activity was apparently knitting dishcloths. The newbie occupational therapy assistant had the job of unravelling the dishcloths after the session so they could be knitted again the next day. Those days have gone, thank goodness.

The new 'Recovery' model starts from the understanding that a person's mental health will improve if they have a fulfilling life. It has to be said at this point that the word 'recovery' is misleading as it implies that the person will go back to exactly how they were before any symptoms occurred, but this may not be the case. The purpose of the exercise is to get the person to live the best life they can with whatever skills and abilities they have, which is all any of us can do really.

This process starts by identifying in some detail how the person feels they are managing in various areas of their life and how they see themselves moving forward. This is driven by the person with the mental health issue, rather than other people's ideas of what they should do – which can be a bit of a challenge to accept, especially for the family.

If you consider what would be a good life for anyone in realistic terms it would include:

- Enough money not to have to worry about it too much
- A reasonable place to live
- Something to do which makes you feel positive or satisfied, whether that is creative, helping others or earning money
- Friends, contacts, people to talk to that you like and feel safe with
- A sense of who you are and where you fit in the world
- Maybe a spiritual sense, connecting with nature or a religious belief
- Some hope and trust that the future is going to be OK and worth living

This list is far from complete. Carers are probably thinking here 'I don't have most of those' and there is a good chance that the family lifestyle has been shaken up and is currently pretty fragmented. How much more does someone's safety network get destroyed when they have a serious mental health issue? Friends, money, job, identity, hope for the future, etc. all thrown up in the air and often out of sight.

The recovery model considers how these factors can be restored by working on them and offering opportunities to rebuild. This is a slow process but is much more 'person centred' than the old approach, which did things 'to' someone rather than 'with' them. I remember careers advice at school where I was told, based on my exams, that I should be a teacher or work in a bank. Thanks. No one ever asked me what I hoped for (which was just as well as I had no idea).

When someone has come out of the other side of a mental

health crisis and things are looking a bit more predictable then the rebuilding work can be started. This might be a short programme of a staggered return to work or it might be rebuilding from the beginning. Ideally this is led by professionals such as occupational therapists and support workers. Unfortunately this help is not available for everyone, the teams who work with younger people tend to have more resources, less for the older adults. Voluntary organisations may be available as an option or it can come down to family and friends to help.

Two important aspects of this work are the need for the person to have their ideas treated with respect and for there always to be a sense of hope underlying the process. These key factors should be central for both professionals and families but both respect and hope can be hard to maintain over a long period. It is easy to slide into the 'Why don't you just...' and 'That's a silly idea!' or 'Really? You think that will happen?' sort of comments. Respect doesn't mean everything that the person suggests has to be agreed with, but sometimes the family just needs to stand back and let someone try their ideas. They also need to have a little faith that things will move in the right direction eventually. More on that later.

How can a carers help this process? The first thing is to find out what the person is thinking and what might interest them. This can be a slow process. I imagine that a lot of these conversations would follow similar lines to the ones I used to have with people at the centre, in my best 'being helpful' voice.

'So, Andrew, things seem to be going very well with you now, you seem to be ready to try something new. Had you thought at all about what you might have a go at?'
'No, not really.'
'Well, you have said you get bored a lot and you would like to do something different?'

'Yeah, well I would.'

'So, what do you think would be a good place to start?'

'I don't know.'

'What did you used to do a few years ago?'

'I worked in a call centre and I hated that.'

'I can understand that. What about hobbies or skills?'

'I drank a lot and watched a lot of films mostly.'

'OK. No ideas at the moment then?'

'No, I guess not.'

This can be a bit of a thankless task. Possibly there may need to be a bit of detective work in noticing clues in their everyday conversation. If they say they feel they are bored of being stuck in the house or can't face picking up their guitar again then this can open an opportunity. What would it take to make one step in that direction? Where could they go that might mean they would meet people in a safe environment? Do they need to start shopping by themselves in the nearby quieter (and more expensive) corner shop or are they ready for a voluntary job? Would watching videos of people playing guitar help bring back some enthusiasm? Ideally these steps will be small and manageable. They must be thought of, or at minimum agreed, by the person with the mental health issue and what they say is final.

Some may be raring to go and ready to try anything, it may be more a question of slowing things down and trying to keep them from exhausting themselves. This may be especially true when someone has bi-polar and gets overly excited and enthusiastic at times. There may be more of a role of watching and waiting, with a sense of anxiety, while they launch themselves into something new.

If the person has delusions and their view of the world is unrealistic at times, this recovery process can be particularly challenging. If they are fifty-seven, suffer chronic asthma and want to go to Manchester and become a DJ, or they want to help the world by bringing it a special message, then there is a fair chance that they will not succeed with either ambition and will face disappointment. Telling them not to try may not help the family relationship or encourage confidence though. Can these delusional ideas be used positively? If they want to be a great DJ can they attend a class, or go out and watch other DJs for ideas? If they have a special message for the world can they learn how to make a good video or put something on YouTube and risk the 'trolls'? Is there a small step that fits with their idea and which also get one foot back into the real world?

Suppose they feel conscious of having lost all their friends and want to make new social contacts, so they do something that everyone suggests, such as go to an evening class. This could work out well and be an exciting first step or then again, they could have a miserable evening and not go out again for six months. Suppose they go to the pub but end up drunk and then have a relapse in their mental health. Making a move is sometimes risky, but not to make those moves is to stay where they currently are, possibly for an awfully long time.

This is called 'positive risk taking'. It does have lots of parallels with having an adolescent in the house, but it is more widely accepted that substantial change is necessary in order to become an adult, this inevitably has risks attached. The challenge with mental health is to accept that the person also needs to regain lost skills and take on new challenges, and that is just as risky and just as necessary. A great deal of advice in mental health focusses on keeping stress levels down, but without some risk taking the result is an individual in a 'bubble' removed from real life. A stress-free life is not a long-term option except in the most extreme situations. People need to rejoin the world in some way to recover a better sense of wellbeing.

What can really help is to prepare. Some ideas that could be useful to help minimise the hazards in new situations are:

- Have a think through how they would like to introduce themselves, what they might say in response to potentially difficult questions. If someone asks, 'Where do you work?' then they have an answer ready. Replies such as, 'I've had some time off because of stress' or, 'I'm not working at present, had a few health problems' could be useful. It must be them that decides what they say and how they say it but preparing helps confidence.
- Rehearsing situations before they occur can also be helpful. If they are going for an interview or to a cafe for the first time in a while there are always possible glitches that can be thought through and strategies made. This doesn't have to be a heavyweight exercise it can just be a few minutes' thought.
- Have an escape route planned. This might be a call from a member of the family at a fixed time so they can say they have to leave. It may be that they need to be clear how to get home; taxi or bus fares and timetable/apps.
- If they need someone with them when they go out because they are prone to panic, then have a tactic planned that all the family know about. If it gets busy and the anxiety level starts to rise then agree a signal that means 'Get me out of here fast' rather than asking them to explain in the early stages of a panic attack or leave it to guesswork. A tug on the sleeve will do. This signal means 'head for the door and don't stop'.

This sense of making progress, of meeting challenges and overcoming them and of working towards getting back to a reasonable quality of life can do as much for a person's wellbeing as any other treatment. It certainly helps to reduce anxiety and distress, which in turn reduces the rate of relapse.

It is also crucial that family 'hold the hope'. The person with the mental health problem may have long periods when they see no future for themselves and no sense of being able to change. It can sound very contrived and fake to keep saying 'You will be better soon' and 'You mustn't give up trying' when they are plainly despairing. One carer told me that she used to use phrases that tried to show that she believed that things would change but didn't put too much pressure on them. This might be something like 'Won't it be great when you can... again,' or, 'I am really looking forward to the time when you start... again.' I think this sounds about right.

AVAILABILITY OF DIFFERENT TREATMENTS

There are a variety of interventions that can be recommended, which may involve nurses, social workers and occupational therapists as well as psychologists and psychiatrists. Some people get a basic treatment package of medication and a regular review with a psychiatrist. Some get a greater number of different professionals involved and have care planning meetings to keep it all coordinated. It may be that what is on offer changes as the situation becomes better understood or when symptoms change.

Families often request a particular type of therapy because they feel it will help. This may be because of their own research, often online, or the experience of friends. Frustration sets in when this is apparently not on offer for the person they support. Conversations as to why this is not being suggested can be hard to arrange, it would be preferable if they were in confidence because it is important that the person with the mental health issue feels secure about what is happening, not being given the idea that they are being excluded from the one treatment that will definitely work. Having the carer criticise the mental health services can undermine that confidence and after all, it is the only help available (free).

Do the professionals feel that the timing is wrong or that the person wouldn't benefit because of their diagnosis? Alternatively, it may be because it is not available locally or has huge waiting lists. If it isn't available, then is a private arrangement affordable? There is the possibility of buying a therapist's time of course but also a psychiatrist's time and a stay on a private ward. This will mean more and faster attention with better access to professionals but the medication and the treatments on offer are the same as the NHS, just offered more quickly.

It is worth having a conversation about this and getting a professional's viewpoint because spending a lot of money on something that isn't going to achieve much is a generous gesture, but can also create a major knockback for everyone when it doesn't result in change. It may feel important to try anything that seems even a vague possibility, but a good professional may be the voice of reason. What are the odds it is worth the expenditure? In the end though it is the family's decision to offer but the decision of the person with the mental health issue whether to accept.

CRISES AND RELAPSES

Only one in every six carers has had a conversation with an NHS professional about what to do in an emergency, according to the Carers UK '*State of Caring*' survey 2019.

When a person who is experiencing mental health issues becomes highly agitated, distressed or angry to the point where there is significant risk of harm to them or to other people, then they need urgent help. They are out of their own control and are behaving in a way that ignores any possible hazard, even to themselves. This is classified as a mental health crisis. It does not include those whose behaviour is affected by drink or drugs or any reason other than their mental health. Most people never get to this point where they are overwhelmed and lose control, but it may be worth being aware of the options just in case that rare occasion happen.

A relapse, however, is when symptoms return, they seem to be heading back to being very unwell after having shown signs of recovering. This may be because they have stopped taking their medication or have been affected by a stressful life event or it may appear to be random. For some people a relapse may result in a crisis, but that depends on the symptoms that they experience as part of their condition.

Families may well regard the return of stronger symptoms as a crisis, but an experienced professional's perspective may differ.

They may see the relapse as being a predictable and containable process, they don't necessarily rush to the rescue in the way that the carer hopes that they might, which can create anxiety. The usual approach to a relapse is perhaps an increase in medication for a while - or a return to taking it if they have stopped. This will often avoid a major emergency, but it does require the person's cooperation. The mental health team could also suggest an increased use of 'coping strategies' such as reduced social activity and more time spent relaxing.

A crisis is more immediate and threatening. People who are in a highly agitated state may be anxious to get help and cooperate fully with the process, but this is not always the case. The following information looks at options in these circumstances and what can be useful either with or without the person's cooperation. There is a section called 'de-escalation-when it is getting out of control' offering suggestions on calming people down but, presuming this approach has been tried and it hasn't worked, there are other possibilities.

A challenging situation, where there is potentially aggressive or unpredictable behaviour, can be tricky to assess. A priority should be the protection of the carer and other family members; if the person with the mental health issue is not responding and calming down then there is a time to admit that the situation is now out of anyone's control. At this point there are two priorities, staying safe and getting help.

Staying in the room with them might help to defuse the situation but then it might not, having someone else there can dramatically increase the tension. Leaving them alone may be the best decision, especially if they are angry and some of that fury is being directed towards another person in that room. It is hard to argue with an empty room, some possible damage to the furniture is preferable to some possible damage to a person. If the worst happens and someone gets hurt it is a whole different problem, possibly with police involvement.

Crucially, families need to be aware that the mental health team are not an emergency service (neither are social care). Calling the mental health duty officer would probably result in a suggestion to get help from the emergency services, especially if the situation is happening right now. Mental health nurses don't have a 'blue light' car on standby so they may not be the first call; it is important to keep them in the loop and let them know what is happening at some stage. (Let them know immediately if a relapse is starting to become evident though, as what is required then is a clinical intervention rather than risk control.)

Some districts may have specialised mental health emergency care options or twenty-four-hour crisis teams that are on short notice call out, so ask for information if they may be needed. It is worth checking exactly who and what they will respond to. It may only be people on their 'list' that are offered this service and what the family see as a crisis may differ significantly from the team's definition. If it does sound like a potentially useful service then make sure their number is on all the relevant mobile phones.

Call the police if there is aggression towards others, or property, or the person could injure themselves intentionally or unintentionally. This may immediately calm the situation down; it is surprising what a couple of official looking people in uniform and wearing stab jackets can do to deflate even a mental health emergency. Police may take the person to a safe place such as a special quiet room at a hospital or more likely A&E until they can be assessed by a psychiatrist for admission to a psychiatric unit – which could take some time. The person is not arrested and doesn't get a criminal record if their behaviour is seen as a direct result of mental health issues. See the section on the Mental Health Act for details on how this happens.

Alternatively, the police may not be convinced that this

extreme behaviour is a mental health situation at all and interpret it as a domestic argument or a drinking incident. It would be helpful if they knew as soon as possible that the person has a diagnosis, this could be useful in making this assessment. Depending on the severity of the situation they may arrest that person. Or they may decide not to take any action at all which means they go, usually giving warnings about repeat incidents. The person may be angry that the police were called, but this does establish very firmly that the family are not going to tolerate extreme outbursts, they will call in help. This could be a useful boundary to set.

Call an ambulance if there is a serious injury/overdose. They can also take people to A&E if they are very distressed and the family cannot get them there. They cannot force someone into any vehicle though and cannot make them go to hospital. The police will be called if the person becomes too aggressive or distraught to contain safely.

Another option is to phone 111, describe the situation and ask advice, particularly if there are physical health issues too. If they have taken an overdose, and it is clear what they have taken, then this service can give information about the likely effects of this and how critical the situation could be. This does require some time though, maybe waiting for a call back. There is also the issue of how the phone conversation can take place privately while the person concerned may be close by. They can also advise if an ambulance is necessary and arrange for one to come, but this may be slower than calling 999 directly.

The family can take them to A&E to get an urgent assessment. This is often suggested by mental health professionals as in, 'Oh if he/she gets very agitated then just take them to A&E.' 'Just' implies that this is a straightforward process and it isn't always. Firstly, they need to get in the car or taxi which requires cooperation. Then someone has to drive them, sometimes a long way. I have heard a couple of carers describing these journeys with the person trying to get out or grappling with the driver. Then they must wait to be seen, usually in a slightly tense environment. Waiting for a long time in the public area of A&E can be a test of endurance especially if they don't want to be there. The environment can be grim and other people can be in pain, panic or pissed.

A separate room or quieter area is sometimes available in A&E departments after the first assessment / triage so it is worth asking if they have any special arrangements for people with mental health issues as increasingly there are rooms set aside. If they have any physical injuries these will be attended to before any mental health treatment.

If the person being escorted decides to leave, then there are few choices. If they have been assessed as having a mental health condition already then staff or the carer may call the police to look for them, but no one has any powers to make them go back to A&E, or stay until they are seen. If the person is not capable of recognising risks such as running into a road or being inadequately dressed on a freezing night, then call the police and describe the situation and ask their advice. If there is a risk of a suicide attempt or reckless behaviour tell them that immediately.

When they are seen by a specialist mental health practitioner at A&E, they will probably be offered medication and/ or a referral to see someone in the local team at the first possible appointment. Often that is enough, the chance to talk to someone and be heard, to get some sleep or at least a calmer period with medication and a promise of further help in the near future.

Unless they fulfil the criteria for a Mental Health Act section they are unlikely to be admitted into hospital even if they really want to go. Inpatient beds are (fully) occupied by the most unwell people so there is only a small chance that this will be the outcome of an A&E visit, but it does sometimes happen.

The chances are that they will come back home again, hopefully feeling calmer and tired enough to get some rest. To be honest, sometimes the hours spent in A&E can exhaust even the most agitated and hysterical person.

People with the more complex mental health conditions seem to sometimes go through a phase of intense high-risk action with a flurry of night-time visits to the hospital, usually when the condition is at its strongest.

There are a lot of discussions about finding alternatives to A&E, particularly for those who view it as a first line support system to use even when they are not that 'unwell' but need some attention or medication. This is tricky to manage; a straightforward ban is not possible as there could be a time when they really are seriously at risk. Secondly, if they didn't come to A&E would they then become increasingly unwell? There are no other (free) options for attention and clinical support at 4 am on a wet Wednesday in February. An alternative would be an emergency mental health clinic with drop in access; maybe some areas have these.

If trips to the hospital become a regular feature for a while, then plan ahead and have an A&E bag ready. The 'carer' bag could include change/card for the car park, a book, food, water and maybe a blanket or a cushion. The person with the mental health issue who is highly agitated will probably not be able to concentrate much, but it is worth considering their comfort too, especially as it might encourage them to stay until the doctor or nurse arrives. Would a packet of cigarettes / chocolate keep things calmer or headphones and some music? What could work for them?

Visits often lessen when the right medication (and the commitment to take it) happens. The A&E visits can have a positive outcome because they are, overall, unpleasant experiences. This might encourage people to try to hold on and get help at more sociable times if they possibly can. The act of 'holding on' is a useful skill to be encouraged and is a step towards self-managing symptoms.

Just to repeat, crisis related incidents are not a feature of most mental health diagnoses, they happen, but only to a few people whose symptoms result in these extreme moods.

TRIGGERS

This term means 'things that make them kick off'. More technically, this could be described as situations where anxiety level rises, there is a growing fear that the situation is getting too much to cope with and the person becomes highly agitated. The family will get to know what 'agitation' means; it could be rapid speech, frantic hand movements or shouting. They may become irritable and fidgety, or withdraw or 'zone out', or they may start talking about threatening or suicidal topics - the next section looks at this last topic in more detail. At worst it may result in an increase in symptoms for a while.

One of the carer's key roles is that of trigger-spotter. The family will notice as time passes what incidents result in a rise in anxious behaviour and they can help a great deal by trying to remove as many of them as possible, especially during the more sensitive early stages.

This checklist may be a place to start:

- Noise / busy places/ bright lights / crowds
- People asking questions
- Being with people they don't know very well
- Pushing them to make a decision
- Giving them too much information to respond to quickly
- Phones going off suddenly

- Seeing their closest relatives upset or worried
- Asking them to do something they are not ready to do

Then there may be more personal triggers which could be related to delusional thoughts or beliefs; black cars parked nearby, certain letters on number plates, schoolchildren getting too close, rivers, women with pushchairs, hearing Chris Evans on the radio, eggs, thunder etc. These are all real examples from my own experience.

If they become anxious at the thought of having to meet other people, then conversations may go like this:

'Oh Dave, I was going to tell you Joan next door is popping over in a minute to collect those books.'
'I don't want her to.'
'Why not? You've always got on with Joan.'
'Tell her not to come.'
'Don't be silly, she'll only be here a minute or two.'
'I don't want her here. Tell her not to come.' (Voice gets more agitated.)
'Dave, you're just being daft, there is nothing to be worried about.'
'Don't let her in here, I can't do this! You are just getting her here to wind me up.'

This descends into a scene that finishes in a battle which really has no winners. Dave has far more invested in Joan not being in the same room as him, so if the carer forces the situation they will then have to cope with the after-effects of a flare-up.

It may be helpful to think about how the family are approaching situations like this, when the emotional temperature is rising. In the above conversation, the anxious person is being dismissed as 'silly' and 'daft' which are everyday words but to someone with a mental health issue may be very wounding. Secondly, it is a judgement call as to whether they are getting genuinely distressed or are just avoiding having to move, be polite, get dressed or feel a slight but manageable anxiety. If the conclusion is that they really are being a bit dramatic then it may be appropriate to carry on with Joan's visit. This has some risks but through listening to exactly what they are saying and try to reach a compromise the worst may be avoided.

In this situation the carer's choices are:

A. Ask Joan not to come but take the books round to her house.

B. When Joan arrives then Dave says hello and then the carer says, 'Dave has just got to go and answer some urgent emails/ fix the car/ do the ironing,' and he swiftly exits the room.

C. The carer meets Joan in the kitchen and Dave stays watching Netflix on the sofa.

Never do surprises. Forcing them into a situation they dread won't show them they can cope; it will probably cause an argument and may be viewed as a major betrayal.

A couple more examples of trigger avoidance.

An unhappy item on the News causes upset and this is not the first time this has happened. The cared-for person feels responsible for a tsunami on the other side of the world or is just generally depressed by the bloodshed and poverty. Does the family have to watch it on TV, or could they get it from their phone or a paper that can be read in private?

A social invitation.

'You've been invited to Chris and Chelsea's wedding.

Chris really wants you to come, you've been friends since school! It's a quick ceremony and then a disco, you like dancing.'

Instead of persuasion because 'it would be good for you' and an escalation of dread as the time gets closer, the optimum approach is some joint planning. What is to be avoided is an increase in tension that results in a flare-up because the person is too anxious to go but can't tell anyone that directly, or they do say it quite clearly but they are still 'encouraged' to attend. They could become angry if they feel they have been made to go, or disappointed in themselves because on the day they just can't make it, which is a 'fail'.

The wedding is a potential trigger, but forward planning will prepare for peak anxiety producing moments, which will hopefully reduce the impact. It absolutely must be based on the person's own ideas as this will increase their confidence and help with similar situations in the future. The plan could look something like this.

- I will take my phone, charged up, and a taxi number and fare for dire emergencies.
- When I go to the church I will sit near the back so if it gets too much I can leave, call you and be collected.
- If I get to the disco then I won't drink any alcohol. You will call me at 7.30 pm and I can use this as an excuse to leave if I need one. If I need to leave in a hurry after that then I will go outside and call you.
- You will be outside at 10 pm to collect me. If I want to change this time then I will call you.
- If anyone asks me how I am or what I am doing these days I will say 'I have had a few health problems and have been suffering with stress, so I have been off work for a while.

Mobile phones make these plans so much easier. If social isolation can be avoided and some contact maintained with friends and family this will really help in time, it might have to be carefully managed in the early stages to avoid triggering an embarrassing situation where the person panics, a setback which might slow things down quite a bit.

In the early days it seems that deliberate exposure to these challenging circumstances is not beneficial, it won't make it all go away. People with mental health issues may struggle to control their agitated response as quickly as other people might. Deliberate exposure is useful with some fears and phobias, but this is usually done with preparation through learning coping techniques and lots of support from a professional. Having your daughter stick her hand in a box with a big spider in is probably not going to make the fear go away or to create family harmony.

In the early days, the family can help to protect as much as possible. As time passes this can be reduced, with some encouragement and planning, so tackling difficult situations is not avoided altogether, and the skills to cope with them are learnt. The timescale for change is likely to be far slower than would be expected, an enthusiastic but premature push from a carer can result in a dip in progress. As always, a tightrope to walk.

Knowing the possible triggers though can help anticipate and monitor change more carefully. As time passes people will undoubtedly become stronger and learn techniques to help with their own fears – just getting older or getting the right medication can help. As their skill in negotiating their way through worrying situations increases and trigger avoidance is second nature, then they will become more self-managing and less dependent on family help.

PREDICTING A RELAPSE

This is a skill that carers learn as they go through the journey with the person they support. Many mental health issues are relapsing conditions and a negative event, stress or stopping medication can all bring back symptoms, although it could occur completely without any apparent trigger.

Bi-polar is often a lifelong condition but when the correct medication is in place, and as time passes and people get to know themselves, it can be very well controlled. Personality disorders can also calm with age, but the outcome varies greatly with the type and with the treatment offered – and whether it is engaged with effectively. Anxiety and depression issues can be over swiftly or be hovering over someone for many years. Relapses may be a worry for a short time or for some people it is a long-term consideration.

The family will increase in confidence and knowledge as time passes, which means they are often one jump ahead rather than only being able to react to a situation once it has already escalated. It is useful, particularly with the more severe conditions, to be able to see a relapse coming as early as possible. If there is a good working relationship with the mental health team the whistle can be blown and hopefully backup will appear with a bit of extra support and maybe some extra medication.

One carer I knew managed this relationship with the mental health services by text messages. That is the ultimate arrangement, the trust that the carer is knowledgeable and sensible and that the professional will come to the rescue when summoned. I only met one carer who achieved this mutual understanding though, hopefully it is increasing.

In contrast, I have heard many family members express a deep frustration that professionals will not respond until there is a serious situation that the carer clearly saw coming. This makes no sense to an independent observer, that a warning signal is given by a reliable witness, but the situation is not responded to until it is a full-blown crisis. If there are any nurses reading this, please consider this a request for further debate?

What are the indications that there may be trouble coming? The following list has been established over the years. It is surprising that, despite the individual differences and the range of possible diagnoses, there is a lot of common ground, although a lot of these behaviours are particularly relevant where there is psychosis.

- Less able to manage daily life tasks, seeming confused or distracted.
- Tired, listless, quiet, shows no interest in anything and can't concentrate.
- Touchy, more prone to losing their temper or being a bit aggressive, maybe talking about violent acts.
- Negative about themselves, they feel low and useless and this is a frequent topic of conversation.
- Sleep badly, have a poor appetite and stop looking after themselves / washing.
- Move differently, behave out of character or their speech may be hard to follow.
- You can see it in their eyes (I have been told this many times).
- Co-operate less and are stubborn.
- Frequent complaints about physical aches and pains.
- Over excited and increasingly uncontrolled, more disinhibited about sex or being very child-like and 'silly'.
- Talk to themselves and fixate on one or two ideas for a lot of the time.
- They may say they are no longer themselves, that their mind has been taken over, their thoughts are being read and people are watching them and mocking them.

Carers come to know the particular signs for the person they support and often develop a plan to cope which may include reducing activity and encouraging lying low in a state of stress-less quiet whilst keeping all fingers firmly crossed. This can reduce the impact considerably.

If a response proves to have a positive influence then it is worth trying it again in any similar situations in the future, tricks that work are worth their weight in gold. Writing them down can help jog the memory when it can be difficult to focus because of rising concern. It could be a favourite film, long walks, staying in bed, long baths or avoiding TV, there are many personal variations on good calming activities.

The first few times the symptoms are at their most severe it can be absolutely nerve-wracking for the family especially if there is risky behaviour involved. As time passes these episodes become more predictable and less devastating, whether because of growing experience and successful techniques or because there is the thought that 'We survived the last one, there is a very good chance we will get through this one too.'

DE-ESCALATION - IF IT IS GETTING OUT OF CONTROL

The carer can play an important role in situations where a person with a mental health condition is jumpy, highly emotional, critical or aggressive towards objects, another person or themselves. This doesn't happen with everyone so please note that it is a rare occurrence, but it is as well to be prepared. The information may also come in useful at work or with the rest of the family, who knows?

The first time this angry or desperate behaviour happens there is little that can be done except react in the moment. For a few people it becomes a regular occurrence, if that is the case then consider having a plan so that the family feel better prepared and are not backfooted.

A plan may start with creating a list of things that may calm the situation down if caught early enough. These will be unique to the individual, so there is no magic formula. This could be walking, looking after a pet or listening to a favourite piece of music. They could learn some basic breathing exercises or listen to a guided meditation which some find helpful to regain some calm. Things to include on this list may be found out by trial and error.

A low stress environment is helpful when someone is jumpy and on edge. This means that there is stability, things are predictable, routines are kept even if your offer of a cup of tea is repeatedly refused. There are minimal loud noises, the family postpone playing their thrash metal for a while. The person with the mental health issue may play loud music in their room of course but this is under their control (unfortunately).

Having neighbours or relatives around may also be inadvisable. Extra people, even familiar ones, can create stress especially if they have come to 'have a word' about what is going on. Peace and predictability are boring but can keep a fragile person going for a while until the tension passes.

Sometimes nothing apparently proves helpful and suggestions are met with increased anger. It can be that the situation escalates quickly and the stage when a calming intervention could be useful is over too soon to react. This may be due to circumstances beyond anyone's control.

Number one on the list of things to try is 'appear calm'. This is not the same as being calm, no one expects that. But if keep the signs of calmness (which are a quiet voice, talking slightly more slowly, limited hand waving or moving about) is effective. Speaking clearly and briefly may get heard better as the person is probably dealing with a lot of cognitive confusion, overwhelming feelings and a sense of panic. There is a fine line with appearing patronising here, a tip is to listen how this 'calm carer' sounds and maybe practice in the mirror. No, I am not joking.

Assertiveness is also useful. This doesn't mean bossing or bullying them but listening, offering to help, being open to talking but also setting firm boundaries.

> 'I am really sorry that you think I don't care and that I'm not listening to you. I might need help to understand what you are trying to tell me, but you need to know that if you threaten to hurt me then I will call the police. I don't want to do that, but I am really not prepared to get hurt.'

or

> 'You are saying that I am trying to hurt you. That must be very frightening for you and I wish I could convince you that it really isn't true. I understand that you don't trust me at the moment, but it is never acceptable to throw things around. If you continue then I will have to get help.'

Eye contact works but too much can be interpreted as threatening so avoid the full-on stare! While making 'boundary statements', brief eye contact can be useful to make sure they are listening and to make a point.

Sometimes an outburst might turn out to be a false alarm, so the suggestion is to wait as long as it feels safe before deciding it is an emergency and going into 'major incident' mode. Everyone is prone to having the odd flash of temper or bad mood moment. Often it deflates and disappears after a brief rant and never becomes too worrying. As time passes, families can become expert in predicting situations, watching and waiting is useful if the situation is contained. It may all die down and everyone breathes a sigh of relief.

Triggers! Look for situations that spark off bad feeling or increase agitation. See previous section.

Paranoia is a (false)conviction that there is a serious threat from someone or something. It may well be that a family member is one of the people under suspicion of plotting, often those closest are prime suspects. If the person with the mental health issue is currently experiencing this or other delusional ideas, then it is unwise to challenge these when they are distraught or lashing out.

One useful tip if there is distrust is for each person to describe what they are doing as they go along so there are no 'hidden' actions. For example, a family member might say, 'I am just going into the kitchen to make a cup of tea. Then after we have finished that I will start on the dinner'.

It's useful to become aware of actions that are often misinterpreted. If a phone rings but the person who is answering it immediately goes and takes the call in the next room then that could easily cause increased anxiety. It can be useful to keep phone calls and computer time brief and either in full sight or offer to call back later.

They may suspect that someone is trying to poison them – this may be caused by a hallucination that is affecting their sense of taste or smell. Can they help with the cooking or at least be in the kitchen so they can witness what is happening to their food? Would a ready meal create less suspicion? Keeping them informed may be all you can do to reduce their anxiety levels.

If they self-harm, then trying to stop them when they are highly distressed can be counterproductive. The best outcome in this situation is that they cut/burn themselves in a controlled way, do minimum harm and take proper care of the injury afterwards. Trying to stop them will probably not work, it can produce two possible outcomes in my experience. Firstly, they harm themselves in front of the carer in more confrontational and angry mood than before, which may result in a greater level of injury. Secondly, they promise they will not self-harm, go somewhere private and do it anyway because they are angry with themselves now. This means the action will be hidden and no one can keep an eye on things. Tough as it is, by saying, 'If you need to then go ahead,' may be making life easier in the longer-term. See the section on self-harm if this is relevant.

A few people seem to experience outbursts of extreme emotion that they cannot control. They are overwhelmed by their distress and express this by throwing themselves on the floor, screaming, sobbing hysterically, maybe banging their head against a wall or other uncontrolled behaviour. This can be very frightening to witness, the natural response from a carer is to rush to help, to try desperately to calm them down and to show the understandable emotional response of becoming distressed themselves.

If this behaviour does happen more than once it can help to practice remaining as calm and matter of fact as possible. The chances of them hearing and understanding what is being said at this time is small anyway, so a quiet, calm(ish) presence may be all that can be effectively offered. Instead of trying to hold them, either slight or no physical contact may be preferred, maybe holding their hand rather than trying to hug them or restrain them.

As soon as the person calms down then giving them maximum attention afterwards, rather than during the episode, this will reward their efforts to control it themselves, and recognise that it takes a lot of willpower.

If this frenzied behaviour happens regularly it could be worth starting a conversation when they are in a quieter mood, along the lines of:

'You know when you get so distressed it is hard for me to know what to do. Is there anything that might help when you are so upset?'

One carer I met used to talk about being in the park, the pond and the ducks, while her daughter had hysterical crying sessions. Her daughter had suggested this, she said that it helped.

I have met families that leave people alone when these outbursts happen, but they don't go far away. They feel that if they are not too close the person will calm quicker. This is one option worth trying, but is not for everyone.

Some outbursts are driven by anger, but this is often linked to fear, is this emotional outburst rooted in anxiety rather than fury? For example: a woman believes that she has been infected with a fatal disease and that everyone she touches will die. Only she knows this fact and she is trying to warn people. Her family respond by saying that there is something wrong with her mind and she should take medication. She absolutely knows without any doubt that it is a genuine threat and that time is running out, someone could touch her by accident at any time. Consider her viewpoint, what would you do when people refuse to listen? Is this anger or fear?

In this example, perhaps the woman would be less distressed if she were left alone or stayed on the sofa and no one else came anywhere near. This would be a short-term fix offered because it helps her stay calmer, not because the family is colluding with the delusion. This requires that the person experiencing this belief is listened to carefully and helps to think of ways to make the situation less overwhelming for them.

Saying that you can see that they are truly angry and upset may help them stay in control. But 'I can see you are feeling angry' can be said in a lot of ways and can easily sound like a cliché. It is important to find a way that sounds authentic rather than strained, so it comes across as (and hopefully is) genuine.

If they are angry about someone or something that is not present at this moment, then listening is a vital tool. This is not the listening that involves interrupting with lots of good suggestions about how to handle the situation. This is the listening that means that questions are asked such as, 'Can you explain a bit more about that please?' or 'I think I understand, are you saying that you have a special message that these people are about to attack?' If the content is delusional it could be worth looking at the 'Psychosis: hallucinations and delusions' section.

There is a time to debate whether this is a mental health issue or not, or how ludicrous it is to believe that there are aliens in the local village that no one else has noticed. When someone is angry to the point of losing control an attempt at a rational discussion may well inflame things. Be prepared to sit in silence for a while, their brain may be working a bit slower than usual so when people dive in quickly with unhelpful advice it can be frustrating and increase the rage factor. There is a detailed section on 'listening' further on.

I have always worked on the basis that being terribly angry is totally exhausting and if it is possible to listen and genuinely try to understand for long enough then people will calm down as they tire.

If they are getting angry with the person they are talking to, rather than with someone or something else that is not currently present, then avoid long discussions or defensive arguments. There may be a horrible list of hurtful accusations coming across, but it is not personal, it is a response to the frustration and fear which is often a result of a mental health issue. Conversations about their viewpoint are better had when they are calm. Responding to an angry outburst by getting tearful or shouting back will probably escalate the situation. They are not going to hear what is being said anyway, no one listens well in an argument.

Direct threats to anyone's safety need to be approached differently. The priority then becomes to keep that person and anyone else in the house safe from a flare-up that could get aggressive. It may feel that it is the family's role to stay with this person and calm them down, but this could become high risk. If things are escalating and the anger is personal then everyone should leave, it's hard to sustain an argument with an empty room. If that is not enough then getting behind a locked door (bathroom) or leaving the house are the only options. If these episodes are a frequent occurrence have a kit stashed ready which could include a snack, a book and a charged mobile phone. Sitting in the car is a possibility or go to a cafe and eat ice cream. Give it a good while to calm down before attempting re-entry.

This action of leaving the room makes the situation safer. It also saves the person with the mental health issue from being pushed into the mental health or criminal systems in a crisis that leaves them labelled as 'high-risk' of being aggressive. Leaving has three possible outcomes; either the person will calm down or they will vent their anger on inanimate objects, which is horrible and expensive but are easier to replace than people are. The third alternative is that they hurt themselves.

If they will answer the phone, then calling them before coming back can help to assess whether it is safe to return. If this is not possible perhaps consider if there is any back up available, or at least have a phone to hand with 999 on speed dial.

If there is a high risk that they have hurt themselves seriously then it is possible to call the police, but they may not come immediately which could increase any risk to them through their injury. The worst outcome is that the carer returns and finds the person hurt, then calls an ambulance if it is necessary. This is a traumatic experience but there could have been more than one person hurt if they were not left alone, which would undoubtedly have been even worse.

If the person regularly arrives at the house in an angry state because of drink or drugs then having a spyhole in the front door can allow the family to prepare, or to put the chain on. This situation is not the same as one caused just by mental health symptoms, it may require more drastic action such as simply locking them out or calling the police sooner.

Dealing with serious outbursts and violent lashing out is highly stressful and creates an atmosphere of fear especially if it happens frequently. There is a message in whatever response is given by the family. If aggression, threatening behaviour or even physical harm is tolerated then the person is protected from having to face any consequences of their actions. The long-term goal is to get them back into the ordinary world where this aggression is completely unacceptable and possibly criminal, so it must be controlled eventually by some means.

The majority of those who suffer these distressing outbursts do manage these feelings more effectively as time passes. The family's role is to support them to get that control, not to tolerate their behaviour. This may include police involvement, or the mental health team or even giving information that allows the person to be 'sectioned'. This can feel like a betrayal but in the long term keeping the secret is keeping the situation going. There is a better incentive to get control if there are negative outcomes.

This all sounds a bit of a lecture but that is what it is. I have seen what happens in families where extreme behaviour is tolerated and it usually leads to an unhappy 'dictatorship' which then becomes the norm and the other member(s) of the family then become very unwell or anxious themselves.

One example I heard about involved a couple who had an adult son living at home. He was prone to paranoia and was highly suspicious. His belief was that his mother was planning to kill him. He stared at her if she entered the room and started shouting if she dared to stay in there. Sometimes there was a trigger event, perhaps she said, 'the wrong thing', then he would lunge to attack her. At this point his father would grab him and hold him down until he calmed, which could take hours. This had been going on for months. Both parents were over 70 years old and not in great health.

This example illustrates what happens when a well-intentioned approach to keeping things safe has backfired and become a habitual response that gives offers no incentive to stop, it also presents an opportunity to get his parent's attention for long periods which rewards the aggressive behaviour. This family were not unusual in doing their best to calm the situation but effectively protecting the person from the consequences of his actions.

The bottom line is that you can't control their behaviour, you can try to avoid making it worse and try to help the calming process but neither of these may work. Getting help if things get out of hand is not weakness or a failure as a carer. It happens because the person is so overwhelmed by the symptoms that they experience that they require help sometimes just to protect themselves from the consequences of their own actions.

Hopefully, you will have read these few pages and thought, 'I can't see any of this happening to me'.

MISSING PERSONS

This sounds a terrifying prospect to consider but there are a percentage of people with mental health issues who go missing, sometimes on a regular basis. Again, this information is preparing for the worst even though the chances are small that it will ever happen.

There are lots of different circumstances which may lead to people 'disappearing'; they may want some peace and quiet or some wild excitement. They may be lost and unable to get home or setting out with the intention of committing suicide. The first time it happens a family may not be clear as to the reason but if it does become a regular occurrence there is a good chance that there will be a pattern behind it.

Families have told me stories of finding their relatives many miles away, they may be following a delusional idea or be using their own particular logic. There was a young woman I heard about who would travel all over the UK looking for her 'mum', who she believed was a famous singer. She was convinced of this although this singer was less than ten years older than her. It was her real mum who had to go and collect her from towns two hundred miles away in the middle of the night and be met with insults and rejection when she arrived.

People have gone missing abroad. One of them I got to know quite well, we shared an office for a couple of years. He told me that he had gone to see his GP and said that he had a lot of energy (he had bi-polar in fact) and wanted to get fit. The GP told him to go for long walks so he got on a plane to India as he thought the walking there would be more interesting. He had a credit card, a passport and no luggage.

I live quite close to a major suicide spot and this seems to act like a magnet for some people. There are preventative measures in place, but this doesn't make it any easier for the carer when they find out where the person they support is going. There are people who go there once and there are 'regulars' who seem to want to go there often when they are feeling fragile, maybe to consider their options.

The bare facts are that a person cannot be stopped from wandering off or going to high-risk area without getting into some complex ethical issues about imprisoning people against their will. In extreme cases the only option is to use the Mental Health Act.

The police are the obvious service to call if someone is missing – not the mental health team as they are simply not equipped for a search party. Police will need information which will help them to assess the situation. Whoever calls them needs to make it clear if there is a level of risk (to the person or to other people) or vulnerability. Being diagnosed with a mental health issue helps define someone as an at-risk person.

The first time it happens it will undoubtedly cause the family to feel very worried, collecting useful information to help the search may be challenging in all the panic. If the person goes missing on a regular basis it would be worth being prepared as it could help the police speed up the search. What have they taken with them? Have they got any money, do they have bank cards, what is their account number? Do they drive and what is their car registration number? Are they going to post on social media and, if so, what are their account details? Do they have a passport with them? Top of the list is having a photo that can be given to the police, any description is going to be less useful than a clear, recent photo.

A useful list is found online under the 'Herbert Protocol' – this includes a form which was originally developed for people with dementia but can be equally useful if someone is prone to running off and is at risk (as was the original Mr. Herbert). This form enables the family to record all this useful information and either have it to hand or lodge the form with the local police so the search can be triggered in the quickest possible way.

If the police assess the situation as high risk they will take immediate action, medium risk will also be acted on but less urgently. They can scan town centre CCTV and send up helicopters for the most worrying situations. Usually the person will be behaving in a way that makes them conspicuous somehow, so they will come to someone's attention.

It is important to realise that when a person is found the police cannot automatically return them home if they choose not to come. There are no legal powers which can be used to make someone come home just because the family are worried sick. If they are acting in a way that causes the police to suspect that they are at risk due to their mental health, maybe they are on the top of a multi-storey car park or acting recklessly in the middle of the road, then the police can use Sect. 136 of the Mental Health Act to take them to a 'place of safety' and then get a mental health assessment. That is the limit of their powers.

Another situation that can arise is when a person lives independently, say in their own flat, and the family have reason to be concerned but can't quickly visit themselves. Perhaps they usually phone each other every day but no-one has heard from them for two or three days, or they have put worrying messages on social media and then gone quiet. If a neighbour has called to say the curtains are drawn and the usual signs of life are not there, again the police may help.

In these circumstances they may agree to call round and do a 'safe and well' check, which could include breaking into the house if they feel it is necessary. There must be evidence that the person is at real risk so it would help to have information ready prepared and include details of any mental health issues.

Most people who run off are found and supported or return without mishap. Sometimes it can result in a Mental Health Act section but then, if they are in hospital, at least the family know where they are and that they are safe.

SUICIDE

This is the fear that underlies many mental health diagnoses. It's true that the suicide rate in the more severe mental health conditions is higher than the national average, that is one of those lurking shadows that many families live with.

How many suicidal acts are as a direct result of someone's mental health? That's hard to quantify but it is true that there doesn't have to be a mental health issue to commit suicide. Statistics can only include those with a known history and diagnosis of course, but just being desperate enough to kill yourself does not in itself mean that the person was mentally unwell.

I have known about fourteen people who had long-term mental health issues who died by suicide and a lot more who made (frequent) attempts. Those that I knew well I could see that there was some logic in their decision in some cases but sometimes it was a complete shock as they appeared to be on the road to recovery. I counted once that I had worked with over 350 people with a psychotic condition, so the odds of it happening seem low, going by my limited experience.

If there is a plan that is either happening now or just about to happen then the police or ambulance should be called. Medical help will be needed if it is not clear if they have taken too many pills or what they are. Other forms of suicide often require equipment, so if that appears then shout for assistance. If it is a threatened trip to a local suicide spot then the same applies, the police would be the better service here. It is not worth hesitating in these circumstances because keeping them safe may just be impossible without some help.

There is a saying that if people talk about committing suicide then it means they aren't going to do it. That isn't true. If this is mentioned then there needs to be a rapid assessment of the situation; if they are talking about it for the first time then there is every reason to take it very seriously. If it's the conversation that comes up every time they are feeling angry or upset but there has been no (recent) attempt and no immediate plan, then there seems to be less reason to get the blue lights flashing. There is more on this later.

This is the eternal quandary as a family carer of someone who has tried suicide, who maybe frequently still tries or who talks about trying. Taking it seriously every time will soon wear out the patience of the mental health team, of A&E or the GP as well as exhausting the carer. Some people consider suicide very frequently, it seems to be reassuring in the sense that it provides an option if all else fails. The family may not feel confident in assessing the level of risk themselves though, because the one time they take no action may be the time there is a successful attempt.

What helps is to notice and probably write down what triggers a suicidal episode and if there is anything that can be done about avoiding this situation. Is it drinking or peer pressure online? Is it hormones? Is it being reminded of their 'failures'? Identified triggers are useful information to tell the mental health team or GP who may be able to help. For example, if Christmas is a difficult time, as it is for many, could there be a temporary increase in medication or plans made to keep them company more of the time over the festive season?

When they are not in a suicidal state it could be helpful to raise the topic in conversation, as difficult as this sounds. One question that can be a place to start is whether they really do want to die, or do they just want their current life to change? If they want change then have all the forms of medication and treatment been exhausted or is it worth one more push to try something new with the mental health team? Is there an opportunity that might help them hold on, whether this is socialising more, getting a dog or trying a different support service?

It can be easy to get into the habit of not addressing the subject of suicide directly, perhaps in the belief that if the topic is brought up it will remind the person that this is an option and they will be more likely to make an attempt. A badly depressed or distressed person will have thought about it, many people consider it at least briefly at some stage in their lives. If the person is currently considering suicide then talking about it is probably going to be helpful, either because the family will show support and/ or the professionals can offer extra help. If they are not in that dark place then having a talk about it will show them that the family care about them, and everyone feels reassured. Mentioning it in conversation is unlikely to be enough by itself to drive someone to this.

The conversation can be quite direct depending on the relationship the carer has with that person. Some conversations may be more helpful than others though.

'Are you OK? You seem really out of sorts.'

'I'm fine.'

'I'm not sure that's true. You do seem very depressed. I always worry since you took all those pills a while ago that you might try that again. You shouldn't think about that stuff you know; you should focus on how you are going to get better. You're not thinking about it again are you?'

'I do think about it sometimes.'

'I thought so, I can always tell. You know we all love you and it would upset us all terribly if you tried again. You need to think about all the things you have to live for.'

'I can't help it; everything seems so hopeless.'

'Hopeless? Never. Remember what the doctor said. You have to keep trying to fight this thing.'

'OK.' (Retreats into silence.)

This conversation might make the carer feel better, but I suspect it hasn't done much for the person who is feeling bad – except to show that their family cares about them. The carer has said their bit but not found out what is going on. They have effectively closed the topic down by saying that the person should be looking on the bright side and should not worry the family. They should control their thoughts so that they only think positive things. That is a lot of 'shoulds' - which is effectively giving them orders.

As no-one can stop a thought coming into their head, this is asking the impossible. It is like saying to a carer 'don't worry', it's a complete waste of breath. No one can control their thoughts; they can only control how they react to them.

Does this attempt at a conversation sound better?

'You're looking very down; in fact you've been really low for a while. Can I help at all?'
'No, I'm OK.'
'You sure?'
'I am feeling bad really.'
'I'm worried about you, especially because you took all those pills a while ago. Does it feel that bad again?'
'Yes, a bit.'
'What do you think might help you to get through this?'
'I don't know. I just feel there is no point hoping.'
'Do you sometimes think about taking more pills or something like that?'
'Yes, sometimes.'
'Do you think you actually might try it again?'
'I might. I can't see how else this can end.'
'Is there anything that anyone can do?' Can you think of anything that could make it a bit less hopeless?
'No.'
'That sounds a desperate place to be. Are you sure nothing will help? You could take some stronger medication, or we could look for someone who you could talk to?'

'I think about it a lot. I just don't know'
'Well would you try some more help before you make a final decision? Shall we see if we can think of something?'
'OK.'

That conversation is still very worrying, but the carer has left the door open, has not gone into a panic (well not in front of the person anyway) and has offered to try to get some help.

The offer of a place to talk about this topic without being judged could make a huge difference. Crucially the carer must try to rein in the natural instinct to persuade and plead, which is really tough in these circumstances, although it is natural to want to show them how much you care about them. Again 'I' statements are useful such as 'I know this is a terrible choice for you but I want you to know that I really hope that you decide not to do it' or 'I realise that you feel as though you want your life to end but I will do everything I can to help change your mind'. Staying chilled and allowing them to explore what they are thinking without a strong emotional response is asking a lot. Professionals find this easier for obvious reasons.

Some people will not talk about it, there will be no chance of a conversation. There are signs that can indicate that suicide is being considered including:

- Behaviours such as stockpiling pills or their browsing history on 'how to' sites.
- Giving away their belongings or writing 'goodbye' letters/ notes to people.
- Posting messages on social media that have a different, worrying feel to them.
- A dramatic increase in risky behaviour, which could be sexual promiscuity, drug use (including alcohol), defiant and disruptive behaviour (at school or elsewhere).

- Increased self-harming.
- Socially isolating themselves, cutting off from everyone. This might include physical distancing or reduced social interaction by phone or online.

There is no guarantee that there will be a clear indication, there may be slight or no warning signs.

When a person makes a serious attempt to die their reasoning it is not always easily understood. There can be delusional beliefs but even without those they may seem to have fixed on one idea, maybe 'the world would be better off without me'. All the information they know about people who love them and who are desperate to help them just seems not to have any influence at that time. Depression stops the mental debate; the person just seems to focus on the pro-suicide argument and lose track of the other factors. This can feel particularly painful for the family as they may believe that they didn't do enough, but according to many accounts of survivors the recurring idea seemed to be, 'I just didn't think about that, I just wanted to die.'

Suicide is even more painful when there is a mental health problem preventing the person from making what most of us could understand as a rational decision. I find it a bit easier to accept that a lot of elderly people find ways to make an exit and that seems to me, nearing that time myself, to be pretty reasonable for some that have major health problems that aren't ever going to go away. It is much harder to accept when the person concerned would struggle to look at the wider picture and make a balanced choice.

It takes a great degree of courage to complete the act of committing suicide, taking pills is often considered simple but it requires a lot of swallowing, and then resisting calling for help straight afterwards. The more instant methods, where there is no way back, seem much more worrying because they can be an impulse; no time to reconsider and change your mind.

There is a strong possibility that any person considering suicide both wants to and doesn't want to, at the same time. I want to get thin and I want to eat cake. I want to carry on drinking and I want to have healthy liver. Which side wins? If you put pressure on the 'you shouldn't do that' side of the argument, then the person may focus more strongly on the 'but I want to do that' side. It is suggested that it is more helpful to allow them to think about both sides of the argument equally freely without too much of a dramatic reaction.

Someone who smokes knows that it is harmful to their health, but this goes up against 'I can't possibly manage without my cigs'. If a friend gives them a lecture on lung cancer they are telling them what they already know and are currently successfully ignoring. Being open to the reasons why they think they cannot get by without cigarettes may help more. Listening to someone talk about why they want to die is asking a lot but there may be a point that is open to negotiation or where a delay could be agreed, just to see if anything more positive does turn up. 'If you wait three months then you will know whether things actually can change,' may be more persuasive than, 'Don't do it because you'll regret it and the family will be upset.' Hopefully if a delay is negotiated then the person will feel different, forget or move on in that time.

Another real challenge is accepting that whatever happens no one can prevent this, if people are determined they will find a way. It isn't the carer's decision to make, they can offer help and support, that is all they can do.

If the worst does happen there are special counsellors available to family members who can help to work through the process of coming to terms with this devastating loss.

REPEATED THREATS OF SUICIDE

This is a different matter. For a small group of people suicide is not a sensitive and difficult topic but may become a regular part of their conversation, most probably as either a veiled threat or blatant warning. These are often people who make serious or maybe not so serious attempts. Perhaps they take medication that they know is not going to be fatal or they do something dramatic but ensure that someone knows where they are and what's going on so that they will get rescued in time.

This puts the carer in a difficult position. Do they take these repeated threats seriously knowing that there is always a risk that an attempt may succeed? They may end up going along with whatever the person wants even if they believe that this is not helping them in the long run. This can be a feature of personality disorders. The emotional needs of the person are so strong that they develop desperate strategies to get them met. Finding that they get a flurry of attention following a suicide attempt becomes a means to an end. If talking about killing yourself gets what you want, then that is a useful strategy. The fear is that if these demands are not met then the person will have to make a more serious attempt to prove they meant it or to 'punish' the offending person.

The decision to not collude with this behaviour needs to be based on evidence that is gathered over a period of time. If the threat of suicide appears to be used to achieve a specific end, then the carer may have to consider their response. 'If you tell anyone about my self-harm I will kill myself,' is a not uncommon ultimatum, so the carer stays awake half the night worrying after a bad cutting session and then has another miserable and resentful day while the person appears perfectly calm and happy. The long-term implication of this, if it is a regular pattern, is that the person with the mental health issue is 'stuck' and the family are exhausted and losing patience.

It is tough to decide to change the response to a threat and to carry it through. If the situation needs to be changed then it will probably have to be the carer that changes it. It can help if there is support or advice from other carers or professionals. There are also PD websites that give useful information for families, (rather than the personal blogs).

If no support is available then one tip is to think through what advice would be useful if this were a situation where a friend with an identical issue was asking for help, what would be their best option? It might also be helpful to look at the 'problem solving' section.

The next time this 'if you tell anyone about my self-harm I will kill myself' ultimatum is given then one option is to follow this sort of plan - although it is not without risks.

1. Recognise their feelings:

'I understand that you don't want me to tell the nurse, it really frightens you that the mental health team might do something you don't want them to do. I do realise that this is a very scary thought for you'.

2. State your feelings:

'I am not doing this just to upset you but I can't carry on knowing that you are cutting yourself, sometimes badly, and I am not doing anything. I can't cope with this on my own. I am worried all the time about what will happen, and it is making me exhausted and unhappy'.

3. Tell them what you are going to do:

'I am going to sit in the car now and phone the nurse and tell him. I shall tell the truth about what happened last night'.

4. Make it clear that what they do is their choice and not your responsibility:

'I really, really hope that you don't kill yourself, I care about you too much and I would be devastated. But it is your choice, you have control over what you decide to do.'

5. Stand firm in the face of opposition

'I am sorry that you are upset and think that I am letting you down, but I feel this is making me ill and I cannot cope alone any longer. I care about you so much and I want you to stay alive, but in the end it is your decision. I hope you decide to live and that you understand why I need to do this. I will see you when I get back and we can talk about it.'

Do it.

Deal with the consequences.

This will probably mean coming back to an angry sulking person but that over time this more equal relationship can be built on. Showing that there is a line being drawn, and that it is going to be permanent, can be helpful particularly with PD where the person may struggle to contain their behaviour themselves.

Possibly this 'betrayal' may lead to them hurting themselves again, followed by a period of agitated and distressed behaviour. It may seem unsafe to 'inform' on them again for a while depending on how serious this injury is, but if it is a regular behaviour pattern that has become something that has to be managed across lots of other situations too, then the decision might be more straightforward.

It is crucial that being controlled by threats is never an open-ended prospect, self-harm and suicide should not be used as emotional blackmail and must be challenged at some stage. This is an impossible situation where the carer has to have faith that a new behaviour can be established in the longer term and this action is necessary to protect the wellbeing of others in the household, including themselves.

The most feared situation for a carer is if they return and the worst has happened, the person with the mental health issue has killed themselves. Any attempt at reassurance from friends and relatives will be swamped by guilt. The chances of this happening are exceedingly small, but it is a possibility that cannot be ignored. There are a few key points that might be worth considering if this did happen.

- A great deal of time and energy has been put into looking after them and keeping them safe.
- There was an impossibly difficult decision to make, the dangers were considered but it was clear what would happen if the situation carried on as it was. There would have been constant risk and the rest of the family would have become worn down and unwell themselves.
- Everything that could be done was done and in the end the decision was completely theirs.

There are special counsellors that can help people bereaved by suicide, it may be useful to find one to talk things through if this situation ever happens. There is no quick way to get over this loss, but it can help to acknowledge that the family carer did what they thought was right with the information they had available.

MENTAL HEALTH LAW

This Act is the legal means by which someone can be made to go to a 'place of safety' and be kept there until they are permitted to leave. They can also be made to accept treatment. This is the only law that can deprive someone of their liberty without finding them guilty of committing a crime so understandably it may seem threatening, but it is used cautiously.

I have met several people who live in fear of the Mental Health Act and families can also be confused about what is possible. The result of this confusion can be lots of unnecessary fear and worry, which is why it is worth having a quick look at the basic facts.

Psychiatric units are no longer the old places of cruelty and chaos, but they can be stressful as would be expected when there are very unwell people there. Although not always havens of calm and tranquillity, they are usually very safe (safer than trying to keep highly distressed people at home) and monitored by trained staff. If someone needs to be admitted they will be kept in for as short a time as possible because this is definitely best for them, for the person waiting for that bed and for the hospital's budget. So although the section may be for up to twenty-eight days they may be home after three.

The Act has different parts which are called sections, hence the term 'being sectioned'.

The criteria for being assessed under the Mental Health Act is that the person presents a significant risk to themselves or to others. This could be through suicide attempts, self-harm, lack of regard for danger or extremely poor self-care. They may threaten to be, or already be, aggressive and violent. The situation must be critical, some evidence of extreme behaviour needs to be produced that is definitely occurring because of a mental health issue.

Families cannot 'have people sectioned' as the final decision is always taken by trained professionals. They can give information and can say what they think is appropriate, but they do not make the final decision.

The process usually requires three professional opinions. Two are doctors, usually psychiatrists or maybe the person's GP, and an 'Approved Mental Health Professional' called an AMHP for short. These are often social workers but could come from a range of professions such as nurses or psychologists. They have had specialist training and their role is to organise the procedure, gather evidence from involved people and ensure that the least restrictive action is chosen. In other words, it is their job to make sure that all the options are explored and that taking this person to hospital against their will is absolutely the last resort.

If a carer said they could keep the person at home, keep them safe and make sure they kept appointments with the psychiatrist then this would be less restrictive than going into hospital. However, the three professionals would have to be convinced that the carer could realistically deliver this safe option and keep the person out of danger.

Getting these three people to where the person is can be a lengthy business and can take many hours. In the meantime, the family may be left in a very tense and tricky situation but can call the police if there is any significant danger during the waiting time.

If someone agrees to be admitted into hospital they cannot be sectioned, it is only applied if it is against their will. If they go into hospital as a voluntary patient and then try to walk out again then staff can use the law to keep them there, if they are considered at risk, until they are formally assessed. Then a section can be put in place.

Being sectioned has some long-term implications, i.e. job applications, visiting some countries, but it does not carry any criminal implications, there is no criminal record.

People detained under a section can be made to accept treatment. This sounds harsh but, in my experience, this is not used lightly. Staff know that forcing medication on people is a short-term solution. If the 'patient' is not convinced by the idea they will stop as soon as they get home, then they will go around the circle of relapse and admission again. It is in the best interest of everyone to try and get the person to understand why they need the medication, rather than force it on them in the short-term. Most 'patients' quickly pick up that they are more likely to go home if they take their meds, this can make people strangely compliant, at least in the short-term.

People may be sedated, using force if necessary, but this happens only when they are aggressive or violent (perhaps towards themselves). It is dramatic when a group of staff pounce on someone and hold them down. They usually inject them in the buttock, which can also look brutal. I can't say that this power is never abused but I do know there is a great deal of paperwork and justification to be done after each incident. The reason several staff are used in these actions is because the situation is then better controlled, this prevents the person getting into a scuffle where either they or someone else gets hurt. This system has been developed over time as the most effective option and should only be used where someone has becoming out of control and a serious incident is likely.

Hospitals are to keep people safe and to observe them so better judgements can be made about treatment plans (rather than the 'cure' expected from physical health wards). On the whole that is what they do: they offer an opportunity to assess and to plan treatment which continues after the patient leaves the unit, this should be monitored in the community by the local mental health team. People may be discharged 'on leave' but still under a section so they can be recalled quickly if the situation deteriorates.

MENTAL HEALTH ACT SECTIONS

The different parts of the Act have different implications, this is a quick reference. Anybody involved in any procedure especially as the 'Nearest Relative' (see next section) should be given appropriate information at the time. The main point of including this information is to make it clear that being detained has time limits, each section is regularly reviewed and if the Act is used inappropriately there are serious consequences for the professionals involved, so it is used very carefully.

Section 2 is a period of observation and is usually used first. After being assessed there will probably be an offer of treatment which could be medication and/ or talking treatments. Section 2 lasts up to twenty-eight days, but the person can be discharged at any time.

Section 3 usually follows a Section 2, only if the person is not considered safe to discharge after the full twenty-eight days. Section 3 is for up to six months, may be renewed for six months and then yearly. Again, it needs two doctors and an AMHP and the Nearest Relative (see next section) must be consulted.

Under these sections people can be made to stay on the unit and to accept treatment, which includes medication and other talking treatments but not ECT, which requires the patient's specific consent if they have capacity, or a second psychiatrist's opinion if they are not able to understand the implications themselves (the family are often involved in this decision too).

Sections 135 and 136 are used by the police. Section 136 is used in a public place and 135 used if the person is in a private house - in which case the police need a court order to go in to get the person out, which takes time. I have heard that experienced officers may try to lure the person out onto the pavement (come and have a breath of fresh air/ cigarette/ see our new patrol car) so they can use 136 and act more quickly. Family can help with this.

Police take them to a 'place of safety' for up to twenty-four hours, this can be a '136 Suite' (special room in the hospital) but these may be busy. Police cells are avoided these days, thank goodness, so often the option is an A&E department with a police escort which is obviously not ideal. Technically a person's home or a family home is legally acceptable, but this is rarely used as it is too complex to manage safely. A full clinical assessment is organised during that twenty-four hours and it is converted to a Section 2 if the criteria are met.

Community Treatment Orders (CTO) can be used after a Section 3. This allows the person to live in the community by setting conditions such as taking medication regularly, living in a fixed place and keeping appointments. It is mostly used when someone stops taking their medication as soon as they are discharged from hospital and then they get involved in either criminal or risky behaviour and this pattern is repeated many times. If they do not comply with the conditions of the CTO they can be returned to hospital immediately. It lasts for up to six months, may be renewed for six more months and then yearly, it is approved by the psychiatrist in charge of care and an AMHP.

NEAREST RELATIVE (NR)

This is a legal term which gives a relative or friend certain important rights under the Mental Health Act. It is worth knowing about this if it looks possible that the person with the mental health issue may be sectioned at some point. There will be appropriate information supplied as the section proceeds but sometimes in these stressful situations it is easy to miss details.

The NR is not the same as the next of kin and not the same as the carer. Of course, one person can be the next of kin, carer and Nearest Relative, which makes life much more straightforward.

The person closest to the top of this list is the NR under this law:

Husband, wife or civil partner
Son or daughter
Father or mother
Brother or sister
Grandparent
Grandchild
Uncle or aunt
Niece or nephew

They must be over eighteen years old. If partners (including same sex) have lived together for six months or more this counts, partners/spouses who are permanently separated are not. With two 'equal' people, perhaps father and mother, the eldest would be appointed and similarly full blood relatives over 'step' ones. Those who live abroad are not included as they are not likely to be involved in the situation to any great degree.

There are more complex rules and details which can be

easily researched (the national charity MIND website is helpful) but most relevant information is given at the time.

If the NR is not suitable in some way they can be removed from that position. An AMHP can apply to the court to have them removed if they have a health problem themselves and are unable or inappropriate to carry out the role. This removal can be challenged in court.

A NR can delegate someone else, but they must put it in writing to their chosen person and to the NHS Trust involved. The patient can also apply to have their NR removed but this is also a county court process. They can also nominate someone if they don't have a NR, or one that is prepared to get involved, but again, this needs to be agreed by the court.

This may seem unnecessarily complex but not all close relatives have the best interest of their cared-for person at heart and this helps to protect those who live with damaging relationships or with abuse.

If you are the NR what does that mean?

Most importantly they can request that a person is assessed under the Mental Health Act. This doesn't mean they will automatically be sectioned and admitted, it still must be approved by the three professionals, but it can start the process. An NR can request an assessment by letter or verbally by contacting the duty worker in the Assessment and Treatment service (ATS). The person, probably a social worker, who investigates the situation will ask for the NR's evidence and then check with the GP and other involved people. If the person is already known to the mental health team then they will look at their records. If they decide there is enough evidence to proceed then they will then get the section process under way by arranging for two doctors and an AMHP to see the person with the mental health issue. Or they may decide there is just not enough evidence and it all stops there.

Other NR rights include:

- To be informed if your relative is detained under Section 2. The AMHP will ask your opinion on what should happen in most circumstances, but legally the NR just need to be told that it is happening.
- To be consulted if Section 3 is being considered. This means that the sectioning process should consider the NR's information and opinion.
- They can request discharge under Sections 2 and 3 and under CTOs. This involves presenting a case to a psychiatrist that a safe alternative is available such as caring at home, but the psychiatrist has the final decision. If the NR 'request to discharge' is refused, then it goes to the hospital managers who are independent people who hear these cases. They take evidence from professionals and from the patient themselves, whenever this is possible.
- NRs should be given notification of the end of a section as often this will mean coming home, unless the patient's psychiatrist feels they need to stay in hospital and they are willing to do that without being sectioned again.
- Regarding confidentiality, the patient still has a right to withhold consent to give an NR any information about them; the NR has no more rights here than any other carer. (See the patient confidentiality section)

Everyone who is detained under the Mental Health Act has the right to an independent mental health advocate (IMHA) who will support them to get their viewpoint heard. A NR can seek independent legal advice too if they want to, especially if they feel the section process was not carried out properly.

A common experience is that the person who has been

sectioned becomes aware that the carer has been consulted, maybe they have agreed with the section process or at least not put up a fight against it. They may also quickly find out that their NR is entitled to request their discharge. Mental health units often have experienced patients who helpfully tell new people these useful tips. The result of this may possibly be a great deal of anger and pressure on the NR to get them home. Failing to do this may be viewed as an act of personal betrayal.

The fact that this person desperately needs to be in a safe place and get some treatment does not mean that they will appreciate the NR's part in proceedings, they may well be hostile for some time afterwards. It helps if other people can be around to remind the carer /NR why it was essential to do this, it is easy to start doubting any decision under pressure. If the professionals all agreed then it was very probable that a section was necessary, and although being on the unit may not be the most pleasant experience it may be the best option in the circumstances.

EVERYDAY CHALLENGES

Supporting someone with a mental health issue is not a constant battle, it isn't that at all. However, there is not much to say about the straightforward bits when everything is coasting along reasonably smoothly. This section considers a selection of 'non-crisis' situations that may or may not arise.

REFUSING MEDICATION

One of the issues that is worth a mention is that of getting the person to cooperate with any treatment plan. Medication is not the only treatment of course, but when someone is extremely unwell it may be the only option. This section is again more relevant to the more complex conditions although many with anxiety or depression struggle to cope without a prescription.

No intervention means that the outcome depends on the person with the mental health issues shaking off their symptoms, either physically or psychologically or both. If they appear to be improving then this is less of a gamble, if not then help may be required.

It is a major step to acknowledge that things are bad enough that 'something needs to be done'. Friends and relatives of this person may be putting pressure on the main carer to make this happen, and perhaps on the person themselves too.

It isn't an easy decision for the family, research on medication can be frightening as the side effects can look horrendous. It takes a while to accept that not all of these happen to everybody, they do tend to lessen after a time and if it is too unbearable then the medication can be stopped (although not suddenly, there should always be a planned and gradual withdrawal). Medication may be all there is that will help in this high stress situation.

For the carer it is obvious, having studied the aspects of the situation that is worrying them, on websites or whatever is available, and all the searches say, 'get medical help'. They have accepted this as inevitable. However, many who experience the symptoms of a mental health condition will not consider the possibility of getting medical help, it is just not on their radar.

What happens now? For many families there can be months of cajoling, bribing, blackmailing, shouting and getting really, really upset and/or angry.

'But a doctor could help you feel less stressed.'
'I'm telling you that you need some help, why can't you admit that?'
'Lots of people get help with their mental health, there is nothing to be ashamed of.'
'There isn't the same stigma these days, look at (insert name of suitable celebrity here).'

The carer can also end up screaming
'For ****'s sake can't you see what's going on?'
'Why are you being so ****** stubborn?'
'Don't you care what you are putting me and the rest of the family through?'
'How can you be so selfish?'

These reactions all fall well within the normal range in my experience.

There may be lots of theories as to why help is being refused. Are they frightened of accepting that they might be experiencing mental health issues? Is it embarrassment or fear of the treatment, of strait jackets, mind-altering drugs, being locked up? Is it just denial? Is it that they actually feel fine? Is it that they won't do it because they just don't believe or trust the people around them?

People with low self-esteem may believe that they are not worth being helped or that nothing can possibly change. For highly anxious people the fear of seeing someone and talking about this personal issue is extremely threatening.

Often winning the battle to get someone to the GP and possibly then to the psychiatrist, with the added hurdle of getting them to be honest about their situation, results in being issued with a prescription. They get the little packet(s) of pills and everyone involved has the reassuring thought that at last things are going to improve. Several storylines can unfold from this point.

- They take the meds and have awful side effects and suddenly stop taking them but tell no one. Several weeks later a stash of nearly full packets is found somewhere, or a little yellow pill appears floating in the loo. This can result in the complex negotiation to get a different prescription and try again, or the total refusal to try anything else ever.
- They take the meds for several weeks/months and feel better. They are now sorted out, right? So why carry on taking them? They stop and the symptoms return soon afterwards.
- They never even take one. This can be because they feel better from talking to the doctor or they only went to the

doctors to keep everyone off their backs and never had any intention of taking them anyway.

- They take them, the side effects aren't too bad, they feel much better.

You have some options at this point with the first three outcomes.

Firstly, the family want this person to give medication a reasonable try so why not bring up the subject on a daily/twice daily/ hourly basis, repeating how sensible this would be, it's got to be better than feeling so awful hasn't it? Back to begging, pleading, emotional blackmail, bribes and threats. The family remain desperate to grab this lifeline, but the person seems willing to tolerate the distress they are apparently experiencing and the upset they are causing the people around them.

Option two: look online for methods to get a dog/cat to take pills and wonder if it would constitute assault on a family member. Decide that it would.

Thirdly, get other people involved if there is anyone who can be trusted. Others who have experienced mental health issues are especially valuable or relatives and friends that the person likes or respects. A major intervention with the whole extended family, the local newsagent and their teacher from primary school may be too much. Picking gentle people who can be sensitive to how difficult this problem is will make the conversation less pressurised.

Lastly, shrug off the sense of desperation and hang on to the fact that they may try them later if they have a change of heart, or the situation changes.

Or all of the above in no particular order.

Follow up appointments with mental health practitioners seem to be frequently met with ineffective persuasion too. The professional may have a short conversation with the person pointing out the benefits of the medication, which may be followed with the statement, 'Of course, we can't make you take them.' Why did they say that, it is legally true but that's no help at all?

The fact is that the professionals have no more power than the family does to make someone take their meds. The exception to this rule is using powers under the Mental Health Act which can compel people to take treatment. This is used only in extreme, high risk circumstances. Threats of suicide, self-harm or aggressive behaviour are not always enough to justify using these powers even if the family feel it's obviously needed. It could be so easily misused and then the Human Rights issues would be frightening.

Taking medication can be such a hurdle for some people, it should be borne in mind that a large percentage of medication for physical health issues also never gets taken. There are added implications to taking mental health meds as they are often seen as 'messing with your mind' or as a sign of weakness. (If it is so straightforward then why do so many carers only take anti-depressants as a last resort when they really have no other alternative, and are clearly slightly embarrassed when they say they take them?)

It helps to keep any comments on such sensitive subjects brief and calm, they are more likely to be heard and to not create a highly emotional situation which could then lead to what is technically known as 'a wobble'. This won't help anyone.

Things will either get better, or they will get worse and then some further action will have to be taken.

Where there is a severe mental health issue such as bi-polar or psychosis then there is one other possibility. There is a symptom called 'anosognosia', which seems an unnecessarily obscure word but useful to impress people at dinner parties. If the person you support seems completely unaware of the unusual nature of their behaviour and thoughts (delusions) and sees no reason on earth to consider medication, then read on.

They think they are fine, everyone else thinks there is something very wrong. This leads to a stand-off between these two viewpoints, 'You're not well, take some meds,' and 'You're persecuting me, I don't need your help. Go away!' Many years can pass with repetitive arguments, bad feeling and no progress.

The man to research is Dr Xavier Amador who personally went through this process for several years with his brother who had a diagnosis of schizophrenia.

What Dr Amador suggests is that this apparent inability to acknowledge what is happening is a direct result of the mental health issue. The person is unable to update their view of themselves, so as far as they are concerned they are just as they always have been. This is not a psychological defence mechanism ('I know there is a problem but I'm not admitting it'), this is a cognitive inability to process the fact that they have changed. It would be like me looking in the mirror and genuinely 'seeing' myself as being thirty years old – fat chance. Some people with psychotic conditions get stuck at the time when this 'update who I am now' switch got turned off, so to them they are still fine and there is no need for treatment.

People who have had a stroke and lose the function of a limb can display the same symptom, hotly denying there is any damage, they just don't feel like moving their arm right now. People with dementia may appear completely unaware that they have any loss of memory function or are doing things in an odd way. It seems that this symptom may also occur in the more severe mental health issues.

Dr Amador not only describes this in easily understandable terms, he also suggests a way of approaching it. This involves a careful and deliberate strategy:

- Listen to the person, which is no bad suggestion in any circumstances, and is described more fully in the section on 'listening'
- Find out what their goals are in life
- Use these to motivate them to take their medication

This is a lengthy process, which involves months of not pressurising them and creating trust. If they come to feel safe when talking to the carer then they may chat about how they would like their future to turn out and be open to a conversation about what may help them to achieve this. These need to be their own inspirations and aims, not necessarily the slightest bit related to what the family feel may be best for them.

For example, they said they wanted to find a partner, have a relationship like other people. A discussion about how the medication might help with this could be more persuasive where all the family's sensible facts and rational arguments have failed. The carer might propose that the meds would make them a bit more confident so they could meet people through internet dating and cope with having a coffee with them without appearing anxious.

This is also a useful strategy when someone is experiencing delusional ideas. For example, if they wanted to be a professional singer, because there is now a degree of trust they may begin to talk about becoming famous as though it is a certainty and going to happen soon. Talking about it one day a carer could say, 'You might need to go to an audition at some stage if you want to be spotted. I know you don't like big crowds, maybe a bit of medication could help you cope with that?'

Perhaps they feel that they are being interfered with mentally and that there are rays being beamed into their brain. Could the medication be something that would strengthen their own cognitive processes, if their brain were feeling stronger would it help them feel more in control and less worried about this?

Notice how no example directly colludes with the delusion by saying, 'You will be famous,' nor does it say, 'There are people interfering with your thoughts.'

There is no short cut here, you can't get to the end result by having a quick conversation. It is a result of trust building and a slow, gentle discussion. (see also 'Encouraging change: talking about it' section)

This is a complex process and not easy to describe so watching Dr Amador's TED talk on YouTube or try the LEAP Foundation website or buy/borrow his book called *'I Am Not Sick I Don't Need Help! How to Help Someone with Mental Illness Accept Treatment'*.

You may choose not to follow this advice, but it is worth being aware of the ideas in it. It does at least create the possibility that it may not be the family who are failing to help this person understand their situation, it may be that they are unable rather than unwilling. After all there is no reason to take medication if you are not unwell.

STAYING IN THEIR ROOMS / BEING NOCTURNAL

It seems to be that many people who experience the more severe mental health issues come out of their rooms only rarely and then it is often at night. Their internal clock seems to slip until they sleep most of the day and become active only with the hours of darkness. It is not difficult to guess why this happens, but it is only a guess.

Maybe there is a difficulty in coping with a lot of stimulation such as daylight, a busy kitchen, the phone ringing. Perhaps it is because they prefer being unobserved, which may feel safer. It might be that medication is causing them to sleep for long periods or that a feeling of depression means they just can't find the strength to get out of bed. It may be much easier to leave their room for the bare necessities of life when everyone else is out of the way. This way they can avoid difficult conversations about how they are feeling, what should they be working on, are they going to see the psychiatrist on Wednesday or just not having to confront the fact that their mind is either far too full or far too empty to have a conversation of any sort.

The choices for the family seem to be:

- Knock quietly on their door and ask them if they would like some lunch.
- Knock loudly on their door and march in, tell them to get up and do something.
- Avoid addressing them except through the door or by text but leave them food and water outside.

In the end it may be that these all get tried but realistically no one can make them come out and be more sociable. When they do appear, the trick is to greet them calmly, quietly and cheerfully with no hint of the hours of worry or frustration that the carer has been through. If their appearance causes a negative reaction, as they see it, this may reduce the probability that they will emerge again when there are people around, given a choice.

If they are staying in their room all day it is important that they don't get dehydrated, so a water bottle can be useful. Other than that, food is the main way to tempt them out, but this doesn't always work particularly if they have taken to scavenging in the kitchen during nightly excursions. This will be yesterday's chicken that you were saving for a curry, chocolate bars, bread and peanut butter or crisps. There is a strong possibility that the salad bowl will remain unscathed. There may well be a trail of mess left as well.

Several medications can make a person very hungry, particularly for carbohydrates. If this is the case – check with a pharmacist if necessary – there may be some drastic weight gain. This can be unavoidable although the professional advice is to leave out healthy snacks such as raw carrot. Yeah! That is going to work, but it is worth a try.

Strategies for mess reduction that I have discussed over the years include:

- Leaving out pre-packed food. Advantage, the mess is reduced. Disadvantage, they lose their ability to cook. If they are not currently using any cooking skills this can be a useful option.
- Defining an area of the fridge as theirs. Advantage, they still need to make a meal. Disadvantage, if they are hungry enough the rules go out of the window and tomorrow's cream cakes are not safe.

Family tensions can also arise because the person has no understanding of the word 'quietly'; they may clump down the stairs, wake the dog and bash about in the kitchen at 3 am. Would a large notice opposite their door that says 'Please Sssssh!' remind them to tiptoe? Can the dog go elsewhere?

They may also play their X box games or favourite grime music or the 1812 at full volume. Usually there is a compromise, will they keep the volume below 11 and everyone else wear earplugs? Will they wear earphones, at least at night, so they can listen as loud as they like? Will they limit the noise to a couple of hours and the rest of the family retreat to a safe distance with their own distractions for that time?

It may be possible to do some joint planning if an opportunity arises. People may just not be aware of the tensions they are causing in the house and it may be difficult to bring these topics up, especially if you are concerned about an emotional reaction that results in a dip in their mental health. A positive approach is to say,

'There is a problem because .... is happening, can you suggest a way this could be improved?' Picking the right time on the right day is a skill that is learnt by trial and error. Of course, if they are just never seen because they are holed up in their room then it may be a communication through notes, texts or WhatsApp.

This night-time wandering and eating are mentioned frequently in any group of carers. It is always a fine balance trying to accommodate them and the rest of the family. They should not go unchallenged though if it is causing disruption, there is usually some way to make it a bit less antisocial. It may be a question of thinking outside the box, have a look at the 'problem solving' section for inspiration.

LACK OF MOTIVATION

There may be a whole variety of reasons why someone is apparently unable or unwilling to try anything new or even just to do everyday tasks. It can be tricky to find out what the reasons are for this inertia, they might include:

- They are not able to find the strength to get going, they feel too overwhelmed with depression or hopelessness
- They have forgotten how to do these things; the task seems too complex to manage
- They are worried they will try and then fail
- Their medication is making them very tired
- Their mental health issue is making them tired or unable to focus and think things through
- They know if they wait then you will do it or at least stop asking them to
- There is nothing in it for them, their attention is elsewhere
- They feel that because they have this diagnosis it is unfair to expect this from them

This list is not encouraging, I am aware of this. There is also a big difference between being stuck for a short time and the longer-term hard-to-shift habits. Any action rests pretty much on whether the carer feels that they are ready to move forward or now seems like a bad time. Understanding and accepting that there are good reasons why someone may find it enormously difficult to tackle even the smallest action, especially during the times when they are most unwell, can lead to a more accepting and therefore peaceful life.

Often the only way to find out is to question the situation gently and see what happens.

> 'I have been meaning to talk to you about looking for something to do during the day. I am worried that being around the house all the time is not interesting for you. How do you feel about looking for something new to try?'

If it works and the reaction is not totally negative, then cause for celebration. If it doesn't then observe what happens next, if your request causes a noticeable increase in genuine anxiety then it is definitely not the right time.

If it seems it is becoming a longer-term habit rather than just their mental health symptoms, then there is a difficult decision to make.

The key is to identify a motivator which outweighs the many reasons they have not to do things. This means that it is either something that they feel is important or that there are negative outcomes for them if they fail to do it. It could be working towards recovering or perhaps recognising what will happen if they fail to make any changes. This may mean offering incentives or a frank discussion about possible consequences if nothing shifts, basically bribery and blackmail.

There must be obstacles to any changes, it is helpful if these are understood, which requires some patient conversations. If they won't come out for a walk is it for fear of being seen by someone they know or is it just too much effort? Is it the medication making them tired or do they feel fat and unfit, if that is an issue? Would moving the walk away from the local area help or a 'start small' programme of just a quick stroll round the block? There can be incentives such as a film afterwards or an ultimatum that no one will buy their favourite biscuits unless they walk to the shop too.

Alternatively, it could help to think through a situation and prepare what to do in any tricky bits. If they have a plan to cope with an anxiety producing situation or they can approach it with back up the first few times that could help get things moving. For example: if they want to go to an art class could a member of the family join too and then quietly drop out after week three? If they want to contact work colleagues is there one person they trust who could either go in with them, or be in the Zoom meeting at the same time?

Change does happen but it can be very gradual, sometimes success is overlooked because the steps have been small and gradual. That is why it can be encouraging to keep a diary, an occasional look back to how things were a while ago might identify where progress has been made and keep the family feeling positive.

For further information it could be worth looking at 'encouraging change' section.

SOCIAL MEDIA AND GAMING

There seems to be an increasing worry in the last few years described by desperate carers whose (usually but not always) sons or partners are spending all day on various screen-based activities. They are concerned about their poor sleep patterns, eyesight, loss of social skills, lack of physical exercise and in some cases, addiction.

These people are literally screen watching from getting up at lunch time until the early hours of the morning. This is, of course, not just a matter that affects people with mental health issues. Is it a problem? On one hand there is some mental activity going on and some virtual social contact, but on the other hand those long hours and the exclusion of all other activity is not a healthy way to while away your years. This lifestyle may also potentially affect mental health, it has been suggested.

Often these screen junkies are living with depression or anxiety, they may lack social skills or have struggled with school or work and lost confidence. Before the online life existed these people may have been more isolated, far lonelier and lacking in purpose. Perhaps sitting in front of the laptop is one way of feeling that you fit in with your peer group. As the communication with others is 'virtual' there is great scope for anonymity and creating alternative personas. Some people use social media or gaming as a means of passing time and it can be helpfully distracting, or it can feed their sense of fear or paranoia. There is nothing so inventive as the internet if you are looking for conspiracy theories. So, is it an asset or a liability?

What are the alternatives? What would they be doing otherwise? Would they honestly be throwing together a healthy salad in their kitchen or walking in the local woods? Maybe and maybe not.

The challenge maybe is to get a bit more of a balance in how each day is spent. Like everything else it seems sensible to try, but the carers I have encountered haven't had much luck. Maybe it's a new enough issue that no one can say confidently, 'They'll stop at some point when they have had enough,' currently that reassurance is not available.

Peer pressure on social media is seen as contributing to self-esteem issues, impacting on confidence and causing distress. Would cutting off all online contacts be preferable? This undoubtedly would be safest but not necessarily a genuine alternative, for many people that would be simply unthinkable. It can be a real source of support and comfort after all. If there was a guarantee that all their online activity was positive and helpful it wouldn't be so worrying, but this virtual world doesn't work that way. What would replace this rather hazardous social contact in their lives if this were not available?

Sites that encourage increased self-harm or suicide attempts can be particularly worrying, they can be very persuasive, causing untold damage when someone is vulnerable.

Gaming is potentially more constructive, perhaps. It requires an active brain and may include interaction with others, which requires no (real) personal information to be exchanged. Many of these games appear to be based on violence though; some opinion implies that viewing a lot of brutality may decrease the normal inhibition to being aggressive. On the other hand, this popular activity may give a sense of belonging to something bigger and perhaps a sense of achievement as well. That excitement is difficult to duplicate in the real world when you've had a serious knock back such as a mental health diagnosis. If only it could be for three hours a day rather than sixteen.

Another big issue is porn. Viewing what are often cruel or degrading images for hours every day has got to be unhealthy. Perhaps the lack of a real sexual relationship may feed into the desire to watch this stuff. Perhaps the medication has caused some impotence issues, this is some form of compensation for this. It seems that sizeable proportion of the population looks at porn anyway, it has to be considered as normal behaviour now.

Vulnerable people can evidently fear that they are 'perverted' or a paedophile because they are 'turned on' by these images.

Those people who spend more time in the outside world may be able to observe their own reactions and see them as normal and just get on with their lives. That's a lot harder when you haven't got other ordinary blokes (or women) to compare yourself to.

Maybe there is room to negotiate if their online life has taken over. Will they join the family for a meal, or come out for a short walk? It may be that there is just a wall of refusal but there are only limited options that the family can try. The online life may be all the person feels they need; this is now their comfort zone.

What about child-safe protection on their computer? This sounds a simple option, but they will undoubtedly notice and for a thirty-five-year-old it's not going to be well received. If they have access at all then it is probably going to be impossible to limit what they choose to do.

There is the option of turning off the broadband of course, maybe for a short time. This may produce a strong reaction swiftly followed by a decision that it just is not worth it, the level of anger or distress is too great. It may be worth persevering if there is any successful communication during that time. Thirty minutes downstairs with the family being attentive might just work.

Perhaps the best outcome that can be achieved in the short term is a relationship where they talk about what they have been doing and ask for advice if they meet an issue that worries or upsets them. This may require that their time in front of a screen is accepted and negative remarks about it are few. Showing an interest in what they are doing or asking them to let other family members play against them may open the door to some communication even if these suggestions are refused. The crucial tactic is to avoid any judgemental remarks.

This is a slow burning strategy that requires a lot of patience; listening to even the most worrying information and responding calmly without judgement may create a chance of being able to influence this online life in the end. The 'I' statements could be helpful, maybe 'I wish that we could spend more time with you, I know you get a lot out of spending time online but I would love it of you would come and have a coffee now and then!' (See 'listening' section). That's the only suggestion I've got that may even vaguely work!

It may be that there is virtually no relationship with them because of their self-imposed isolation, perhaps it is based on occasional texts or brief visits to the kitchen for food, but few words. If everything possible has been tried by the family then consider whether this is time for Plan B. This online time can be the carer's time to get on with their life. It is not unknown for family members to sit and wait for this person to emerge bleary eyed, even though they haven't for weeks. If it becomes clear that they are not going to join the family and be sociable but they are safe and occupied, then this is a good time to go out, leave the black cloud hovering upstairs and go and do something completely different and distracting. Staying downstairs twitching at the smallest noise from their room is not making any changes happen.

THE FOUR PILLARS OF CARING

This is one of the few useful bits of direct guidance for family carers that I have discovered:

> 'Mental health professionals recommend that the four most important needs of patients that family members should meet are:
>
> predictability
> reduced stimulation
> appropriate expectations
> sensitivity to a person's self-esteem'

(Harty M.A. (2001) p 226)

This book isn't really for family carers but professionals (that is why it says 'should' so much). This list sums up what the family can be aiming for however, particularly when the person being supported is very fragile and sensitive, so it is worth looking at it in more detail.

PREDICTABILITY – the person with the mental health issue needs to know what is likely to happen next. This means establishing routines, being reliable and consistent and keeping them as informed as possible. A carer gave me some wonderful advice about supporting a person who was very psychotic and paranoid. Anxiety increases as the person they depend upon appears untrustworthy and plotting them harm. She suggested a bit of a running commentary, 'I am going into the kitchen now to make lunch, I'm making ham sandwiches. Then I am going to call your dad.' 'I'm just going to take the dog out; you can come if you like but it is raining. I'll be back before half past.' These bits of information can take the edge off the unease for someone who is expecting something terrible to happen at any moment.

In less extreme circumstances, predictability can mean setting routine mealtimes or times when the carer goes out and comes back. It could mean setting boundaries that if person's behaviour crosses certain lines, the reaction is always the same. If they make a major mess in the kitchen then they are not getting their favourite curry until it is cleared up, or if they are overly aggressive then the police are called.

Predictability helps people feel safe. It doesn't mean that things should always stay the same, but that change is discussed, flagged up before it happens and is gradual and slow. No surprise parties.

REDUCED STIMULATION – this really follows on from predictability. When a person is experiencing psychosis they can feel flooded by noise and activity. People with high levels of anxiety can be hypervigilant like a sentry meerkat, constantly monitoring what is going on to spot potential danger. Those who are feeling low may not be able to keep up when there is a lot going on, they can feel left out. All in all, there are lots of reasons why a quieter environment is a good idea. There is more detail in the 'keeping it calm' section.

This might be a problem if there are people in the house who like making a lot of noise or having visitors all day. The needs of the person with the mental health issue may seem more important, but in all but the most severe periods of fragility a compromise is important. Is there any way to manage the noise, such as if a family member likes to practice their rapping, are noise cancelling headphones at all helpful?

Another useful bit of planning could be to establish a set of signals that can be used in any environment. If the person feels suddenly overwhelmed by the situation then the family pre-arranges a quick sign that everybody knows about. Some ideas:

> Grandma is about to launch into an interrogation, so Tina rubs the end of her nose violently while looking highly anxious. Her dad swings into action to rescue her by saying, 'Oh! Tina, don't forget you promised to parcel up that jumper to return this afternoon, do you want to go upstairs and work on it while me and grandma have a chat down here?'

Or

> Simon frantically tugs his sister's coat sleeve in the frozen food aisle of the favoured supermarket. She looks up from the bags of chips at this previously arranged signal to see he is just about to have a panic attack. She puts the basket down and walks just in front of him in the straightest line possible to the door. Walking a bit in

front clears a way and he can 'hide' behind her. They get outside and then do some breathing exercises together as previously practised.

These signals are most useful in the worst times and could be gradually reduced as the person recovers and is better able to communicate under pressure. A sense of being prepared will reduce anxiety for everyone. An undemanding environment and an escape plan when it becomes too much to cope with, that's point two done.

Thirdly in the list there is **'APPROPRIATE EXPECTATIONS'.** This is about adjusting to a realistic assessment regarding what the person with the mental health issue can do today or might be able to do tomorrow. This would be so simpler if there was an algorithm, a set of reliable rules. The family have their observations of the cared-for person's behaviour and mood, that is all the professionals have too.

The giant obstacle to this exercise (which the professionals don't have to deal with) is that the family knew them before all this happened. There was undoubtedly a lot of hope invested in their future and the kind of life they would have, whether this is a child, a partner or a parent. This expectation can take a long time to adjust, there is a bit more on this in 'Grief and Guilt' section.

'Appropriate expectations' are a fine line between being too pushy and actually holding them back by being too attentive and over helpful. The carer may 'hold the hope', by expecting positive changes to happen and for them to get a better quality of life, but this must be at their pace, however long it takes.

If the family have no belief that there will be change and no sense of hope that it is possible this can be a subtle but effective negative influence. This means maximum carer alert to protect them from every mistake that could cause the smallest ripple in their world so they can stay safely just where they are. Letting them move at their own pace may require some risk taking but this is a necessary part of the process. As always it is a tightrope to walk!

Not managing to meet the family's expectations acts as a constant reminder of their failure to succeed – and make others proud. They may have dropped out of Uni but getting back to being a student may have to wait a while. Perhaps they are not managing to bring a wage into the house right now. It will happen for some but may not for others. They may have been a highly paid executive with career prospects but if they lose their job because of anxiety they will feel bad enough without someone sending them three new jobsite links a day.

One way of staying hopeful without exerting pressure is to say things such as:

- 'One day, I'm sure, you will feel strong enough to go to the shops. I hope it's soon because you must miss it.'
- 'I wonder if you will go back to your old job or do something different. It will be interesting finding out what you decide to do.'
- 'Now you are working on those strategies the therapist told you about, so hopefully you will see a difference soon. You will have to let me know when you notice a change?'

These sound a bit stilted, it is important to sound natural, but the essence is that there are no deadlines, no pressure and just a sense that there is a firm belief that things will definitely move towards the light at the end of the tunnel – in their own time.

One of the biggest challenges is to avoid showing disappointment and frustration when things don't improve for a while. The situation has many variables, progress can be subtle and slight; knockbacks often attract more attention. The optimum attitude is one of being patient and positive, easy to say but hard to maintain.

The fourth factor in being a good enough carer is **'SENSITIVITY TO A PERSON'S SELF-ESTEEM'.** Please see previous paragraph about appearing positive. This again is a battle with the frustrations of the recovery process. Rather than delivering another lecture, it is easier to consider any occasions in life when people have been the slightest bit critical or pointed out an error.

'Thanks for doing that job for me. Well up to your usual standard, I expect great things from you. I was a bit surprised by that misprint near the end as you usually notice them early on but apart from that it was great.'

What does anyone take from this positive feedback? That this is praise for a usually excellent worker who has made one mistake but is still very much appreciated? Or that you made a big fat mistake. You idiot. Think about it all evening and replay the mistake and the feedback a hundred times until you finally fall asleep at 4 am.

If someone is already aware they have a mental health issue, that they have fallen behind their peer group, they don't know if it was all their own fault and have no idea what the future is going to be like, then any sense of being judged will hurt even more.

So, predictability, reduced stimulation, appropriate expectations and sensitivity to a person's self-esteem. Maybe the carer could include sensitivity to their own self-esteem too and allow themselves permission to have bad days, slip ups, total meltdowns and long moans to anyone who will listen without judging.

THE QUIET LIFE

This section covers a range of issues that are part of the low stress times, when things are ticking over reasonably well. This may be the recovery period after a one-off mental health crisis, the lull between relapses or a longer stretch of time when the medication is reasonably sorted but the person is still very dependent on the family.

These topics are ones that were frequently mentioned to me by carers because they caused them concern. Sharing coping strategies on these everyday issues were often just as important as dealing with a major crisis.

EGGSHELLS: WALKING ON

This is a state of carer anticipatory anxiety, waiting for something bad to happen. Living through a completely nightmare-ish experience when the person with the mental health diagnosis is very unwell and maybe at risk, it isn't surprising that the family feels the need to remain on red alert and ready to react in a split second. This means that there is a raised level of adrenaline in the house and everyone is in full meerkat mode. People then get tired and irritable but find it hard to relax, while the person everyone is worried about is apparently managing quite well.

This may also result in an unnecessarily strong over-reaction to what may often turn out to be small, inconsequential blips and minor wobbles. The truth is that this state of perpetual readiness doesn't help in achieving the goal of appearing calm or successfully coping if something does start, additionally it wears the family down in the process.

If everyone is monitoring this person closely and waiting for signs and signals, is there a plan what to do if they should happen? The experience of going through the difficult times does provide useful information which can be drawn on, just as a professional might, to consider what to do if things seem to be sliding.

This is one option. Suppose the carer, and other family members if they are involved, develop their own 1-5 scoring system. This is a made-up example so won't apply to everyone.

1. He is very calm; he is eating enough and he is sitting downstairs without any obvious uneasiness.
2. He is quite calm but a bit agitated. He seems OK until something startles him or upsets him.
3. He is all right but pacing a lot and won't settle to anything. He is very tense but not shouting at all or talking about the black cars outside.
4. He is very agitated; he is shouting at the neighbours again. He is talking about the cars outside and finds it impossible to sit down. He doesn't seem to know if anyone else is in the room or not.
5. He is aggressive and loud. He keeps running outside and is being rude when anyone tries to talk to him. His eyes have that look again.

If a scale is developed it doesn't need to be written down, if it is then please hide it well. An assessment can be made whenever it seems appropriate. This will quickly become a useful tool that is used to monitor their mood and to identify what apparently makes it shift from one level to another (if there is anything external causing it). It can also help with family communication.

If they are at 4 or 5 it might be time to inform the mental health team, especially if there is a suspicion that they have stopped taking their medication.

If they are on 1 or 2 is it time for a small challenge? This could be an opportunity to go out for a coffee with them, or alone, or ask them to help with lunch. It could be having a conversation about a tricky subject or reminding them about an appointment they don't want to keep. It is only through trial and error that progress is made, and even mistakes are opportunities to learn.

This is about cultivating a professional distance, becoming more like a practitioner who makes an objective assessment and plans how to handle the next step using the information they have available. The carer learns how to handle the tricky days the same way - also by reminding themselves that difficult times have been managed before and survived.

In the early days the family carer may find that their emotional state is closely tied to that of the person they support:

- The person gets agitated
- The carer notices, they get agitated
- The person notices their carer is agitated and gets more agitated
- The carer sees this increasing agitation, this increases their agitation.

If the carer can say in a reasonably confident way, 'Oops, looks like a level 3 day. I'll try a walk, a promise of game of Monopoly this afternoon, and run her a warm bath and see if that works,' rather than be frightened by a thought in their head that is saying, 'Oh no! It's getting bad again! What can I do? It will be like last time! I just can't cope.'

All this leads to a better sense of control, not over them but over the situation. If it's a number 5 day, then by all means remain in alert mode. If it's a number 1 then it is time to put your feet up or do something enjoyable. Confidence comes from having faith that if it changes it will be quickly noticed and a plan will be put into action with some tried and tested responses.

This confidence is not about being irresponsible, just because it worked last time and another period of level 5 distress was survived doesn't mean the next time will be easy. The process of observing what upsets, what calms, what helps and what makes it worse will help the family cope and gain certainty. There will always be factors outside anyone's control, and mistakes, but assessing from a professional distance helps to monitor what is going on, rather than just being buffeted by worry and fear, with roller coaster anxiety levels.

DAY-TO-DAY CONVERSATION

Supporting someone who is experiencing a mental health issue, regardless of the diagnosis, seems to produce an expectation that the family should encourage them to talk about how they are feeling. This has an unavoidable outcome which is that there will be an obligation to listen. Often it can be a satisfying experience to have a conversation with someone who has been unable to communicate for a while. Sometimes it can be a tense because they are stressed or angry.

Listening to carers talk about the conversations that they were having led me to suggest the following different categories:

A. Everyday talk about everyday things. Particularly important.
B. Really useful talk. This is information about how a person is feeling, what is going on for them, how they

see themselves. It will help the family get to know what is going on for them and form a supportive relationship. There are some hints on how to get this sort of conversation going in the next section. This kind of talk cannot be made to happen, like all things the art is to create the optimum circumstances and then hope; interrogation doesn't work.

C. Talk around delusional or flawed belief systems. These may be conversations to get your support or agreement or just because it is the world they live in and that is an accepted and interesting topic of conversation for them. (See 'delusions' section)

D. Repetitive talk. This can be realistic or not but, whatever the content, it is on a loop. It usually focuses on one or two topics, often events in the past or health issues.

E. Abusive remarks made about people in general or about members of the family / friends.

F. They are saying nothing, you would be incredibly grateful for any of the above.

There frequently seems to be limited capacity to talk about celebrities, the weather or politics, this will depend completely on how severe the mental health issue is, but this general chat often seems to be scarce. No great loss perhaps but listening to someone talking almost exclusively about themselves and their issues is tough. This challenges the usual rules that focussing the conversation solely on 'me' is highly anti-social and selfish.

One theory is that a mental health issue causes the brain to respond as though it is under threat and, as a result, all the person's attention is devoted to monitoring the self, their physical and mental health and potential sources of threat and harm. Their world is now only what directly affects them. This is not a choice they have made but their brain's survival technique.

Introducing more variety in the conversation may be a long-term goal but it can be an uphill struggle.

Repetitive talk can be a total nightmare for the family. I well remember the individuals who attended the centres where I worked who had a set conversation piece, with encores that were pretty much the same thing again. I was paid, so I felt bound to persevere with trying to listen but also trying to change the subject, long past the point of common sense. This is not intended to insult or belittle this behaviour, but no one is able to pay attention to a conversation that is stuck on one (apparently selfish) topic without getting irritable, a bit sarcastic or simply turning off and planning tonight's dinner.

'Mum, my leg hurts.'
'Does it dear? Now there's a surprise.'
'No, it really hurts. I think it's blood poisoning.'
'Blood poisoning? You've said that every day for three weeks and if you were right you would have only one leg right now.'
'It really hurts. You don't care.'
'I cared enough to take you to the doctor last week, again, and she said there was nothing wrong, again.'
'She didn't look properly. She thinks I'm making it up.'
'Really? You think so?'
'How do you know there is nothing wrong then?'
'You just ran down the stairs, is that not enough evidence?'
'You just don't care. You never listen to me, it could be a fracture or cancer, etc.'

This sort of conversation achieves nothing and adds a strain on any relationship. The carer needs to survive though, and no one can focus endlessly on an unhappy person without being ground down.

One option is to time limit conversations, so there could be an offer of a fifteen-minute slot twice a day where they get undivided attention and someone who is really listening. Fifteen minutes may seem a short time but in reality it is long enough for a detailed conversation. Thirty minutes is an option but there is a good chance that any talk will stop before the time is up.

This time of attention involves not passing judgement or belittling anything they say – but not necessarily agreeing with it either.

Something like:

'Susan, it's five o'clock. What do you want to talk about today?'

'My leg hurts again.'

'Does it? That seems to happen to you a lot.'

'It really hurts. I think it's blood poisoning.'

'If you are worried about that what would you like to do?'

'I don't know. Maybe I should see the doctor.'

'What do you think she will say? We did go last week remember?'

'She thinks it's all made up.'

'You think she doesn't believe you?'

'No, she isn't listening.'

'What would you like to tell her about your leg?'

'I don't know. I told her it hurt last week. I'll just have to wait until someone takes it seriously or I die of blood poisoning.'

'Can I help at all? '

'No, you can't help, you're not a doctor.'

'I guess we will just have to wait and see then.'

During the day particular topics can be saved for that time, 'that sounds like something we should talk about later when I can give you my full attention'.

That doesn't mean that there is no conversation outside of this time but that is limited to neutral or practical things rather than their obsessional thoughts or anxious worries. But this is not an easy option, the carer or other family members must give undivided attention at the promised time if it is going to be accepted as a fair strategy. This total concentration is a reward for waiting - which can also help them to learn to manage anxieties for a while by themselves, rather than immediately dropping their worries onto someone else and then getting more agitated when that person appears not to be instantly concerned.

If they won't cooperate with a time limit and the talk just keeps on coming, it is fine to say 'stop!' in a calm but firm voice, maybe with eye contact and raised hands in front of you. This is better than screaming 'Shut up!' – or the more sweary equivalent – because anger or frustration has taken over. Unless they are in a very agitated and distressed state it is appropriate to say that this is enough. A lot depends on how it is said.

Useful phrases could be:

'I think we have talked about that a lot already. I'm sorry, I don't have anything new to say about it, I can't really help. Can we talk about something else please?'

'I don't know how you want me to respond to that idea. You talk about it every day; I think I understand what you are saying now but I don't have anything I can add.'

'You keep talking about this. I'm really feeling that we have said everything we can on this topic. We are going around in circles and it is making me a bit tired and irritable. Can we do something else?'

Or even eventually after all else has failed:

'You keep telling me the same thing over and over again, I have listened to it a lot of times. I really don't have anything else to say about it and I keep asking you to stop. If you keep on talking about it then I am going to go to my bedroom / turn the radio on/ put my earphones in/ go for a walk.'

It is important to bear in mind that the topics that are repeated frequently may be a genuine worry to that person, or they may be struggling to think of anything else to say, or they may have a real challenge getting past the repetitive thoughts themselves. Seeing it as a shared problem may help the tension levels and still address the problem.

'We seem to spend all our time talking about this one topic? We don't seem to be getting anywhere, what do you suggest we do?'

This may produce a rather miffed response, after all, any request to stop is a form of rejection but hopefully a conversation could be started that involves joint working and negotiation, which is always preferable to an emotional outburst from either person.

Finally, a look at some responses to abusive remarks. Rudeness or insults are often made about family members or certain groups in society that the person appears to dislike. One aspect of some people's delusional system is a total sense of 'grandeur' which can make them very insensitive. There is a conviction that for some reason they are highly superior to the rest of us, which can make a relationship with them exhausting and challenging.

I met a wonderful, quite frail older woman who cared for her son who apparently experienced these 'delusions of grandeur', he saw himself as part of the gentry. She would clean for him, even when he became unwell enough to smear excrement on the walls. She would do his washing and some of his shopping as well as paying out of her limited income for someone to come in and give him extra help. He called his mother 'the old washer woman'. This was not him just being horrible (I hope) but the delusions that came with his psychosis.

I also remember a very pleasant man who was usually extremely sensitive to the possibility of hurting other people's feelings, he was kind and sympathetic to those around him, but his racist opinions were unbelievable. It wasn't so much that he was rude to people or even directly about them, but it appeared that he had a deep-seated conviction that being white was an unquestionably superior position. My favourite for sheer bad taste was 'I was really surprised yesterday to see a black man carrying a Marks and Spencer's bag, I didn't think they went in there.' I know this was the 90s but even then the vast majority of people would have considered this a completely inappropriate remark. He was totally unable to recognise that his attitude was socially unacceptable, let alone morally wrong.

Whatever causes these embarrassing and anti-social statements the family can only:

- Point out when they are being offensive – the person with the mental health issue may just not know
- Let them know that the family consider these remarks to be unacceptable and that other people will think the same
- Ask them to stop
- End the conversation and walk away if they persist

If the remarks are said with anger or a sense of threat are directed at individual people, then make sure the mental health team know, if they are involved. If it all gets a bit tense then have a look at the 'de-escalation' section.

LISTENING

People do this all the time, right? I once thought to myself in a moment of blinding honesty that I only really listen to people when I am paid to, but don't tell my family that.

It is interesting to consider what goes on in anyone's head when they are apparently listening. Maybe they are preparing the next wonderful remark to top the other person's story. Maybe they are judging what is being said and planning how to tell the other person what they should be thinking instead. Perhaps they are thinking about getting the boiler serviced. That is normal conversation.

People can tell when someone isn't listening to them. Subtle glances at the phone or watch, eyes elsewhere, hands fidgeting – all signs. Having a conversation with a counsellor, if they are any good, sets a useful example of how it can feel to be really listened to.

No one is suggesting that a carer must become a counsellor although it may feel like that at times. This section has some tips to having a different sort of conversation, which needs a bit of practice but can really bring benefits even if it is only for a few minutes now and again.

The advantages of having some real listening time may include a better sense of trust in the relationship plus more important information about what they are thinking and feeling. Getting that understanding can radically improve how effectively the family can respond. It also helps to know what the person with the mental health issue is wanting to happen, because working together on these hopes can make positive change more straightforward. (see 'encouraging change' section).

This is a description of the bare bones of a technique that is taught to people who listen for a living. It is a useful skill in work and home situations regardless of whether there is a mental health issue in the situation or not. There is a lot more on 'active listening skills' online or join an evening class and meet some lovely people.

First rule of listening is that there is no wandering of attention, it is about being completely 'present'. That means focussing only on what the person is saying and trying to understand it, rather than following some other distracting thought or planning the reply. Any straying off this subject should be met with an internal prod and re-focus.

Techniques that help this concentration and at the same time let the person know they are being listened to are:

A. Keep some occasional eye contact, and either nod or say small encouraging words such as 'right', or 'I see'. The trick here is not to get stuck in a rut and start to sound like a parrot, so not always the same word in the same tone of voice.

B. Ask open questions. This is a question that doesn't have yes or no as an answer. So instead of saying 'Did you get upset when he said that?' say 'What did you do when he said that?' This sounds easy in theory but hard to get used to doing, especially when the answer may be obvious. This technique encourages them to talk and offer explanations which might help to understand how their mind is working. 'How', 'why', 'what' are the key words.

C. Repeat back what they said last, either in their words or in your own.

D. Every now and then do a quick summary.
'So the car came round the corner and the man really looked at me. I could tell he knew who I was, so I was really scared. I walked quicker but didn't look round in case he was behind me.'

'You didn't look round because you thought he was behind you?'

Or

'I went into the surgery, but the doctor just kept looking at his computer and I sat there for ages. He didn't seem to care that I had come in, so I just sat there feeling really stupid. By the time he turned round and started talking to me I was already fed up and ready to walk out.'

'He just ignored you and left you sitting there, so that made you angry before you even started?'

E. Be speaking for less than one fifth of the total conversation time - I have never ever achieved this. Never.

These techniques let them know that the listener is concentrating and trying to understand, they can say if something has been misunderstood. It also helps the person to hear what they have actually said coming back to them, and this encourages thinking about it at a deeper level.

If it feels too unnatural then don't use it, there is nothing worse than somebody repeating back your last few words with every sentence. Children do it to wind people up and, in fact, it is a symptom of some mental health problems called 'echolalia'. If it feels a bit daft then practice on an unsuspecting relative or neighbour until it feels about right, but it is important to sound 'normal' and not as though the answers are being read out of a book.

Having a more severe mental health issue may result in a slowing of the cognitive processes, ideas can take a while to be put together because of the fogging they may be experiencing, which may be down to symptoms and/or medication. Long pauses for thought could be required even in everyday conversations, maybe even returning to a topic after they have had enough thinking time, maybe days later. Silences may feel a bit unnatural but may make it more comfortable for them.

The pressure that carers feel during chats is often self-inflicted because at some level they feel they should know the answer to every sticky situation and go into 'life coach' mode. It can take a while to accept that listening without making suggestions is definitely time well spent.

Most 'helpful' comments feel like a judgement. Carers often get a lot of well-intentioned remarks from other people who are trying to be useful. 'You should make them go to the doctors,' or 'why don't you get them to take medication?' or similar. There is an implied judgement in these well-meaning statements that people can be sensitive to:

> 'You are too daft to have thought of that by yourself'
> 'I know better than you do as to what should be done here'
> 'You are a bit incompetent that you haven't done these things already'

If a carer has been at the receiving end of this sort of remark it can be useful to remember how it felt to get unwanted advice. That is why it is not always a great idea to be full of suggestions, even if they are sensible. If the person clearly has no ideas themselves or asks directly for help in deciding what to do then that is different.

If they have ideas but they seem to be unsuitable or unworkable a good question to try is, 'what do you think would happen if you did that?' and then try to talk through the consequences.

> 'So, let me make sure I've got this right. You think it's a good idea to stop taking your medication because you are putting on weight.'
> 'I don't want to feel this fat. It's so depressing.'

'What do you think will happen if you stop taking them?'

'I'll be fine. I'm fine now aren't I? There's nothing wrong any more, I just feel so fat.'

'Can you remember how it was before you started taking them?'

'No, not really. I've been on them for ages and I just want to stop, I'm getting enormous.'

'I can completely understand why you want to stop but I am worried that if you do that terrible time you had last year will come back again. Will you at least wait until the next appointment with Dr. A so you can ask him if there is a different medication you can take, or if it is safe to just stop taking them suddenly?'

This illustrates the ideal of asking them their plan and then only suggesting an alternative when it becomes clear that there is a flaw in their reasoning. They have control over the choices they make and rightly so, following their own ideas through, whether they work or not, is a useful exercise and how everyone learns life's lessons. The carer may have a better sense of what will succeed but being right all the time might not be the most effective support that can be offered in the long-term.

CAN CARERS BE THERAPISTS?

A family member or friend may be close to the person with the mental health issue and provide a great deal of emotional support and reassurance. They may listen to them for hours or many times a day. They may be the only ones who know their secrets (or sometimes the last ones to know). But should there be some limits on what is discussed? Should the family always try to find out more?

There is a logical sequence of thought here:

- Talking is one of the main ways of helping someone with a mental health issue.
- The carer is the person who knows them best.
- They need to change what they are doing / thinking if things are going to get better.
- The professionals are not offering anything / they are on a lengthy waiting list
- Someone needs to do something right now and there isn't anyone else

Therapy is 'the treatment of mental or psychological disorders by psychological means' according to the *Cambridge English Dictionary*. Mental health practitioners train and practice a lot of times before they get their accreditation. Carers probably lack formal training and are forced to practice on their only client, learning through trial and error. Nevertheless, there is a strong pressure to 'get to the bottom of this thing and sort it out'.

I always remember hearing this speech from a very worried father:

'I talk to my son every night and I tell him that he has to calm down. I've told him how to relax and how he needs to think more positively about himself. I try to get him to talk to me but he just keeps on saying the same thing, how he can't go back to college, he can't meet any of his friends, he just can't do any of college work right now. All can't, can't, can't. I tell him every night that he needs to do something soon or else he will be missing out on life and it will be too late. He doesn't listen and nothing has changed.'

This is not therapy, and it probably will not result in any improvement in this young man, but dad may feel he is doing all he can and his son will be aware that he cares, and that is very important in itself.

Any carer who sees themselves as taking on responsibility for providing 'therapy' is potentially setting themselves up for some disappointment. Trying to delve deeper into how the person with the mental health issue is feeling or what exactly is going on in their heads may have the opposite effect from the intended one.

When a group of experienced carers discuss this topic the usual answer to the question 'can a carer be a therapist?' is a resounding 'no'.

Therapists and carers do have something in common, they cannot make people change. The art of creating circumstances in which someone may choose to change is a complex one and has many years of theories and research behind it.

There are many reasons why any individual's recovery from a mental health issue may not follow a straight path. Even with lots of positive help and support people can get worse for a while. This can leave the carer feeling that they have failed and can knock both party's confidence in the relationship. No family member let alone a partner or friend has the final control over how another person develops and changes, not even when the relationship is a parent-child one.

If the carer becomes intensely involved, dedicating an endless amount of listening time (and always having an answer), then this can result in an unhealthy level of dependency. With a professional therapist worrying topics have to wait and be contained until the next appointment; having immediate access to this form of support can reduce both the motivation and the ability to hold on, or to work it out for themselves.

Families can offer clear guidance of what is expected on the average day, on life skills and coping with ordinary events. They can work together with the person to help bring about change in their ability to manage their stress and worry. It is the more intensely personal, emotionally charged stuff that perhaps is best left to people outside the family - although what each family sees as appropriate could vary considerably.

My own 'Hmm, maybe not' list of topics would be:

- exploring the person's personal history especially if being asked to take sides
- analysis of emotional issues (just how did you feel when your dog died?)
- theories about what caused their mental health issue (families will obviously think about this but perhaps privately?)
- in depth analysis of the person's private thoughts (so when you say you are afraid of dogs is this actually a representation of your father because he was a boxer?)
- probing the thoughts and beliefs that are a direct result of their mental health issue (especially topics such as voices, or the threats that underlie their OCD)

General guidance could perhaps be summed up as:

> 'Don't ask any question unless you are absolutely certain of how they will react and you know the correct way of responding, no matter what that the answer might turn out to be.'

The therapists available through the NHS are often wonderful ones. Getting to the point of being offered this choice and then joining a lengthy waiting list can be a disheartening experience though. There are private options of course but it can be complicated trying to get one the right one. If this can be funded, it can be useful to look at the British Psychological Society (BPS) website as this includes each therapists' special interests and all of those listed have trained to the Society's standards. It may be a question of seeking out a counsellor, psychotherapist or CBT practitioner who has a specialisation in depression or bi-polar or whatever is required. This will cost a fair amount of money so it may be worth considering whether the 'client' is genuinely up for this at this time. Will they engage with the process and have the necessary awareness to work on their difficulties? Not everyone is in that place, especially in the early days of any mental health condition.

There is something about talking to someone you don't know in a safe space that encourages honesty and courage. This is a new situation, with the attention of an expert who is there for them alone and there is no 'history' to get in the way. Carers who have had counselling themselves may be in a better place to understand this relationship, it isn't easy to duplicate. Family members might feel the need to take on the therapist role at times, but they are often just too emotionally involved. They want it to happen so much, any relief of these distressing symptoms, and this makes it even harder to be patient and avoid analysing and theorising with this distressed person.

A carer can be best placed to reassure and to help calm things down, they can be the main reason why a person makes it through a mental health issue but they may not always be the right person to tackle the mental health issue head on, they may simply be too close.

LIFESTYLE, FOOD AND ALTERNATIVE THERAPIES

There is a strong but sometimes confusing message that eating right, exercising and sleeping well will sort anybody out. If this fragile person takes enough supplements, eats enough kale, gives up gluten or does enough yoga then any negative matters will disappear. Living on a diet of burgers, beer and Xbox is undoubtedly going to influence anyone's wellbeing. If the person with the mental health issue had diet of salad and oily fish and meditated twice daily would things improve? There is an increasing interest in the relationship between diet and mental health, with gut health as a major factor. However, improving this requires a highly restricted diet, is this really going to happen?

Number one problem here is the attitude of the person in question. Some medication makes people constantly hungry, particularly for things like bread and potatoes. Will a plate of salmon with a watercress garnish go down well? Other lifestyle changes that are recommended include a minimum of seven hours sleep with relaxation techniques. They may want to sleep a minimum of fifteen hours and then wander for a while snacking on six packets of crisps. Or they may be struggling to sleep for five hours. Is this a healthy sleep pattern and, if not, then how is anyone going to change it?

As a family carer it is all too easy to become convinced that an answer is out there. Google says if they take enough of one vitamin or another then they can come off their medication and if it worked for that nice bloke on YouTube then it's worth a shot, surely. This is a positive impulse with good intentions, but it can create a lot of bad feeling.

This is not meant to be a knock-back, families can get very enthusiastic about finding a means to help someone, it offers new hope but can also set up a source of tension. This is especially true if it produces either no effect or a negative one that they can then hold the carer responsible for.

If they won't cooperate then you have two choices, to step back and forget it for a while or increase the pressure so that whatever time is spent together is overshadowed by the need to convince them of this light at the end of the tunnel. This may soon feel like nagging, even if with delicate handling.

'Hello dear, come and have some breakfast.'
'OK, God I feel grim. What's that on the table?'
'It's those vitamins I was telling you about.'
'(Groans) You do just keep on, don't you?'
'I didn't say anything!'
'No, but you put the packet right by my plate.'
'Just give them a try sweetie, I am sure you would feel…'
'Haven't we had this conversation before? I've told you I am not taking any more pills. I'm on loads already. I can't see the point.'
'Yes, but these are different.'
'Cos you got them off Amazon?'

It's similar to taking medication, they follow their own path and the carer can only wave frantically and point.

If there are professionals involved they may be less than enthusiastic about trying something different. Realistically it must be very risky for them to endorse any approach which has not received the blessing of the NHS or NICE guidelines (the lead organisation that says what treatments should be offered for each condition). What may be frustrating is that ideas sometimes do get adopted after they have been thoroughly researched but this may be several years after it has been recommended elsewhere. One carer I knew spent years trying to get nurses to give omega-3 oil to her son and being generally regarded as either a nuisance or a complete idiot; now some psychiatrists prescribe it in certain circumstances.

It is safe to say that eating healthily, exercising moderately and avoiding alcohol and other non-prescribed drugs is bound to be a good move. Attempting to get these positive changes to happen is important but it is going to be far easier with some people than others, depending on their existing lifestyle. One consideration must be the potential conflict and the damage it can cause to everyday relationships.

Anyone who experiences anxiety would be better shifting to decaffeinated coffee and tea. Is a quick substitute made in the hope that no one notices or is there a conversation that could go either way and result in them suspiciously checking the cupboard?

It's easy to nag about drinking alcohol as it carries such health risks, particularly in mental health. So many people, including the average carer, may well use alcohol to get by, it is hard to escape from its influence. For the person with the mental health problem the positive aspects of drinking may be:

> 'It blots out a fair amount of time when I don't have to deal with anxiety / pressure / boredom / thoughts about how awful my life is.'
> 'It is what other people do; can't I do something that is normal?'
> 'It gets you to talk to me.'
> 'I have forgotten how to not drink - you keep telling me I should stop but I don't know how.'

If drink is a big problem then there are some suggestions in the 'addiction' section.

Alternative therapies are valuable and are increasingly being accepted into mainstream practice. For example, acupuncture works wonders for certain issues and hypnosis is powerful for some and can really bring on change. 'Eye movement desensitisation and reprocessing' (EMDR) is often available on the NHS for PTSD but would never have been considered mainstream twenty years ago. It consists of a lot of strange movements and eye rolling, which sounds weird but it really works for certain symptoms.

Among the over the counter products, 'Rescue Remedy' is a useful calming agent and Bach's Flower remedies can also really improve someone's mood (including the carers?). St John's wort for example is often considered helpful for depression but it can affect anticoagulants, anticonvulsants, and contraceptive pills. It is also not clear if it is safe if you are pregnant or breastfeeding. Just because it has a picture of an innocent looking weed on the packet doesn't mean it isn't powerful stuff. These are strong substances not to be used casually, they may not produce the reaction that is required and could make things more volatile. Anything could potentially interfere with other medication or cause the situation to worsen.

If something looks as though it might be useful, especially for someone else who might not be so accepting if it goes wrong, it is worth getting proper advice. This is definitely not from the people in the shop who have had three weeks training and are trying to sell you something anyway. Finding those with proper qualifications and allied with professional bodies is key to getting reliable information when so much depends on it.

If they suffer with anxiety in any form, most people with mental health issues do, then activities such as yoga, chi gung, tai chi or meditation seem to be brilliant and at minimum can do no harm. I practice mindfulness; it fits well with my character and I can't think of any circumstances in which it isn't helpful. Some NHS trusts offer mindfulness training for their staff which is a recommendation in itself. There is information on a wide range of relaxation or mind focusing techniques through videos and books, if classes are too much for the person to cope with. Ten minutes with a guided meditation or some simple breathing exercises can provide a coping technique that succeeds where all else fails.

It isn't straightforward, there are glitches to overcome. It may say online that large quantities of omega-3 fatty acids can reduce the chances of psychosis, but it may cause diarrhoea. Tough call. It could be challenging to ask someone with a bi-polar fuelled high energy to 'sit still and just relax'. They may need a specialist class or some individual advice on taking it a bit more slowly. They just may not have the self-control or the willingness to persevere, especially in an everyday class.

If a new source of help is suggested, researched and then tried for several months there should be some signs of change. The person may say it is helping them or the family could notice some improvement. If this doesn't happen then throw them away or remove all pressure to keep going. Just like any other therapy monitoring and evaluation is necessary, if there is no noticeable outcome there is no point in just carrying on.

Some things work because we believe they will. This is as true in mental health as well as other fields. It may be optimistic to look for a cure but if anything helps to calm them either directly or through believing that it will, this is a positive outcome. If they say that standing on their head and whistling makes them feel calmer, then who's to argue? Maybe try it?

One of the big challenges of being a carer is accepting that at some stage the search for a magic speedy solution might have to be abandoned. Having a stable and calm relationship through all this mayhem may be one of the foundations of their wellbeing and recovery, and if determination to find a wonder cure gets in the way of this it may be more trouble than it is worth.

KEEPING IT CALM

One thing a family can do which undoubtedly helps is to keep things pretty chilled. An environment that is constantly quiet and predictable may be unappealing to the rest of the family but may help anyone with a mental health issue, at least for a while. So why and how?

Some conditions, such as those that include psychotic symptoms or the 'high' feelings in bi-polar, can really affect the person's ability to manage information. It is impossible to filter incoming data, the sights, sounds and smells, or they can be agitated and overwhelmed by busy or noisy situations. Anxious people can panic at having too much to cope with. For vulnerable people who have little defence, what may be manageable for most people, such as a supermarket, can be truly overwhelming for them.

If it is apparent that they become agitated by busy situations or seem anxious to leave places where there is a lot going on, it may be helpful to try and make life quite dull for a while. The long-term plan could be to gradually build up their tolerance to noise and confusion; medication and coping skills will help. So may a growth in their confidence.

If their safe place can be peaceful and the number of visitors few, then that may be appreciated. If the phone is too loud or the TV/radio/laptop too intrusive then perhaps these things need to be in another room. Often there can be compromise with other family members such as earphones or laptops for private viewing. Avoiding circumstances which can produce an increase in anxiety makes life easier for the person who is currently hypersensitive, and therefore for the rest of the family too.

There is one sort of agitation which can be a major trigger, this involves the whole family and key figures in this person's life. This is about 'expressed emotion', getting angry, distressed or even too 'involved' in the presence of the person with the mental health issue.

It is perfectly natural for family members to be very affected by the realisation that one of them has a mental health issue. It

is understandable that they may become distraught about this –
and sometimes by the apparent lack of what appears to be speedy
and appropriate help from the mental health services. It is totally
normal for the carers to bounce between exhausted, tearful,
angry, pleading and unable to speak. They may be reduced to
shouting at the person because they can see what they need to
do, but they just won't do it. They may become highly agitated at
the frustration that they can apparently do so little to keep that
person safe and well. They may become irritable and upset with
each other.

If the carer seems to be distressed then the person with the
mental health issue may feel unsafe, they may be dependent on
others to cope on their behalf and if they don't seem to be doing
that then their anxiety will increase. Having a dramatic scene
with a big row or desperate crying will probably cause a sizeable
upset to the person whether they are directly included or not.

The family carer may want to be highly involved by constantly
wanting to know what is going on for this fragile person. They
can feel so strongly that they know this person best and they are
legitimately acting as their representative, after all they cannot
possibly speak or decide for themselves in their current state.
The carer must be included in every conversation with or about
their relative. The person is cossetted and protected, excuses
are made for them and little is expected of them. It's protective
caring but going too far.

If reading this is making you feel a bit uneasy because you
have done either the shouting or the over protecting, then
welcome to the club which has pretty much every mental health
carer as a member.

The only bit of research I found that suggests that families
can have a direct negative effect on the wellbeing of a person with
psychosis, although it may be important in other diagnoses as
well, is about this expressed emotion. (This excludes direct abuse

of course). Families who remain calm and largely unruffled in the company of the person they are supporting create a healthier environment for them at this time. This leads to fewer relapses, and these are less severe.

So the family can help by staying relaxed, but this may feel like yet another reason to be judged. The situation of being a carer would make even a stone statue angry and upset. It is a reasonable response to having someone you care about in trouble and not looking after themselves that well either. Humans have anger and distress as a normal reaction to worrying and frightening situations.

It's about overriding those natural reactions especially for people who 'do a bit of drama' and usually show emotions in a loud flamboyant way. Turning it down a bit can be achieved through deep breathing and counting to ten rather than exploding either at them or at other people when they are around.

Saying, 'OK, I'll leave that up to you,' a bit more often is also worthwhile. Stepping back a bit can feel risky, but this must be addressed at some stage or the situation becomes horribly stuck. (see the 'skills for independence' section)

This is really hard work, particularly for some personality types. Exuding calm and remaining relatively unmoved through it all is a real achievement - but that tension must go somewhere. What happens when the cared-for person is not around is totally a matter of choice, screaming at the dog is permitted. Exercise helps a great deal, as can getting support from the right person, preferably another carer. Punching a pillow, or wild dancing is great. Medication is an option for the carer too if it all feels overpowering.

There will be times when the natural responses to these stressful situations just break through. It might be a question of putting that moment down to experience and not being too self-critical, it is going to happen now and then. You don't have to be calm and in control, you just have to look it. No pressure.

BOUNDARIES

This term seems to be used repeatedly in mental health as a sort of mantra. 'You need to set boundaries' are words of wisdom often given to carers by mental health professionals. There is not usually any further information as to how to do this.

This is one of the hardest aspects of being a carer in mental health. It is tricky enough to attempt to limit the behaviour of a partner or parent and tell them what to do. This excludes normal marital rule setting (or nagging as some call it) where hopefully both have some say in the outcome. Caring for an adult child the situation is no easier, parenting 'power' is no longer valid, in most situations both parties should be virtually equal by now.

Boundaries need to be established to control behaviour that is either risky to the person with the mental health issue, or someone else, or bringing about other serious negative outcomes. If the carer is the one who has, at this moment, got a better idea of what to do then it may be their job to say 'enough' sometimes. Some people seem to find this harder than others.

One wise carer I talked to said that when he was considering saying 'no' he tried to:

- See situations from his wife's perspective before talking about it with her.
- Considered why he wanted to stop some behaviour, was it for her benefit or his?
- If it was for her benefit, then was he sure it was absolutely necessary?
- If it were for his benefit, then could he justify this in terms of

his own health or state of mind? Was it a mild inconvenience or was it really keeping him awake at night?

There needs to be a statement made at this point that self-harm is not one of those situations to be 'boundaried'. Attempting to limit this directly may well increase pressure on the person because it is taking away one of their coping skills. Saying 'promise you won't cut yourself while I'm out' is going to turn up the anxiety and probably produce the opposite of the desired result, it is something a carer cannot control directly. That doesn't mean that boundaries can't be set around other behaviours but be aware that the possible short-term reaction may be an increase in self-harming. The question is whether this is worth it; that can be a tricky decision.

Generally, the most effective and calmest approach to boundary setting is to negotiate, particularly with the situations that are not life-threatening. Is there something that can be offered in exchange for a different behaviour? Is there a compromise? If the matter is not too dramatic and more of a nuisance, such as nocturnal fridge raiding or getting off their phone/laptop for a short time every day, then bargaining has the best chance. What is potentially a good offer in exchange?

A stronger approach is to withdraw something they value. This requires consideration as it is bound to cause bad feeling but may be a last resort. The regular outing to the all-night garage for some chocolate may be stopped if they don't turn their music down after eleven o'clock. Paying their phone charges is withdrawn until they spend less on alcohol. Be aware, however, that withdrawing chocolate, phones, cigarettes, alcohol etc, may mean a mood shift which then has to be tolerated. See the 'problem solving' section for more thoughts on this.

It is also useful to try some of these phrases (in your own words) calmly expressed at a time when tempers are not high.

'I am really not happy about this; it makes me terribly upset.'
'I wish that you could find a better way of… it seems to be unhelpful to you and that makes me worry.'
'I would like to talk about this problem. I hope we can find a way to work it out because I don't want things carrying on as they are.'
'I am asking you to think about why I want this behaviour to stop, why it is making me so exhausted'

'I' statements are a reminder that someone else is affected by this behaviour, they have feelings and they care enough to want to work on the problem. They are not a magic solution, but must be better than a load of 'What you need to do is …' or 'What on earth are you doing that for?' Using the 'I' word helps when the mental health issue may make it difficult for the person to see things from somebody else's perspective.

A boundary needs to be held consistently, if it is only applied now and again then it creates confusion. People with a personality disorder or an addiction issue particularly need to know where the line is drawn and that it is not open to challenge or change.

Trying to persuade them to adapt might well not succeed, that means there is little hope of immediate results. The challenge now is not to let it become a major obstacle that is dwelt on a resentful, seething sort of way.

The situation should be dealt with differently if the behaviour that is causing concern has a risk attached, where it is potentially causing hardship or risking injury.

Examples might be:

- Taking money from someone to spend on alcohol or drugs
- Threatening or aggressive behaviour, even if it is currently minor
- Doing damage to furniture or the house

Just to clarify that this sort of unpleasant activity is not a part of most mental health issues but there are complex reasons why other people may be identified as hostile or threatening, or there is a desperate need for something that is more important than their relationship with the family at this moment. If this risky behaviour is not as a direct result of their mental health issues, then the police may need to be brought in sooner rather than trying lots of tactics to make it stop first.

Any aggressive or threatening behaviour cannot be allowed to go un-checked and often the person with the mental health issue is not able to make that change alone. Most importantly this should not be a secret kept within the family. Involving others can be frightening as there can be worry about consequences or shame that it has all got so far. Stating that someone else is going to be involved creates a good chance the situation will escalate in the short-term, but the long-term outcome is improved.

Being faced with repeated hostility, theft or criminal damage means there are some extremely difficult choices to make. Mental health professionals will probably tell a carer to call the police, so would I, but it's the family that must live with that decision.

If the police come, then one of several things can happen:

1. They can do nothing, see it as a 'domestic' and after conversations with the people involved, they will exit.
2. They will arrest the person and start criminal proceedings.
3. They will invoke their powers under the Mental Health Act and hold the person until they have been seen by mental health professionals. Following this they may be forced to go to hospital or be offered treatment as an outpatient or – nothing if they appear calm and in control at the time of the assessment.

If it is 1, this is not altogether a bad thing despite the fact the person is probably going to be angry and feel betrayed. There is a clear message that the police will be called if their behaviour crosses the line and the family are not going to conspire to protect the person just because they love them. Their actions will (always) have consequences.

If it is 2 then ask the police to consider that the person has a mental health issue which may have influenced their behaviour, if this is the case. This can substantially change how the police act but there are no guarantees. If they are arrested, then let the mental health team know and gather evidence for a health report. It may be a family decision whether to press charges but that isn't always an option. Conduct which results in a criminal action may require a dramatic response to prevent it from either continuing or escalating.

If it is 3 then the outcome is treatment rather than punishment, but of course they may not see it that way. Family carers have the difficult task of trying to work to long-term goals while the person they support lives very much according to their current mood and the needs they feel in the present moment. This is always going to be a source of tension. The family sees psychiatric treatment as a road back to recovery, the person with the mental health issue might well see it as enforced and unnecessary, the brutality of the 'system.'

Both 2 and 3 result in an omelette / eggs situation and the family relationships can be damaged in the process. Letting them do whatever they want, regardless of their and other peoples' wellbeing, also has serious consequences especially long-term. If they are to move towards an ordinary life, then they may have to be reminded that this requires fitting in with society's rules and that these are boundaries that have consequences when they are broken. Someone experiencing a mental health issue can change too if there is a clear and definite consequence to their actions.

PROBLEM SOLVING

Only the dedicated few will read this bit because it sounds like one of those weird self-help ideas but it is a very practical and reassuring approach which can greatly reduce the stress of deciding what to do in potentially worrying or complex situations. It can create some order when life seems to be full of challenges.

The question is, how can anyone be sure that they are making the right decision in any given situation? The answer is of course they can't, but this technique is the next best thing. The process needs to be followed, with no short cuts.

The process is:

1. Define the problem. This can be tricky; it needs to be taken right back to its roots.
2. Generate as many options of things that could be done as possible. Avoid evaluating them as they are added to the list, this is particularly important as it distracts and interferes with creating new ideas. The list can include any apparently ridiculous or silly options as they may lead on to other thoughts. Ask for help from other people if that is appropriate to get a fresh perspective. This can take several days, allow time to ponder.
3. Go through the list of options and score them out of ten as to whether they look as though they may work.
4. Put the highest scoring one(s) into practice.
5. Evaluate – is it working? If not, then try the next one on the list.

Why bother with all this palaver (or pavlova as my dyslexic daughter once called it)? It seems so obvious yet often the 'headless chicken' approach is adopted, trying lots of things randomly and then not knowing which, if any, works. A carer using problem solving technique can say, possibly to themselves, that they have looked at every angle with all the information available at this time. This gives more of a sense of control rather than feeling at the mercy of daily events.

An example might be:

> Dave lives with his partner, Jean, who is very depressed and anxious at present. She stays in her bedroom and seldom comes out while he is home. When he comes in from work she has usually made herself sandwiches and heated soup in the microwave, the mess is all over the kitchen. He is tired and hungry but feels he must clear this up before he can start on his own meal. It makes him angry and he sits and seethes for much of the evening.

The problem is that Jean is not clearing up after herself. But is she currently able to do that? Maybe if she can make a sandwich, which takes a bit of thought, then can she at least put stuff back in the cupboard and wipe the worktop? Does she put the butter back in the fridge? If she does then she can put other stuff away and at least put plates in the sink even if washing up may be too much.

If Jean is not really making sandwiches but just grazing out of the fridge or cupboards, maybe she can't do more complex tasks yet. Maybe she just feels too muddled or exhausted. It's worth thinking about what evidence there is around what they can realistically manage to do, rather than presuming that they just won't do it because of laziness or because they 'can get away with it'. Maybe they haven't done any housework for a long time or maybe someone else always does it, so it is out of sight and out of mind.

Defining the problem isn't that easy at all. Dave must use what evidence he has to decide how much Jean can really manage. Let's say that he feels that she is capable of cleaning up at least a bit, he has evidence that she puts some stuff away and has occasionally at least put one or two things in the sink. He defines the problem as

'Jean is not clearing up after herself in the kitchen as much as she could'.

What are his choices? He comes up with the following list of possible options. While he is coming up with them, he doesn't stop to consider the possible outcomes of any of the suggestions but just keeps on trying to think of things.

Dave's ideas:

1. Stomp upstairs and have it out with her straight away and let her know in no uncertain terms that he won't tolerate it any longer.
2. Leave the mess to pile up in the kitchen and hopes she'll take the hint.
3. Break every plate and mug he finds dirty and make a pile of the pieces in the kitchen.
4. Buy prepacked sandwiches and powdered soup in a cup and nothing else.
5. Put locks on the cupboards and the fridge – being hungry might persuade her to help more.
6. Use paper plates and disposable cutlery.
7. Waits until next time she seems ready to talk and asks her to do a bit more then.
8. Leave her a note in the kitchen to remind her.
9. Just accepts it and decides it's going to happen for a while, he shouldn't let it upset him so much.
10. Observe what she usually eats and prepare a packed lunch so there will be no need to get lots of things out.
11. Leave home.

Then he goes through and scores each one looking at the possible outcomes and whether he has tried it before etc. He decides that 7 and 8 are worth a try with 10 as a back-up plan. This allows him to calm down a bit and to feel that he is tackling the issue rather than just getting angry about it.

If Dave had decided that Jean just wasn't able to clear up much, he might have defined the problem as

'I am letting the mess in the kitchen bother me when at the moment there is no way to avoid it'

He might have to accept that his only current option was number 9. How could he stop it from spoiling his mood every evening? Problem solve the choices!

This can be a useful exercise to help a family cope together and make sure everyone, with the person with the mental health issue if possible, is included in creating options.

ENCOURAGING CHANGE

Most carers undoubtedly spend a great deal of time trying to get the person with the mental health issue to change their behaviour. It seems unethical to be constantly trying to get someone else to live their life differently (unless it is a flat-share or a couple, of course). The nature of many mental health diagnoses is that the reduced supply of energy, motivation and empathy, and/or the ability to identify risks in the situation means that someone else may need to drive any effort for a while, or else progress can stall.

Some changes are vital and some are minor, the phrase 'pick your battles' might become important.

There needs to be a clear understanding from the outset that changing someone else is not straightforward. If it were easy then everyone would be nearly perfect, we would all do bad things once then someone would put us straight, from then on we would never do it again. Changing behaviour is a huge, intensely researched topic with no magic formula.

The bottom line is that all anyone can do is try, but the amount of effort that is put into trying does not relate in any way to the results achieved. Parenting is the best example of this, it comes with no guarantees.

A person with a mental health issue presents a complex situation because it is not always clear what elements of their behaviour they currently have control over. If they are staring out of the window for many hours, is this a choice or a necessity? Is their anxiety or psychosis really overwhelming them and making them incapable of any action? Could they take a shower if they wanted to? Could they really stop smoking weed? Could they get out of bed?

It requires a bit of detective work to establish whether they can do these things if motivated, or if it is currently just not possible. Severe mental health issues can bring cognitive confusion, with an extra layer of medication-induced woolliness on top. This means that there are times when normal activity is not going to happen. However, if they come out of their bedroom at night and watch TV then it's not impossible to hope that they could, say, come out for a short time in the evening with the carer if the house is quiet. Could this change of routine help them regain confidence and get them used to being with other people again?

Most carers try any or all of the following in an effort to change something:

- Bribery
- Begging
- Blackmail
- Persuading
- Rational discussion usually focussed on the future
- Getting angry

This is not a complete list, inventive carers have usually tried a wide variety of approaches, some succeed and some don't. A lot depends on timing.

The golden rule to avoid an escalating sense of frustration is, 'if it's not working then stop doing it'. If these attempts are going nowhere then all that is happening is the carer's increasing exhaustion. The two options at this point are to wait and try again later or to try the 'problem solving' technique if that hasn't already been used. (see previous section)

It's always worth thinking through why the family have decided that this particular change is important. Say it is about the state of this person's room, then is this an unrealistic expectation at the moment? The house is clean and tidy, their bit is not. They really don't care; they are not aware of any mess. Is there anything in this grubby situation that is really a threat to their health? A clean person can presume that there is a risk, but have they actually had food poisoning, or fleas, or whatever it is that comes from a dirty room? If it is just because this chaos offends a clean and organised carer perhaps it needs to be them that lets it go just now. There is a lot to be said for just closing the door. Could it be a battle to be fought when they are more capable?

If there is clear evidence that they are well enough to make some alterations in their lifestyle but are simply reluctant then there are other options.

CHANGE: DIRECT ACTION.

When one person really wants someone to change and it is equally important to the other person that they don't, then there is stalemate. The carer can only make it happen if that shift is one that can be controlled by their own behaviour.

For example: the carer is in the house all day because the person they support becomes hysterical and threatens to hurt or kill themselves if they mention going out. This is not being judgemental about behaviour that is a result of a mental health issue; the person is working to manage their overwhelming feelings and is convinced they are unable to cope without their safety net constantly available. At some point they become used to having support readily accessible and presume that they cannot survive without it.

Staying in all day is hard if it is not a choice. If a carer feels like a prisoner then this will affect their mood, their health and their relationship with this person. It may come to the point that the situation becomes unbearable and cannot be sustained. If the person with the mental health issue appears to be in a relatively calm and positive place but the carer isn't then who takes priority?

The first step as always is an assessment of risk. Being controlled by threats it is not a healthy situation long-term for either person. Total dependency on someone else is a poor quality of life and the carer's health is suffering too. Things have become 'stuck' and unless there are some enforced alterations they will stay in this damaging place.

The question is this; if this change is pushed through what is the worst that can happen? It is largely guesswork but informed guesswork. Is it worth taking the risk that they will self-harm or make a suicide attempt? Is this happening anyway and if so, then how much risk is involved? Sometimes these dramatic gestures become manageable because they are routine or seem to be kept within safe margins. It is a highly individual judgement.

If the decision is to go ahead then this is one possible approach:

> The carer makes a clear statement that they are going out, they need some fresh air so they are going to the nearest shop or for a walk and they will be exactly fifteen minutes. (It may be better not to make this statement too far in advance as this will allow anxiety to build). They will have their phone with them and when they return there is an offer of a cup of tea perhaps with a cake from the shop, and complete attention and a dedicated talking time.

Then the carer walks out of the door ignoring the threats and comes back at *exactly* the specified time. The person who has been left alone will probably be furious having spent this period in an advanced state of panic – and the carer will possibly know what that feels like as they have been pretty tense too, but they are going to try to hide that.

Crucially there is the promised time together straight after coming back, with an opportunity to express anger or anxiety without the carer belittling their fears and, if possible, giving some positive feedback about the fact that they did cope and held on.

Returning to find that someone has self-harmed or taken pills creates a hard decision. If these actions are happening in other situations and at other times is it advisable to persevere with the change, given that the family are probably experienced at dealing with this by now? This is a question of balance, the health and wellbeing of the carer / family against the possible risk to this vulnerable person.

An additional factor is that if they are to 'live their best life' then their ability to tolerate stress and develop coping skills is going to be crucial. Learning to self-soothe, to manage their own anxiety levels without help from others is a key element to rehabilitation.

Basic relaxation techniques such as breathing exercises or visualisation can be useful, they could practice these preferably together with the family so everyone knows what they are and can call on them. Putting together a schedule of relaxation exercises to do while they are alone or leave them playing a guided meditation tape or watching YouTube classes, will that help? There are lots of good ideas online that everyone in the house could join in.

There needs to be a regular routine established, time limits are kept to the minute unless there is an emergency and then the person is informed by phone. Once the major meltdown on the return home becomes just a small gesture then the time out can be extended, by ten minute intervals perhaps. There can be a bigger treat or a phone call halfway through as the time gets longer. This gradual increase in time allows for levels of anxiety and anger to be adjusted slowly rather than expecting a sudden jump. It is also important to recognise that this process requires great courage on the part of the cared-for person, their bravery should be acknowledged.

A carer I knew tried this method and, as advised, stuck rigidly to the time he said he would come back home. This meant that one day, when he was ten minutes early, he waited at the end of the road in the pouring rain. A puzzled neighbour stopped and offered him a lift which he refused. Probably caused a great deal of local gossip but it had to be done!

The carer is under considerable pressure, attempting to drive through a change like this. Getting support and advice from family, professionals and anybody who could be trusted would help especially if the decision involved taking an acknowledged risk. There is more on this topic under the 'suicide' section if the ultimatum includes a threat to take their own life.

CHANGE: TALKING ABOUT IT.

Trying to make changes can ruin communication. Carers often say that they end up going round and round, constantly returning to the same topic by different routes, and each time it is brought up in conversation the result is the same.

'Hi Sarah, how are you this morning?'
'I'm all right.'

'You know I was wondering about that counsellor, you know the one we were talking about yesterday?'

'The one you were talking about you mean.'

'Well anyway, I think it would be a really good idea. You could talk things through, and it would all be completely confidential. Don't you think it's about time?'

'Not really.'

'Why not? You could at least try it!'

'Nope. I'm not going.'

'What's wrong with having a go to see if it improves the situation. You're getting nowhere at the moment, wasting all day doing nothing.'

'Will you just stop having a go at me!'

'I'm sorry but it worries me that you seem to have got a bit stuck, I'm just trying to help. How can I help?'

'You can leave me alone and stop nagging!' (Stomps off to her room- again.)

People with mental health issues are no different than the rest of us, they are reluctant to respond to people who keep telling them they ought to be doing something that they don't want to do. They have the symptoms, the medication and the self-esteem issues to deal with, none of which lend themselves to tackling something new. The carer is trying to help but the person is not responding, the result is frustration and irritation on both sides.

Normal conversation is often about exchanging information in an established pattern; Person A talks about themselves and Person B politely throws in a positive remark and then talks about themselves, and so on.

'Hi Lucy, how are things?'

'Fine, I've just had my hair done.'

'I can tell, it looks great. I'm having mine done next week, I

am thinking about changing the colour.'
'That's exciting, I wanted highlights but lost my nerve. I just had a cut and blow dry'
'That's a shame, that would have been great for the summer. I think I might go a bit blonder.'
'What a good idea. Maybe I should have the highlights next time.'

The pattern is verbal ping pong and it is what people are used to on a day-to-day basis but doesn't work as a means of encouraging new ideas or activities.

'Active listening' creates a different relationship, one with more trust and openness; this may take weeks. After a time, gradually and gently, the carer can put their point of view across. There must be trust that they will not 'take over' and tell the person with the mental health issue what to do.

Tactics that help to focus listening and encourage more open talking are covered in detail in the 'listening' section, there is also a short summary here:

- Asking questions, especially ones that don't have 'yes' or 'no answers.
  'I'm not sure I understand what you're saying, tell me a bit more?'
  'So, what happened next?'
  'How did you feel after that?'

- Letting them know you heard what they said and have understood it by repeating it back, perhaps as a question.
  'Then you went in to see the nurse, but she looked very busy?'
  'You woke up in the night and thought you heard someone?'

- Picking out the feelings in what the person is saying:
  'That sounds very frightening, you must have been really scared.'
  'So she said you didn't need to change your medication? Was that a relief?'

No suggestions or judgements or comments, just focus on what they are saying.

Suppose the earlier conversation was more like this?

'Hi Sarah, how are you this morning?'
'I'm all right.'
'You know I was wondering about that counsellor, you know the one we were talking about yesterday.'
'The one you were talking about you mean.'
'You don't seem keen on the idea. What puts you off trying it?'
'I just don't want to.'
'You don't want to try it at all?'
'Nope. It's not going to happen.'
'You seem pretty certain it's the wrong thing for you.'
'Well you wouldn't want to go talking to some stranger who might get you put in the nuthouse would you!'
'You think they might section you?'
'Yeah. They can't be trusted, if they think you're crazy then they'll call in the white coats.'
'That worries you then, that they might put you in hospital. They can do that can they?'
'Well I expect so. That's their job isn't it.'

What has been learnt here is that Sarah is worried about being sectioned if she talks to anyone who is a professional, which is not an uncommon fear. Knowing this opens some possibilities for conversation in the future, perhaps finding out how people are sectioned or why. Also, what she means when she says 'crazy' and why does she think it applies to her? There is a great deal of misunderstanding out there, some people believe that if they think at all about suicide they will be locked up. If that were true then there would have to be some exceptionally large psychiatric hospitals.

Spending time getting to understand what is going on in the mind of the person with the mental health problem is an investment.

If the carer wants to push through a new idea then the person they support needs to know exactly why this is necessary, it is equally important to understand why they don't want to make the change if there is still resistance. The optimum outcome is that they solve the situation through their own ideas. The carer could ask:

'So, if this doesn't change what do you think might happen? Is that ok?'

'Have you got an idea about how this might get sorted out?'

'What do you think you could do to help this to happen?'

If they have got ideas about what they would prefer to do then it may be worth supporting them or, at minimum, leaving them to have a go. Trying their solutions first shows respect for their opinion and consideration of their input as important, which helps their self-esteem too. If their plan works then fine.

If it doesn't or they don't have any suggestions, then they may be more open to alternatives – which could be the carers ideas. (Using the problem-solving technique together can be useful if they are up for it but the person with the mental health issues gets to rate the choices, alone).

This is a bit complicated so a quick summary may be helpful.

A. Listening carefully over a long period of time, without advice or judgements, helps develop a better understanding of their side of the picture and less sense of confrontation.

B. Asking the person to solve any problems and giving them every opportunity to do this is the optimum outcome.

C. If this doesn't work or they have no plan then the carer can make suggestions, but they still cannot progress without agreement.

There is one more 'change making' strategy if none of this works. Active listening often means that someone will talk about their hopes and future plans. What are they thinking and what do they want to happen? What do they look forward to? If they have ambitions or wishes, even ones that might spring from delusional beliefs, then these could provide an incentive to bring about the required changes.

'Using' highly personal thoughts and ideas as a means of persuasion sounds awful, perhaps it is better phrased as 'trying to see from their perspective' and then finding a way to make the change appealing to them.

Again, just the bare bones of this idea; is it possible to adapt their goals to make a change the carer feels would help? There is more information under the 'refusing medication' section.

EXAMPLE A

Their goal - to go back to college.

Carer's goal - stop them spending so much time gaming online.

Suggestion - will they consider an online course as a warm-up to college?

EXAMPLE B

Their goal – to get on Britain's Got Talent

Carer's goal - to encourage them to look after themselves better

Suggestion – being on TV makes people look ten pounds heavier, and there is no escaping a close up shot. Is it worth working on looking as good as they can in preparation?

EXAMPLE C

Their goal – to have more friends

Carer's goal – to get them to clean their room

Suggestion – talk about how, if people come to visit, they might want to chat in their room. How could it be made comfortable for visitors?

The carer is motivating the person by using their personal plans to create a change rather than imposing their own priorities on them.

It is worth repeating that no one can make another person behave the way they want them to, they can only control their own behaviour and hope that any alterations they make will encourage change in others.

FAQS

This is an attempt to make short answers to complicated questions that seem to feature regularly in conversations with carers from all backgrounds. Some of this information is covered elsewhere but this is a briefer version for people in a hurry.

IS IT MY FAULT?

Parents have this innate sense of guilt but also partners and older children can hold themselves responsible when someone in the family becomes mentally distressed. People want to know why it happened and were they in any way a part of causing it?

That is a difficult question as there are some families that really do hurt each other. There is obvious abuse – physical, sexual or emotional, which clearly causes damage. It is not uncommon though for a carer to feel that they have not been sufficiently supportive, spent enough time, offered enough encouragement or always been sensitive to this person's needs. Perhaps there is an underlying awareness that the relationship isn't perfect; that they were not the favourite child, or that parents have been through a lot because of their behaviour or that there has been a regret for a long time now that this relationship ever started.

These nagging thoughts can be another stress to deal with when more pressure is really unhelpful. There may be no one to talk to that can be trusted. Perhaps asking someone may result in answers that confirm the worst suspicions.

The causes of mental health issues are not yet fully explained, more detail is given in the section called, strangely enough, 'what causes mental health issues.' The brief version is that there are several possible causes:

- Biological / genetic causes such as neurotransmitters that don't behave as they should or processes that are damaged during pregnancy or birth.
- Sociological aspects, which is what happens to people because of the world they find themselves in, including their family/partner.
- Psychological factors, the way a person thinks and their attitude to their experiences. Some people seem to be able to easily brush things off where others get deeply wounded by small worries.

Just to make it more complicated this internal coping ability may be influenced by the biological factors so someone born more generally anxious could find it harder to calm themselves in a crisis.

There is another complication that a traumatic experience such as a redundancy or a bereavement may then cause physical changes and those changes become harder to reverse; what is initially a life event then develops into a permanent change in the body chemistry.

It is just not possible to establish in any one individual what exactly caused their mental health to change, but it is known that some diagnoses are more biologically based whereas some are more about personal experience or thinking habits. Mostly it is a mixture of all three in varying proportions, but no one knows what combination in any one individual.

The sort of reasoning that might go on in any carer's mind could be something like:

- He was bullied at school by that awful boy with the bad haircut. (Social)
- He was always too withdrawn to cope with other kids, even when he was young. (Biological/Psychological)
- He got dumped by that inconsiderate girlfriend during his exams. (Social)
- I drank when I was pregnant (Biological)
- I went out to work and left him with that odd childminder. (Social)
- His dad used to shout at him far too much. (Social)
- His dad's auntie was on medication for her 'nerves' and was clearly the batty one of the family. Then, of course there was my grandad. (Biological)
- I just didn't listen to him when he was young and wanted to be a musician. (Social)
- He got in with those awful friends at college and did all that dope. (Biological)
- He was always the moody type; he was bound to fall apart at some stage. (Psychological/Biological)
- He was in that car crash when he got knocked off his bike and hit his head. (Biological)

Being a parent leads to a natural tendency for self-blame but don't be in too much of a hurry to see it just from that perspective. It doesn't help that in the early 1970s there was a stage when it was fashionable to point the finger at the family as being the sole cause for all the flaws in anyone's personality, especially mental health issues. This approach has fallen out of favour for a good reason, it can be a factor of course but how extreme does it have to be to cause permanent damage?

Parents often mention divorce when talking about causing stress for their children. A family splitting up does cause all kinds of ripples but surely most divorces happen because they need to. If this family had stayed together would it have been a less stressful and more stable environment? Would every member of the family have been better off emotionally? Given the divorce rate, if it were always a key factor in creating mental health issues surely the number of people diagnosed would be even greater than it is.

Most families that I have met, many holding themselves responsible at some level, are without doubt as normal and unexciting as the rest of the population. They had rows, shouted, lost their temper, called each other names and said things like, 'I just don't know why I bother to try and help you, you ungrateful little wretch/dreadful father/nagging wife', or words to that effect. That is what families and partners do, it is not enough on its own to make a substantial change in someone's mental wellbeing.

There could have just been a change, a shift internally in someone's body 'mechanics' and the family and even the world around them played little part. Maybe they used drugs, they should have been stopped of course, but finding out how to stop someone using substances to make themselves feel better or to fit in with their peer group is, as yet, still an unsolved problem. The alcohol and drugs trade will put a contract out anyone who finds out how to do this though.

There is no concrete evidence that links specific causes and specific outcomes, although people (like me) love to play the armchair psychologist and create an imaginative backstory based on childhood experiences and bullying as a teenager. It may well all play a part, or none at all, so taking on the guilt could be unnecessary distress. Beware the lure of creating a story that explains why, it may be satisfying, especially with friends and family contributing their opinions, but it may also change little. Certainty is unlikely.

The chances are that any part a family member played in this mental health issue was very incidental or non- existent. It is far, far more likely that as a carer the support offered will far outweigh any minor distress in the distant past. Most parents/ adult children/ partners/ friends know if their efforts are 'good enough', it may be wise to allow a little leniency when it comes to the blame stakes.

The time spent delving into past misdemeanours is probably not productive, it changes nothing. What needs attention is what is happening right now.

AM I DOING TOO MUCH?

This is another aspect of being a carer that causes those endless inner dialogues that rumble on for years. It can also create a source of tension with other family members that can cause permanent damage to those relationships.

'You do too much for your dad, you are just making him helpless!'
'You would have him wandering the streets living in a skip or begging in the rain I suppose?'
'Don't be silly, I just think he's not going to get back to doing things for himself if you keep doing them for him.'
'Have you talked to him about sorting out his money? He hasn't got a clue. If I don't do it, he'll be in serious debt.'
'OK, but when do you stop doing it? You going to be his financial manager for the rest of his life?'

From the outset it needs to be said that there is no rulebook that states 'After a month you can…' or 'When she starts doing this then you should do that'. Like most of the mental health game no one has undisputable rules to follow.

Professionals tend not to be around much when a person is doing well. During any crises they may be more available and open to questions. When it all goes quiet then they go and help someone else, that is their job. Getting advice about your individual situation can therefore be a challenge when the most distressing periods are gone, this is now the quieter phase. Other carers are always a useful resource but can't always give detailed instructions as situations are so individual.

Carers undoubtedly can contribute to a situation becoming stuck, it is necessary to be aware of how the family may be colluding with the person's sense of helplessness. This is completely understandable because this person has had a traumatic and devastating time battling through, the carer has had to 'take over'. When there is an improvement in their wellbeing it is incredibly hard to let go because it feels so risky.

I once met a man who said, 'I am the only person in my house who is allowed to unload the dishwasher as I am the only one who will put everything back in the right place.' Now some may nod in agreement, but I suspect that the majority will think, as I do, 'You fool! Talk about shooting yourself in the foot.'

One man I worked with for many years lived at home and functioned at a very minimal level. His parents chose his clothes, his TV viewing, his food and his daily activities. He was usually relatively cheerful but basically made no effort to do anything new. He just wandered around making repetitive conversation. I left my job but bumped into him about ten years later. He was on his way to a workshop with a friend, two concepts that were quite a shock to me, so I asked him how life was now. He said, 'My dad died and I'm much better now.' Shocking as that was, I realised that he was saying that he was stuck before because his family did not allow him to be otherwise. Without their imposed routine he had discovered new possibilities and appeared to be making the most of it.

'If you do tomorrow what you did today, you will get tomorrow what you got today' as somebody famous said once.

Carers are seldom motivated by considerations of their own wellbeing, so it is worth remembering that it does the person with the mental health problem no favours being a 'helicopter carer' and hovering waiting for their every need. To regain a real quality of life, particularly with the more serious conditions but also with the less devastating ones, people need to become as independent as possible as quickly as possible. This means that they either return to how they were before, where that isn't possible then they reconstruct a new life making the most of what they have. The 'skills for independence' section has more on this.

The big question when considering the 'am I doing too much?' is always 'can't they or won't they?' When they are unwell and completely unable to function, the family may do their washing, make their meals, manage their money, look after their medication and take them to appointments and so on. After a while, if they are making themselves the odd messy sandwich or playing complex online games, is it time to get heavy and ask them to clean their room?

Can they really do this task but are choosing not to? Is it because:

- They fear failing and it makes them very anxious
- They are trying to keep the carer closely involved
- They are just lazy
- They cannot think clearly enough to manage the task.
- They define themselves as 'ill' or 'disabled' and believe this means they are no longer responsible for themselves
- They are apparently not expected to do more

Or all the above? A lot of tough questions.

Some people are eager to rebuild their lives and face the

challenges – some definitely are not. Their lack of motivation is understandable. They are probably feeling foggy and fragile, possibly very socially conspicuous and have got out of practice in performing certain tasks.

Take going into a shop if it hasn't happened for some time, there are a series of obstacles to face:

- How do I get there? Can I cope with driving, a bus, walking, all those people?
- What if someone recognises me? What will I say?
- Do I look like I'm crazy, will people point and laugh?
- When I get to the shop will I be able to walk in? If I lose my nerve, I'll have to run and then people will look at me.
- If I get in how will I know where to go, what to choose? There is so much stuff!
- When it comes to paying I might have to stand in a queue, that feels like being trapped. I can't leave without making a fuss, what would I do with my shopping if I ran?
- When I get out of the shop I've got to get home again, I'll be exhausted by then.
- What if I have a panic attack?
- What if I get something wrong and people notice?

If everyone anticipated each daily activity with this sense of dread not much would get done. The way forward, as every self-help book reader knows, is to face your fears. If the carer does their shopping for them the problem is solved – but only for now.

If someone says they can't do their own shopping but will pop to the local all-night garage for a beer now and then, there is a clue. If they start an evening class but come home having failed to make it through the front door of the college and are in bits for three days, there is another one. It's all that professionals can use to make their judgements and the family can only tap into the same resource.

What the family needs are powers of observation and nerves of steel. This means that a plan can be put in place, it helps to focus on developing one or two areas rather than employing the scattergun approach because consistency and repetition may be required

Principles:

- The carer should never do more than they absolutely need to in order to keep the person safe and well.
- When they are wobbly and agitated they will need more help.
- When they are looking a bit stronger there is an opportunity to do less.

Ideally people will be motivated with rewards (tidy your room and it will be a fish and chips night), but in reality there may not be much to offer that appeals more than carrying on being looked after. It may come to some harsher ultimatums.

'You can make yourself a sandwich any time you like but unless you wash the knife and plate and put them away afterwards, and put the stuff back in the fridge, I will stop buying the food you like and it will be plain bread and butter, that will be it.'

No one gets scurvy in a week.

'You want your beer on Friday then you go to the shop and get it.'

This requires an absolute certainty that they are capable of this. Anger about not having a customary beer is not something to be brought on without due consideration. These arrangements can be difficult when living in a family home but there may be a way that a minor inconvenience can be used to bring about a small change, if is not happening willingly.

Positive risk taking is the art of letting them take a chance because it might pay off. It is worth being ready if it doesn't of course. I always think of the time my kids decided they could walk to the shop on their own. I wasn't aware of this until one day they returned unexpectedly minus pocket money and clutching chocolate. The next few times they went I would be biting my fingernails. They had to go of course or else I wouldn't have been doing my job. Hard on the nerves though. It's the same when someone recovering from a mental health issue does something new on their own for the first time.

Professionals survive (or not) by having that distance between them and their patients/clients. They care, of course they do, but only so much. It is manageable caring. They also make tricky decisions within teams or in supervision when they can talk through the options and share responsibility for the outcome. Some get burned out by working too long and taking on too much. It's not easy to leave, but it is always an option for them.

Family carers often work alone, make decisions alone and cannot walk away from the situation without fear of the consequences. Yet that professional detachment can be developed enough to help get through this time. Professionals observe, assess, try things out and if they don't work then they make a new plan. If a carer can manage to detach enough to watch from a safe distance, they can keep one foot on firm ground and avoid being too buffeted about by the process.

The principle of protecting them when they are vulnerable but supporting change when they are stronger is non-negotiable.

The sense of progress is important for them to feel they are getting somewhere, it will prepare them for the time when there might be no one around who is able to do all this stuff. (Does this sound like a nag? Good).

The bottom line is what happens long-term if no one at least tries to help them to do more for themselves?

WHY CAN'T I HELP MORE?

In contrast to the previous section looking at the perils of doing too much, this bit is on why carers seldom feel they are doing all they could. A typical quandary which helps to illustrate why the role is so stressful.

Family carers often use the word 'should': 'I should be able to help', 'I should be the one that finds the answer to this'. What is particularly difficult, I think, is recognising the limitations of their influence, that the outcome is not really under the family's complete control, much relies on external factors over which they are powerless. Accepting that there are circumstances where only the professionals can help, and sometimes they can't either, is worrying. This is a tough idea to accept as it implies that there is a large element of unpredictability, when everyone would obviously like there to be certainty about the outcome.

Can the person with the mental health issue be made to go to the doctor, be honest when they get there, take medication, keep appointments, stop drinking, etc? What control do families have over what mental health services do or how effective they are? Will the GP prescribe a helpful medication? Will there be a counsellor/therapist that they get on with? Will they get appointments when they need them and be supported appropriately in an emergency? Can the family make sure that they are resilient and effective at resisting the symptoms that they experience?

My job with carers involved saying at least twice a week 'you cannot change anyone else's behaviour or thoughts. The only behaviour anybody has control over is their own'. The first response when identifying a new problem, rather than being, 'I have got to fix this' could perhaps be, 'can I realistically do anything in this situation?' When there is a mental health issue it becomes a real skill to work out how much to wade in and how much to sit on the side lines and wait and see what happens. No point wading in if it isn't going to make any difference.

Addiction to illegal drugs is a good example. At one end of the spectrum the carer can pay for and even go and get supplies on behalf of the person with the mental health issue and I have met families that do just that. Go out once to meet a man on a dark street corner to get a wrap of some class A powder and there is a precedent started that's hard to break. On the other hand, there is the full 'tough love' approach; throw them out of the house and cut off all contact. A middle way would be to buy them food, try to keep regular contact and make it clear that the family would very much like them to stop but that in the end it's up to them. Non have any guarantees of working, it's more about what gives the family a sense of doing the right thing.

To answer the question 'why can't I help more?' the carer could choose to review those bits that they actually have influence over. This includes their behaviour with the person with the mental health issues, with professionals and others that impact directly on how the day goes. All that can be done is to review the elements that are under the family's control. See 'the good enough carer' section for a checklist on this topic.

Carers may become aware that many of their conversations with the cared-for person may be suggestions as to how they should be doing things differently, because it feels as though all they have to offer is advice. It is a continual struggle to avoid continuous 'what you should be doing' statements because it may be the only option that feels like it is offering help, although it may be more reassuring for the carer than effective in making things happen. The 'encouraging change' section has more on this.

The progress of recovery in a severe mental health diagnosis can be very gradual, there is no fast track alternative. Families may well be doing a wonderful job but not be aware of the effect of their efforts for many months.

This process of accepting that the carer cannot always write the end of the story, how things turn out is only partially within their power, is not an emotionally satisfactory answer. It feels impossible to let go of wanting to make it right and a kind of admission of failure to acknowledge that it will go its own way, to a considerable degree. It's useful to talk to other carers as it is often easier to observe in others how angry they can become with themselves for not achieving an impossible task.

One carer told me that after some counselling sessions she had decided 'I am doing the best I can, and as much as I love them, I cannot take responsibility for the things I cannot control'.

The words that offer the best comfort are 'I am doing the best I can', after all that is all that is possible.

WHY DON'T THEY WANT TO GET BETTER?

This is a short but necessary point because it is vital to be aware that recovery might mean quite different things to different people. Some people just don't want to get better, it took me a long time to see this. When more experienced workers would shrug and make fatalistic remarks, I thought they were just making excuses for their own inability to help people effectively, but over time I saw the results for myself.

The family really want someone to get 'well'. This is a

shorthand phrase for 'like you were before all this started'. This does happen for some people; the symptoms are a temporary blip that come once or perhaps a few times but on the whole things go pretty much back to where they were.

Some people have symptoms for a lot longer and this might mean that the person with the 'sick' label comes to consider the prospect of recovering as not altogether positive. This applies to physical health conditions as well as to mental health ones. The sick role is largely a passive one, the expectation is that medication is taken willingly, the lifestyle is not too challenging and there is an established comfort zone where the 'patient' is not expected to cope with change for fear of causing a relapse.

The current treatment for mental health requires that the person actively participates. It used to be frequent dose of medication, with a regular appointment to check on side effects and an instruction to 'Go away and live quietly.' In fact, the number of people who lived out their lives in institutions was so much greater even fifty years ago; medication was given out every day from a trolley, nurses looked under tongues to check for hidden pills and everyone carried on living their sedated lives wandering the grounds counting squirrels and knitting dishcloths.

The new medication that started to come in after the 1970s, especially the 'atypical' antipsychotics, lessened this zombie-fication of the severely affected patients. The recognition dawned that what was happening around the person and how they approached life mattered a great deal in their recovery. They needed to build up their resilience, cope with life's tricky bits and manage their symptoms. This requires that they tackle these issues themselves, they can no longer be a passive patient.

In an ideal world someone who has got through their initial crisis should then move on to new challenges and a gradual reintroduction to the world. For some people that is quite a small step, it may be a phased return to work and to social situations. Those who have been more restricted for a longer period may have a lot further to go.

Knowing that an individual's progress does to some degree rely on their own efforts creates a new pressure. Families can get really frustrated when their cared-for person seems reluctant to engage with a new opportunity, whether it's an art class or cognitive behavioural therapy. They should be jumping at every chance to improve their mental health, surely?

A noticeable pattern that can emerge during this rehabilitative phase is the positive move swiftly followed by a negative one. They achieve something wonderful such as going back to college or getting a voluntary job. This could be a brilliant step forward and everyone is so pleased. Why do some people then sabotage this shortly afterwards by then having a huge drinking binge or a major self-harm episode, even a suicide attempt or whatever they do to show they are not better yet so the family had better not expect that they are?

That is the whole point, that the prospect of recovering is just too overwhelming. Possibly this is because being 'well' means functioning competently. It includes working, relationships, managing finance, leaving the shelter of the family and living alone, if that hasn't already happened.

Currently the person with the mental health diagnosis may be leading a rather protected existence; expectations are small and sensitively suggested, there are medications that probably take the edge off things, and there are often nice people to listen to how they are feeling. They may be professionals rather than friends, but they are a safer option. Life is predictable. Mental health symptoms may be challenging and cause distress at times, even great distress, but it is a familiar distress. The mental health issue is the comfort zone.

Therapy and treatment require a change and change increases

anxiety. Doing well means getting discharged from services and a reduction in attention when there are few other sources of this. Some people love going into hospital and to demonstrate that they need this by gestures such as suicide attempts. This is not someone trying to die but someone asking to be rescued. This may become a pattern involving a regular significant overdose or visit to a dangerous place followed by a phone call to be saved from themselves. It is a drastic gesture that means they are not able or willing to cope 'out there.'

In addition, people who have strongly identified with their delusional beliefs may come to realise that this is not a rational view of life, they know at one level that it is a feature of their mental health diagnosis but what is the price of letting go of this other world? Which 'reality' is nicer?

I remember a conversation I had on an almost daily basis with a man who was convinced that he and Princess Diana had an understanding, she would send for him any day now and then they would be married. This was based on a fleeting glimpse of her twenty years previously when she communicated this promise to him through eye contact – he was very psychotic at the time. I got on well with this man and talked to him three or four times a week, he was very emotionally 'stable' now so our conversation was more honest and challenging than it would be with someone I didn't know so well. It used to go something like this:

'How are things going, Keith?'
'Very well, I think the day is nearly here so I'm going for a haircut this afternoon.'
'You mean the Princess?'
'Of course. Any day now.'
'We have talked about this quite a few times now Keith.'
'Hmmm?'

I't's been a long time since you saw her, don't you think if it was going to happen...'

'She's been terribly busy, flying around on tours and all that.'

'Do you remember we talked about how she died quite a while ago and maybe you just didn't see the announcements on TV?'

'Yes, I'm sure you're right.'

'I know she is incredibly special to you but maybe there is something new you would like to try now rather than just waiting for her all the time?'

'Yes, that's a great idea. I'll do something new. I'll think about that.'

'Brilliant. Let me know if I can help in any way.'

The next day

'Morning Keith, did you have a good day yesterday?'

'Yes, I had my haircut so I am ready, she is calling me today.'

My naivety about delusional systems meant that I wasted a great deal of Keith's time and mine. Why couldn't he move on? Perhaps it was partly the way his cognitive processes were working but perhaps there was also an extreme reluctance to let go of this dream. When she sent for him he would be a royal, rich and famous. Without this he was a middle-aged, unemployed, unfit man with no prospects of being restored to his previous white-collar respectability. What is in this 'getting better' for him?

This is not meant to depress or deter any carer who is working hard to make positive things happen. It may be useful, however, to address the topic of how frightening or challenging it is to move forward. If there are ways of offering reassurance that they are not going to be abandoned it may help. It is true that as an individual progresses through the mental health system they will get less support, this is a major worry that they need to face. It could be helpful to acknowledge this and not to presume that increasing independence is equally everyone's goal. Getting these fears into the open could be a useful move.

CAN I STOP BEING A CARER?

The carer's role is tough going at the best of times and at the worst of times it can do some real damage to the family's health and wellbeing. Over time stress can push people beyond exhaustion and despair. Please do not panic at this point if this makes no sense; things are a bit daunting sometimes but on the whole everyone is coping reasonably well with the situation. Crises only happen to some, not all carers are as resilient as others, some have other pressures in their lives or physical / mental vulnerability themselves. Some circumstances can prove too much, at some stage a tough decision is required. Stopping should never be regarded as a sign of weakness, it may just be necessary.

Now that the number of hospital beds has decreased more people are cared for 'in the community' and the burden on families is undoubtedly much greater. This community living is a more successful model than putting people in an institution for large portions of their life (but not necessarily cheaper). If there is a family involved the outcome is likely to be more positive too. It may be the optimum arrangement but, like breastfeeding or caring for your dad with dementia at home, it isn't always going to work out.

A carer can stop at any time. This question should be asked in a 'carers assessment' (see the section on this for more detail) and, in theory, mental health staff and others should be recognising if it is all getting to much and putting plans in place to lessen the impact on the family. In my experience this support seldom happens or if it does it seems to be long after the first desperate shout for help. If a carer decides that they want to stop then it has to be said loud and clear, probably repeated numerous times to the right people who will probably have a wide variety of reactions to this statement, not all positive. If a carer is aware that their mental/physical health is failing they can

- choose to keep going until the situation is decided, probably by a crisis of some sort
- plan to do less but still stay involved
- walk away and cut off all contact, which potentially results in feeling terrible but does offer a chance to recover

I have met a few people who walked away. Mostly they were partners and they took a long, long time to make the decision. It inevitably caused them much pain and guilt. I have met a couple of parents who cut off contact with their adult children but then restarted communication again when the situation improved. I have also known of parents who cut off all contact and never heard from their children again, but these were without exception situations where there was an addiction as well as a mental health issue.

One husband moved to another country to make a fresh start after years in a tortured relationship with his very suicidal wife. I met him again by coincidence several years later when he came back to visit his children. His description of his wife was that she was much improved and more independent now, living in her own flat. It was his children who still struggled with his decision and saw it as running away.

However, every position is unique and other people's decisions may not necessarily be relevant in making the choice. To make the break with minimum regrets there needs to be an absolute conviction that it is the right thing to do. On one side of the debate in the carer's head there may be something like the following list:

- They have been much the same for a long time and there is no immediate threat of a relapse. It feels as though the worst has passed but they are still asking for a lot of attention.
- Now the crisis is over I feel exhausted. I am irritable with everyone and have a constant headache. I am too tired to sleep properly. I think my blood pressure could be up again.
- I know I am not responding to anyone helpfully because currently I just don't have the strength.
- I feel my other relationships are suffering and am worried they may be permanently damaged if I don't do something soon.

On the other side there may be:
- If I try to change anything then I know there will be trouble.
- If they get angry or worried it might trigger some sort of relapse, which could mean the worst bit will happen all over again.
- I'll feel guilty if I'm not there for them. I will never forgive myself if I walk away and something bad happens.

Other factors that might be part of this debate include:

The process of pulling away does not have to be permanent; if the situation started deteriorating then it can be reversed at any time.

The person needs to become as independent as possible regardless of their home situation or diagnosis. Staying highly involved is postponing the separation that may be inevitable one day or may come as the result of unexpected circumstances.

If it is a question of the carer's health and/or the rest of the family's wellbeing versus the person with the mental health issue, then there may need to be compromises preferably before the situation reaches critical level. Whose needs take priority?

No matter how stressful the situation it seems to be that the carer can seldom escape without some guilty feelings. There are no rules, it is a personal decision when to end this arrangement and it often requires as much courage as staying in there.

I have spent many hours with people who were thinking about option two, the partial withdrawal. This required planning and a tussle with their conscience as well.

The main source of tension often comes from sharing a house and the obvious solution is that the person with the mental health issue moves out. An independent flat may be a possibility if the money works out. If there is enough for a deposit and to either cover or subsidise their rent that saves a lot of hassle. This could be a long-term commitment, so the maths and finances need to be reliable.

If this isn't a possibility, then finding out what benefits they would be entitled to and what rent they could manage is a daunting but necessary task. Local advice lines or centres can be helpful with this and often have a great deal of experience. Then there is the challenge of finding a landlord who takes a tenant who isn't working and is on benefits. The local housing department is always worth contacting but the main stumbling block is that if the person currently lives in the family home then they are not homeless. The non-urgent housing list is long, the number of available properties is short.

The homeowner (i.e. their family) can evict them and if the local housing services accept that they have a diagnosed mental health issue then that makes them 'vulnerable.' In these circumstances they may be eligible for help (please check with your local housing authority as I haven't worked in this area for years and this is constantly changing). At best this could lead to being offered emergency housing which can be grim and full of unsavoury people with bad habits. Getting through that experience then eventually may lead to a flat but there is little control over area or surroundings. Some situations can be fine and some dreadful. They may meet wonderfully kind neighbours and, with family support, feel much better. They may live in an absolute tip that makes everyone shudder each time they go in, but they will have a degree of independence which can only help their self-esteem.

I have known of families who have made a 'separate houses' arrangement happen, they wouldn't look back. What is more important is that the person with the mental health issue has also adapted to the new circumstances and has become much more self-sufficient. It is surprising how many people do well against all expectations when they live alone. It has effectively saved the relationship even though the carer may still be heavily involved on a daily basis. There are no guarantees though. It isn't always a possibility; resilience, local conditions and the family finances play a big part.

It is an option to create a bit more space even if both the carer and the person with the mental health diagnosis live in the same house. The ways in which a carer can reduce the impact of this relationship could take several forms, these are just some ideas.

If the person with the mental health issue can't or won't physically move out, then can there be some no-go spaces or times set aside when they manage alone? One possibility is to establish a no bother time, say between 6 pm and 10 pm. This could require preparation such as leaving a (microwave) meal ready or investing in an online source of films for them. This is backed up if there is a space to go to that can become the carer's territory. Is there a room (or a shed – got to love a shed) that can become a sanctuary? This is a non-negotiable arrangement where the only reason to break it is a dire emergency - it could be useful to define exactly what a dire emergency would be so there is no misunderstanding.

If they are phoning every ten minutes, then an assertive but calm reply might be something like:

'We spoke a few minutes ago. I know you are feeling very anxious, but I really have nothing new to say that might help you. You need to find a way to manage this worry yourself. I am not going to talk now but I would really like to hear how you got on after X o'clock.'

Then put the phone down. Repeated this message until it gets through.

Moving apart and reducing dependency is going to cause upset. There is always a risk especially if they are prone to self-harm or suicidal acts but if this is balanced against the probable outcome for the carer then it could be a necessary gamble. The optimum way of doing this is by offering something in return, such as set periods of complete attention or activities together to compensate for time apart.

Getting advice really helps, either from mental health professionals or other carers, so doing less for them doesn't feel like a selfish act. If a carer can see a crisis coming wouldn't they do their best to try to avert it – even if the crisis is their own?

WHAT HAPPENS AFTER I'M GONE?

There are several reasons why any individual stops being a carer at some point, either through choice, illness or the more obvious 'falling off the perch' reason. This seems to be a vague but constant worry for a lot of families, how will it work out when the current support system is no longer an option.

Being a carer means moving along a path with little idea where it may be going, especially with mental health diagnoses that are not progressive, that do not inevitably get worse but fluctuate between relapses and periods of stability. How does the family prepare for the long-term? Is there anything that can be done to put everyone's mind at rest when they are thinking about how things will be when the current arrangement is no longer possible?

There doesn't seem to be a fool-proof plan that comes with warranties, but there are aspects that can be arranged in advance. These points apply more to people who are still dependent on a fair amount of support and who continue to experience relatively severe symptoms.

If the person is under the care of a mental health team then warn them as soon as it becomes clear that things are about to change. The GP may be a good place to start if the mental health team are no longer involved, they can pass the message on. If there is any reason to suspect that things are going to get a bit rocky then they need to know as soon as possible.

If the person with the mental health issue is doing quite well there is no immediate need to classify this as an emergency as long as they have a roof over their heads and can manage day-to-day life, including their medication. If this is not the case and the carer stepping down means plunging them into chaos, then the mental health team should see them and assess the situation quickly. At that point they will decide whether this person meets the criteria for a service, if they are not currently getting one, and what they can offer.

Until the person has been assessed by a mental health professional or the GP there will be no concrete plan as to what will happen next. It can be helpful to ask what might be arranged while this situation is still only a distant possibility, but in nine cases out of ten the answer most probably will be that the decision can only be made at the time that it happens, the mental health services cannot make any promise before then because it depends on:

- How the person is at that time
- What resources are available.

It's hard to argue with that logic but it is also deeply unsatisfactory when carers want a hard and fast guarantee that everything will be fine.

Many carers have hoped that, when they are out of the picture, the person with the mental health issue will be moved into residential accommodation with support staff. This resource exists but is generally reserved for people who have clearly demonstrated that they cannot manage to survive in the community and whose mental health symptoms put them at some risk. There are few places and a lot of demand which doesn't mean it won't happen, but the odds are long.

Usually when someone is made homeless then they end up eventually in a flat. Every attempt is made to keep them going with this arrangement because it is better for them. Only if the independent living fails and they are clearly at risk (from more than the bacteria in the kitchen) will other options be considered. Despite the carer's despair at the piles of clothes, disgusting toilet and burger wrappers this is closer to normal life than a staffed hostel - where all the other occupants are probably quite unwell themselves.

The probable outcome if the carer is unable to continue and there is no possibility of keeping the same living arrangements would therefore be a flat, with some support popping in occasionally. This plan would be monitored until it clearly can be seen to be working; or not.

If someone else in the family is to step up as carer then they should be clear about what they are prepared to do. A common situation is that parent(s) become elderly and frail and an adult child with mental health issues is left increasingly to cope alone. If there is a sibling who will help out that is great but if that person has a young family, another caring role looking after these elderly parents or an exhausting job in the city then they may be able to offer far less support than their parents had. This sibling needs to be firm about what, if anything, they can offer in the way of time and support.

There are two phases in taking over a caring role, one being the setting up of a routine and sorting out of practicalities. The other is the long-term 'being around'.

Sometimes it is no bad thing that people find themselves having to manage with less support, families can get very stuck in a routine. It is not unknown for a person to become more independent and satisfied with their life when they are forced by circumstance to take on new skills. This is not to say it will inevitably be a positive event, losing their main carer, but there may be a beneficial aspect to it. This is one of the reasons there is a constant theme throughout this book that every carer should always do as little as possible in their caring role. The more confident this person is at coping alone the easier this transition will be.

What about the money? One of the major worries is about the Will. If there is a house or a substantial sum of money, then this transaction is worth planning carefully. If there is neither, then the family can be pleased that at least the lack of assets has led to one less worry; there are seldom positive aspects to being strapped for cash.

Leaving the person with the mental health issue a large lump sum could be the source of all sorts of problems. I have fond memories of a man I met who had just been let out of a forensic secure unit as he had murdered someone because of his mental health symptoms. Acts this violent are a rare occurrence but they do happen very occasionally, as the media loves to remind us. This man was quiet and shy, the staff team had to work hard over several weeks to help him to relax and settle in but it was included in his terms of release that he would attend the centre, so he was rather stuck, poor soul. All went very well until the benefits system, in its infinite wisdom, gave him back pay on his sick benefits. He got a cheque for £300 and disappeared. We found out he had got completely sloshed, and I do not blame him in the least.

Although he had not done anything terrible when inebriated he had broken the terms of his release by drinking alcohol, he was whipped back into the forensic unit before his hungover feet touched the floor.

Suddenly acquiring money is a dangerous thing, especially if the person has total control of it and is not great at thinking the situation through. They can go a bit wild with spending or drink, which could affect their mental health, or they can suddenly find they have lots of 'friends'. This can leave them extremely vulnerable. It also messes up the benefits system in a big way.

Again, I recall a woman whose mother died and left her several thousand pounds. She informed the DWP who stopped all her benefits immediately. She was instructed to claim again just before her mother's money ran out but was also told that she was expected to use this windfall 'sensibly'. There was an expectation that there would be no rash spending and that, and I quote, 'all receipts may have to be provided'. This gave her no clue as to how fast or slow the money was meant to be spent, or what was acceptable to buy and what wasn't. It was evidently a matter of discretion by the local benefits office, there were no hard and fast rules. I sincerely hope that this is no longer the case.

So this nice woman who had just lost her mum was suddenly faced with the prospect of having to justify everything she bought for at least the next year or two with the threat that when the money ran out she would be told 'Sorry, you spent that too fast, no benefits for you.' I remember her saying to me soon after this became clear, 'Do you think they would mind if I had an ice cream?' She went into hospital about a month later.

I am not trying to frighten anyone with tales of what happens if you leave money in a Will, just suggesting that the circumstances are thought through. If the cared-for person is likely to be living without dependence on benefits because they work or have a private income, then there is no problem if their bank balance suddenly jumps. If not, then the option is to see a solicitor and set up a trust fund.

The ideal plan is to leave a small sum which they can have immediate access to, and which is insignificant enough for the DWP to allow. This means they can have a treat to help cope with the difficult circumstances of losing their carer. The trust fund will then pay them an income for as long as the money lasts. This again either replaces benefits completely for a while or is a tiny extra allowance so that the basic benefit still gets paid and the person doesn't drop out of the system. A small extra allowance can make a big difference, it can provide some small luxuries that are much appreciated.

This fund can be managed by Trustees which means that the person can go and ask for some extra dosh if a life event requires it. The Trustees can be relatives, this is obviously the cheapest option and it keeps it in the family. Just a small note of caution that if the person with the mental health issue knows that their brother/ aunt / nephew now has power over all their money and is rationing it carefully, this may not lead to a smooth and friendly relationship. How would anyone feel if their siblings inherited cash, but they got theirs only in small amounts and had to beg for any extra?

Another option is to get a solicitor to be the Trustee. Of course this costs money, but it may save a lot of family tensions.

Leaving property is also complicated as there are running costs, insurance and repairs to consider. They will need help to manage all this and that is again either down to family members, with legal advice or a solicitor - for a small fee.

This trust fund is one thing that can be put in place as early as required. It may mean a couple of expensive appointments with a solicitor, but they will also put the family's mind at rest, at least about the long-term financial arrangements.

USEFUL RULES AND REGULATIONS

This is a short section covering four different policies that carers may find useful. These are, in no particular order:

PATIENT CONFIDENTIALITY – what are the actual rules about patient confidentiality in the NHS and how does it affect carers?

SAFEGUARDING – what protection is offered when people are possibly being abused, whether that is someone with a mental health issue or their carer?

CARER'S ASSESSMENTS AND OTHER BENEFITS – how can carers access help for themselves?

CARERS AND WORK – what can anyone expect from their employer?

PATIENT CONFIDENTIALITY

This is one of the major issues that has caused friction between carers and professionals during my working life. True, there are changes happening now which mean this should be less of an inflammatory subject and hopefully it will soon fall into the category of 'what we used to do in the old days.' If a carer lives in an area where patient confidentiality is not yet clearly managed or is unfortunate enough to encounter a practitioner who still hasn't got the message, it may be worth reading on.

There are strict rules in place to protect patient confidentiality and these are highly necessary. If I went to my GP and felt that they may gossip to others about my disgustingly unpleasant ailments I probably wouldn't go. How much more so when you are disclosing thoughts that may lead to a mental health diagnosis. The stigma remains, despite major media campaigns. It is still a massive reason why people feel the need to keep mental distress quiet. All clinical staff are sensitive about keeping a patient's personal information away from other people, this rightly includes their family.

Very early on, during the early form filling at the beginning of any relationship with a mental health service the question is asked, 'Can we talk to your carer?' The reply is logged on the 'Permission to Share Confidential Information' form or some similarly titled document. There are a variety of reasons why the reply could be 'no'. The carer(s) have special status here, there is an obligation to communicate with them, rather than all the random relatives and friends in general. How much information is communicated depends on the answer recorded on this form.

It may be that the person with a mental health issue sees their relatives and friends as being part of the problem, or as unimportant in their survival from day to day. In their view they may be doing fine and the weeks of anguish and worry that the carer has been through while trying to look after them just don't exist. They may desperately want to keep a secret, maybe their drug use or their sexuality or their suicidal thoughts. If they are experiencing psychosis they may feel that their family members are a threat and are trying to kill them, this is not unusual. They may accuse them of abuse and completely believe that to be true. A family member may in fact be abusive, how are the staff to distinguish at this early stage?

Sometimes people who offer a substantial amount of help to someone with a mental health issue are uncomfortable with the word 'carer' because it has many meanings. It can also be seen as offensive by the person themselves, not many people are happy to say that they have a 'carer.' Nevertheless, at the beginning of any contact with mental health services it is helpful if one is identified. The cared-for person may be reluctant to do that, so it may be down to the family member, partner of friend to speak to staff themselves.

The local inpatient services in the area where I used to work rephrased this question 'can we talk to your carer?' and substituted a sentence for staff to read out which said: 'Do you have anyone at home who helps and supports you? Can we share information with them?' This was a useful addition as it avoided the 'c' word completely.

I spoke to a nurse on one occasion who described how difficult it is for them to distinguish who, out of all the visitors to an inpatient unit, is the main carer if they don't identify themselves. Is that very friendly young man who has just come on the unit someone's brother or someone's drug dealer?

The 'patient' has a total right to dictate who hears about their diagnosis, treatment and how they are doing while they are under the care of the mental health services. In reality, a good staff team should only pass on any highly personal information on a 'need to know basis' anyway and usually just give out the minimum information, but the patient is not to know that. Why should they trust anyone considering what is going on?

This is the first hurdle, filling in the form with the person accepting that they have got someone whose support they rely on and that they don't mind information being shared with them. If it is straightforward and the answer is 'yes' then the carer can be immediately involved. I have heard some say that they have still received a brush off even if the form is signed, they think it may be because staff can't remember everyone's confidentiality status, so they play it safe. Knowing about the form and whether it has a 'yes' on it can be valuable information.

Staff are supposed to return to this 'Permission to Share Information' form later if the patient has said 'no,' and ask them to reconsider. The family can remind staff of this if it is causing any problems. A nurse could be helpfully persuasive by saying things like 'it would help your father to know a bit more about what is going on, as he will be around when you go home and he can help to make sure everything is going OK.' Hopefully as the person becomes less distressed then they are more likely to sign the form.

When the patient withholds permission to talk to the carer the staff can be very uneasy about telling anybody anything, even when it flies in the face of common sense.

There is a clause that says that the person can only make the decision to give or withhold permission to share information if they have 'capacity' and they are able to understand the implications of their actions. This remains a thorny area in mental health. There are fewer complications with dementia or learning disabilities because the person concerned will probably have a reasonably static or even a deteriorating level of understanding, which means a more predictable assessment about how much they can grasp. In mental health someone's understanding of a situation can vary considerably, sometimes within a short time. One day they may reject their mother as someone who is trying to poison them. The next day they may greet her as a long-lost friend. This makes it hard to judge capacity, so the default position seems to be a presumption that they are capable of making the decision.

Staff can break this 'no telling' rule when there is a serious risk that the carer needs to know about. This might be that the person with the mental health issue has said, 'I hate my sister so I'm going to set fire to her car as soon as I get home,' or, 'When I get out of here I am going to run away to see my son in foster care'. Theoretically if someone was posing a serious threat they shouldn't be going back home yet, but if there is a clear indication that there is a potentially risky situation then the rules can be broken. This allows the carer to monitor the situation better and be more aware of any dangers.

The local mental health trust my colleague and I worked with made a couple of changes to their policies which were very welcome. I thought they were brilliant, although it took a lot of discussion and meetings. The two changes were:

1. To make a statement when the 'Permission to Share Information' form was being completed that the staff would always tell the family that the person was 'safe' even if they could say nothing else. (This followed from a carer feeding back that she had spent the night wandering around a local suicide spot in the dark desperately trying to find her daughter who was, in fact, in the local inpatient unit. She had called to ask if she had been found but been told, 'We can't tell you anything.')

2. To introduce a third level of disclosure. The patient could agree to the carer being told:
   • everything
   • nothing
   • just not specific topics.

Perhaps the person may be OK with carers being told about appointment times and medications but not any personal information about them. Again this extra option followed feedback that when the person needed the family member to get them to an appointment it was a bit unhelpful if they didn't know when that appointment was, the message may not always get passed on reliably. This practical information may be necessary simply for the benefit of the cared-for person.

The 'middle way' option states that specified personal issues remain confidential. That could be all personal information or just one topic, maybe about suicide attempts or drug habits etc. This means the staff need to be more on the ball in a busy ward when there can be a fast turnover of patients, so it isn't surprising that sometimes they just play safe and say little.

So if you are a carer and are in a situation where you are being told that the staff of an inpatient unit or a local mental health team can't talk to you because of patient confidentiality then there are some important points to bear in mind.

A. There are no rules anywhere that say that staff cannot listen to carers. They may not be able to say much, but the carer can always talk to them. If this conversation would be better held privately then this should be arranged. Staff should have the skills to be sensitive about this. It seems a waste of time to list the reasons why staff should always listen to close family and ask what they know, I'm sure any carer could think of several. The situation seems to be improving rapidly with families being consulted for their opinion right from the start, but not always.

The risk assessment form is perhaps the one that causes the most concern. Professionals must assess how much threat a person presents to themselves or others, especially at the point they leave the care of the services. How they act at appointments or in hospital may not be a true representation of their behaviour, a family carer will probably know a lot more. Without their information any risk may not be assessed effectively.

B. The carer can request that information they pass on to staff should be kept confidential, maybe they are worried that the person they support will see this as a form of betrayal. For example, a carer could tell the nurse, 'He may not tell you this, but he is self-harming again. Please don't tell him I told you.' This leaves the nurse with an awkward dilemma. How can he/she act on this information without disclosing who said it? A good nurse will be creative, maybe ask the patient if his self-harming is still an issue. If the patient says 'no' it may be necessary to say, 'Well your wife says otherwise.' The optimum way of dealing with this is for the carer and nurse to talk about options and agree how best to handle it. Carers may accept that they will have to be the object of some anger for a while.

C. Staff are obliged to give 'sufficient information to care', this is an obligation that is not always kept. They can always in principle give carers 'general information' rather than personal specifics, so there could be a useful conversation about 'people who have depression'; a creative staff member will use this well. They may say, 'People who suffer with some mental health conditions may find it worrying to take medication because of possible weight gain,' rather than, 'Your husband is refusing medication because he is worried about getting fatter.' One of the best examples of this I heard was when a carer called about her daughter who had an eating disorder to ask if she had taken any food that day. The staff member who answered the phone said, 'I can't tell you that, but I can say that no one on the unit went hungry today.' Bending the rules in the interest of common sense.

D. The crucial one. The most obvious but overlooked one. This should be in capital letters really. If the carer knows it already then how can it be confidential?

'Hi, I am Debbie's mum, I know she has said not to tell me anything, but I am very worried. She is coming home soon, and I had an awful time before she came in as she was self-harming so badly. I didn't know how to handle it and I really thought she was going to kill herself accidentally once or twice. What should I do if it starts again?'
'Sorry I can't talk to you, patient confidentiality.'

Disclosure can only break confidentiality with previously unknown information. Ta da!

If you do come across these confidentiality obstacles it is useful to know that staff are obliged to abide by the decision of the patient, except in extreme circumstances, so no point getting upset with them. If they are not restricted by the 'permission to share' status because the person said 'yes' then that is a different matter. Asking them to check what is on the form is sometimes a useful reminder.

If the person with the mental health issue is saying 'no' to sharing information when they are very unwell but are fine with it in calmer times, then there could be another option. Perhaps they would be prepared to help write a letter which could say something along the lines of:

'I know that when I am unwell I refuse permission for staff to share information with my partner. I would like this to be ignored and for my partner to always be told any relevant information regardless of what I may say during those times when I am in hospital.'

Ask them to sign it, date it and keep a relatively recent copy available should they be admitted. It is no guarantee that this letter will solve the problem, but it may lead to a more flexible approach.

Much of the frustration around patient confidentiality appears to be because of staff being nervous of a complaint because of breaching confidentiality, even if the relevant form has been signed. I was told that there are very few grievances made on this topic but there are lots from carers who feel shut out from discussions and treatment plans. This exclusion of family information has led to serious mistakes being made more than once in the past.

If you are facing these complications, it is time to riot. If enough carers come forward with a protest in the places where this is still a problem, asking only that the correct principles are followed, then the carers who come after will be extremely grateful.

SAFEGUARDING

There is a principle embedded in law which says that people should be able to live safely and not be abused, bullied or neglected. Investigating these situations in their early stages can prevent more serious incidents and avoid crises or persistent mistreatment. This is a topic that's worth having a slight knowledge about because mental health could be a factor.

Safeguarding is used to protect adults who are at risk in some way and are vulnerable. This may be because of illness, injury, age or the position they find themselves in; this includes a caring role. These are people who would be unable to protect themselves effectively and would need to support to cope with the situation.

Anyone can report when there is an adult at risk who is being treated in a way that is or could become abusive. If it is a child who is being mistreated the law is different, but it would still be reported in the same way. This safeguarding is a statutory obligation of the local authority, not the NHS, so any potentially abusive situation should be reported to the relevant Social Care services, whose details will be available on the website of the local authority. Social workers will be the professionals who lead any action.

Incidents that may require a safeguarding intervention could be:

- Physical – actual harm
- Emotional – deliberately causing distress
- Threatening harm or harassment
- Neglect – withholding necessary support, or access to what that person needs
- Financial – taking or withholding money that is theirs
- Sexual – forcing without consent. Can be viewing images or direct involvement
- Discrimination – harassment based on gender, race, sexuality, disability, faith or age
- Modern slavery – exploitation, maybe for labour, drugs or sex trade, or false benefit claims.
- Domestic violence –a close family member controlling, threatening or being abusive.

It is easy to see that some of these situations may occur when there is a person with a mental health issue who may not be able to protect themselves adequately. It is worth noting that a person committing the abuse could have a mental health issue and the 'victim' could be an elderly family carer who is being bullied for money, or a partner who is forced into a sexual relationship. It is acknowledged that carers can be the subject of abusive relationships especially when they are not that resilient themselves.

In addition, there is a new category which was introduced in 2014, extreme self-neglect now falls under the safeguarding policy. A lot of families are extremely concerned about the person they support failing to look after themselves sufficiently well and running risks with their health. This may take the form of a poor diet or unhygienic living conditions.

It is worth noting that safeguarding will not enforce any changes if the person has capacity to demonstrate that they are happy to live like this. They cannot be compelled to live a more hygienic life if they don't wish to. It doesn't mean the situation wouldn't be assessed and discussed but there is no method to make it happen against their will unless it becomes high risk. Someone who hoards newspapers may make their flat a fire hazard, which could be assessed as an unacceptable risk if there is no means to get out in a hurry. Week old dirty dishes are not enough.

What happens when a safeguarding incident is reported? The social worker will speak to the 'victim' of the situation and find out what they want to happen, an advocate can be arranged if required. They will then speak to other people, including the person causing the problem, and perhaps other agencies such as a mental health team if one is involved. They will involve the police only if they feel a crime has been committed.

The process is one of negotiation, trying to work out a way forward where the abusive situation will be permanently resolved. It may lead to an agreement or contract between the two parties. It isn't an easy solution with guaranteed results, but it is often useful for someone who is effectively bullying another person to know that there is a third party involved, it isn't their secret anymore.

It isn't a crisis service, if there is a serious situation where there is potential or real immediate risk then the police should be called.

CARER'S ASSESSMENTS AND OTHER ENTITLEMENTS

The local authority (not the NHS) are also statutorily obliged to offer all carers a Carer's Assessment. This is not a judgement of how well the cared-for person is being looked after, whether a Social Worker should charge in and make all kinds of unpleasant changes. What the assessment offers is a chance to discuss the carer's needs in some detail and, depending on this information, decide if they are eligible for some help.

It is the same process that a person with a mental health issue goes through, the information given is assessed and a judgement made as to whether it meets the criteria to be offered a further service. It must be emphasised that this is the carer's needs, not those of the person they support. Help offered will be based on how the caring role is impacting on them and what other demands they are having to cope with.

I hate to sound cynical at this point – and maybe this is a local thing – but I have never encountered anyone who has been totally overwhelmed by what's on offer for mental health carers (except dementia carers where there are sometimes more resources available). The bar for getting help is set high and it has been lifted further recently in line with the plummeting funding.

What help could be on offer if the criteria were met? The options seem to be

- respite (either a few hours weekly or so the carer can go away for a while)
- help in the house, either through equipment or someone coming in
- money
- information

It may vary in different areas please don't get too excited at this point, please read on.

Respite is difficult in mental health because no one can make a person leave their home if they don't want to go and there aren't funds to put paid support workers into their home for a week. In fact, it would be three carers a day if the person cannot be left alone at all, plus 'getting to know' time, a costly option. If there is a tame relative who can step in then that is great, but the best that is usually on offer is a few hours of a weekly sitting service, if the person really can't be left alone for that time.

These 'sitting' services are often run by local community organisations with volunteers who are usually marvellous people. The person with the mental health issue must not mind strangers in the house, which a lot of highly anxious people do. There must also be a risk assessment to ensure they are not going to do anything that the volunteer sitter cannot cope with. So, if there is a level of risk, perhaps the person self-harms, (which means the carer needs a break more than ever), this option may not be available. Other choices are again a kind relative or neighbour. If there is enough money to pay a private agency, they sometimes offer this sitting service, it is worth asking.

There may be other local arrangements that can be accessed via the nearest Carers' Centre including funding to pay for a sitter if the carer has a health appointment for their own needs. The same problems apply as above but it is nice to be able to pay a friendly neighbour to come round rather than asking them to do it for a coffee and a biscuit.

Inpatient beds are generally not used for respite. I knew of one situation where someone was admitted for a week without really needing it because the carer was experiencing health problems and was exhausted. If a carer is truly desperate or needs a major operation it is always worth asking. The biggest problem, even if a bed is offered, is that the person cannot be sectioned if they are not that unwell. If they won't go in willingly then no one can make them. The community team may increase visits and speak to the person by phone if the carer goes away and the person with the mental health diagnosis stays at home, if that will help keep them safe.

Assistance with housework is not always relevant for mental health issues, it is usually provided for physical health conditions where bathing, laundry or shopping could be difficult. Cleaning is often a nightmare though, especially if the person is unable (or unwilling) to do the basics and creates a lot of mess. Again, without wishing to paint a gloomy picture, it appears to take a huge health hazard to get any assistance with cleaning a person's own flat. If it is a family house and the carer lives there too – well it hasn't happened in my experience.

A few years ago, there was a pot of money for carers that was accessible through the Carer's Assessment process. It was for activities or equipment that would specifically target the carers' wellbeing and allow them to get something that would support them to keep going. This usually took the form of money for a hobby, a gym membership or a wood turning lathe, or train fare to go and visit relatives. This pot has been subject to noticeable shrinkage, as has everything else, but it is always worth asking what is on offer. Its primary aim is to help the carer stay well both physically and mentally, it could be useful to have an idea ready if the option did arise.

All in all, a mental health carer seems less likely to get any real help out of the assessment than, say, a carer of someone with a physical health problem that included incontinence, they might get some cleaning hours and a washing machine.

Most mental health carers get offered information. This can be fantastically useful but often takes the form of being handed a pile of leaflets, and quite possibly the next professional encountered will offer the same leaflets again. These could be vital information but it can feel a bit of an anti-climax, as many carers have told me.

Completing the Carer's Assessment can be helpful as it requires details about what is involved in the caring role and what impact this is having. People often carry on for a long time without evaluating what they are offering on from day to day. This assessment may cause some rethinking, whether there are changes that can be made or if there are other options. The downside of this reality check is that it can be both distressing and depressing to pay close attention to the situation, especially if nothing happens except the promise to repeat the story in a year or so at the next Carer's Assessment.

There is a question on the assessment about whether the current situation can be sustained, can the carer carry on. This is a delicate matter, I know of one carer who replied, 'No I can't,' but then had to continue anyway because no rescue party appeared. The person who reviews the assessment may well have no connection with the mental health team so they cannot speak for them. If there is a strong likelihood that the carer is going to have to stop there may be guidance through the assessment process, but it may be much more direct to inform the mental health team as soon as possible.

In fact, it is worth noting that the contents of the Carer's Assessment form may not be seen by any professionals working in the mental health services. Sometimes it is shared, sometimes it is completed by a member of that team, but not always. If the carer feels there is information about them or their role that the mental health team should know then relying on this system to pass it on could be a mistake.

A Carer's Assessment can be requested by contacting the local Social Care service or the Carers' Centre if one is not offered by other means. The GP should also have information available. It may be carried out by Social Care staff (a social worker or resource officer) or a Carers' Centre's staff or in some places by NHS practitioners. There can be a sizeable delay after requesting one, although this varies, but given the current situation it would not be surprising to expect to wait for weeks or even months. Most areas also have the option of filling it in online which is much more immediate, it is usually found by searching for 'Carer's Assessment' on the local authority's website. There may be a local organisation that will help fill it in if that is required, probably via the Carers' Centre.

When the completed assessment is returned it is checked against certain criteria. If the information flags up that assistance is appropriate and that the criteria for this is met, then Social Care would respond. As previously stated there needs to be a demonstration of a high level of need and a service available that can meet that need before any offers are made. It is always worth having a talk with the local Carers' Centre about arrangements locally and what options are around with or without an official assessment.

It should be repeated annually or if there is any substantial change, generally it seems that the carer may have to initiate a reminder or wait for much longer than a year.

What a completed Carer's Assessment does do is inform the local authority how many carers there are in their area and what their needs are, which can generate statistics which affect their expenditure on services. It may also be the best way of finding out what support is available for carers in the local area if this not yet known.

Other entitlements that may come through a Carers' Assessment or be available separately include:

CARERS' ALLOWANCE. There is a benefit you can claim as a carer which is nothing to do with the assessment but will require another lengthy form, this time from the DWP. Again, this is not a source of great excitement, in fact it's best to go very carefully. Currently (but subject to constant change) any benefit awarded may well be deducted from other benefits, possibly the cared-for person's income. The carer is required to declare that they are caring for over thirty-five hours a week and that their net income must be under a fixed amount - but this too is subject to alteration at any time. A reliable source for information is 'Carers UK' who are good at making benefits and allowances simpler to understand, this site is worth a look for carers' rights generally. Alternatively, there is always a Citizens Advice Bureau or equivalent.

A CARERS' CARD. In our area this includes small discounts in some local shops or cafes and a wonderfully big reduction in parking fees at the local hospital. It also helps to have this card in a wallet or purse for identification and information in emergencies.

CARERS' CRISIS PLAN. There may be a local service that will swing into action to help people whose family carer has got stuck far from home or has had an accident. Initially a plan is put together which will inform the person with the mental health diagnosis what is going on and check that they are OK. This may be something like asking the neighbour to call round or call dad etc. which will be put into action if the service is notified by the carer themselves, or by a medic or police officer, to say that the situation requires urgent attention. There is a card which informs anyone who finds it that the bearer is a carer; it gives a number to call to start the process.

If there is no relative or friend who can step in local authority staff may call the person with the mental health issue to make sure they are all right or they may even call round to their house. Other involved professionals will be informed. This service is available at evenings and weekends so is worth putting in place especially if the situation is dependent on a lone carer.

CARERS AND WORK

There comes a time when many carers feel that they are going to have to give up work. 38% of carers reported having given up and 18% reducing their hours in the two years before the Carers UK *State of Caring 2019* survey. This usually follows a lengthy period of trying to cope with work and home commitments and not really making it happen. Exhaustion sets in, there are difficult discussions with colleagues and bosses and then HR get involved because of the sick leave. On one side there is the sense of commitment to the person who needs help and on the other there is an income, and possibly an identity and a sense of satisfaction as well.

If a person identifies themselves as being a carer then it is illegal to discriminate against them at work, but options are limited. Being self-employed or working at home may mean being able to survive longer.

If the carer has worked for the same employer for over a year and if the person they support is under eighteen then they can take up to eighteen weeks unpaid leave before their eighteenth birthday. This averages out at one week per year; it is not clear if that means it is possible to take eighteen weeks in the last year if none has been taken previously, so check with HR.

Under the law, working for a firm for six months gives a carer the right to ask for flexible hours, although this is not an option if a similar request has been made already in the last twelve months. This request needs to be written down and to state what arrangement is required, how it could affect the work situation and the business in general. It can be refused, but the managers need to produce a reason which involves the wellbeing of the organisation.

In an emergency anyone can take leave at short notice if they are needed to deal with a crisis for someone who is dependent on them. This will not be paid unless your employer has agreed to an arrangement in these circumstances in which case it may be written into the initial employment contract. Some organisations do offer more than the basic rights under the law.

If the time comes when there must be a choice between caring responsibilities and work, there is a real dilemma to face. There is the option of claiming Carers' Allowance benefit if working is not possible or there is a dramatic cut in hours, (see the previous section). It is not going to make anyone rich but is better than nothing.

Apart from the financial implications carers often mention missing the company and the job satisfaction. If it is at all possible to create some time and space to try and find a replacement activity it is well worth the effort. Support groups aren't everyone's choice, but they do provide a social opportunity and good tips, especially if it is a mental health carers' meeting. Alternatively going somewhere where there are people who are cheerful, inspiring or who require something that is nothing to do with the caring role could help to balance the week. This could be the pub quiz, the local school governors, the fundraising committee for the local hospice, a favoured political party or a local gardening project. Learn a new skill, there are free online courses to keep the brain active if going out of the house is not an option. Build the *Titanic* out of matchsticks.

These alternative sources of social contact and personal satisfaction help ward off the effects of feeling trapped by a caring role and create moments to escape to a different space and be your 'other self'. Finding the energy is daunting especially in the earlier more frantic period, at some stage some space is going to open up and that might be a good time to consider options. This is what the person with the mental health issue is facing, finding the motivation to try new challenges and get their lives back on track.

CARERS V. THE REST
OF THE WORLD

This is a summary of some of the frequently mentioned glitches in life that carers have talked about. They are, for once, not about the carer or the person they support. It's all about everyone else.

STIGMA

This is the cloud that hangs over some encounters with other people, when there is a suspicion that the situation is being judged based on some presumption or myth about mental health – probably not in a good way. The *Oxford Dictionary* defines stigma as a 'mark of disgrace'.

Mental health conditions have always been subject to public suspicion, possibly for several different reasons. People may have a fear of some sort of contagion or an awkwardness because it reminds people of their own vulnerability. Additionally, society works because we can predict to a large extent how people are going to behave. If I am walking down the road in the dark and there are a group of young men wearing hoodies behind me then I will feel some apprehension, and possibly do a great disservice to a group of boy scouts out collecting litter. If there is a group of older women then I will not get scared. My brain is aware of the statistical probability that a group of female pensioners will mug me - they would probably back off sensing one of their own.

People value this predictability; they know what is expected of them in different situations and as long as everyone plays by the rules it works well. People with mental health diagnoses can break these guidelines. There is always an association between 'madness' and extreme violence even though it is a rare event, but there are other rules that can be broken. I passed a man today who was swearing very loudly as he strode down the pavement, making generally socially unacceptable gestures and smelling awful. He was conspicuously breaking the social rules about not interfering with other peoples' personal space and right to peace and quiet. I heard another man say 'Another ****** nutter'.

A conspicuous person can also be very distressed and clearly needing help. Not many people know how to approach someone in meltdown, particularly a stranger. Is talking to them safe, what will they do? Will they run into the road or scream abuse? Will it end up having to take responsibility for them and getting stuck for hours? Are they dangerous? This is part of the public view of mental health, the obvious and rather threatening rule breaker. Not feeling safe with the obviously unwell people leads to the quiet ones getting pushed into the same category. Unpredictable equals unsafe.

Without a doubt there has been a radical change for the better in my working lifetime, in how mental ill health is viewed by the public. Various media campaigns have helped to combat the stigma over the last few years. This is a very welcome development of course, but the battle is far from over.

Part of this media campaigning is the support for celebrities to produce stories of their struggle with their own 'demons'. Many are clearly genuine, but some make me a little suspicious that there may be some exaggeration involved. No really, there could be. These people have a certain protection afforded to them by their celebrity status, they are doing well after all just to be in the public eye. It brings hope: she was depressed and now she is on a chat show, there is a happy ending.

On the other hand, it may make mental health less real, the versions in the media all seem to be positive endings and the celebrity wins the battle, or they just disappear out of the spotlight and no one notices. This sets an expectation that all people with these challenges should get back to 'normal' and if they don't then they are just not trying hard enough.

The result of this is an increase in stigma, because if you have these issues then you must be weak and or unwilling to fight, where others have bravely battled and won.

There also seems to be a lack of media coverage about the mental health diagnoses that are less responsive to people's own efforts and not totally within an individual's control. Techniques can be put in place to help to relax if a panic attack is beginning and this can lessen the effect or maybe prevent it altogether. Feeling a bi-polar mania phase beginning the available options are less effective, the person may have some control and that only after years of effort, but generally not prevent it completely. Getting a grip on symptoms is far, far harder for some than others, and sometimes impossible, even with medication. This doesn't seem to be acknowledged in the media.

There is probably as much variation in the public view of mental health as there is about gender issues or being a vegan. Newspapers, social media and magazines promote acceptance and understanding, many people sign up to these views in theory. Inside schools, workplaces or in the pub on a Friday night there may be different views expressed.

People still use 'psycho', 'nutter', 'crazy' and similar insults.

Sometimes these words seem to be used very positively such as, 'My friend, she's a real schizo, she's totally wild,' meaning she is great fun, disinhibited or liable to drink too much. It's hard to reconcile the use of these words with the reality of these conditions.

My opinion is that, by now, it should be better accepted that mental health and physical health problems have a great deal in common, except that people are not shunned if they develop diabetes or need a hip replacement. All health problems are about a bit of a person not working as it should or giving up under pressure, yet when the bit that is affected is in the brain / mind the whole thing becomes a much more socially fragile topic.

Stigma changes how people treat you, there are lots of reports of verbal and physical abuse as well as routine avoidance or unequal treatment. The way that people with mental health issues are treated in the outside world or online can add a great deal to the burden of the symptoms that they live with, creating additional depression and anxiety.

The family is also subject to stigma 'by association' which can take the form of direct abusive remarks or it can be more subtle through avoidance, like crossing the street. Maybe there is a fear of saying the wrong thing, of not being able to cope with the possibly embarrassing aspects of any conversation because people may get upset, something like the difficulties of knowing what to say after a bereavement. Perhaps some feel the family have contributed to the situation in some way or failed to deal with it appropriately.

If the person with the mental health issue is a target for any abuse or discrimination it can be taken further – but this is not always the right move, particularly if the person themselves will become stressed about it. If they are up for a fight, then make a complaint or talk to the police/ headteacher/ HR dept/ parents if it was a serious incident. It is a 'hate crime' to be subject to abuse because of belonging to a minority group after all.

Sometimes it can be constructive for a carer to think back to how they thought about mental health problems before they were so personally involved, this can help to feel more forgiving with friends or neighbours that say 'the wrong thing'. If anyone offers help then a carer could seriously consider if there is a way to involve them, not just for their support but to give an opportunity to understand what it is really like to live with a mental health condition.

What are the choices for a carer regarding stigma?

1. Do not mention the subject of your cared-for person's mental health status unless others mention it first. Then appear apologetic and slightly anxious as though the information may cause offence.

2. Be very matter of fact and have a set 'one liner' so that it doesn't have to be discussed in any detail then change the subject fast, 'Yes, George is suffering with some anxiety issues at the moment but he is seeing someone and we are hoping it will improve soon. It's been raining so much lately hasn't it? What do you think about the price of cabbage?'

3. Go in with all guns blazing, introduce the topic and show no sign of wanting to hide from it. Tell everyone like the hairdresser or the newsagent. In reality it can feel uncomfortable to discuss the person with the mental health problem behind their backs, especially with people that might know them. But chatting to a stranger on a train? Go for it.

Many people have told me that they were extremely reluctant to talk about their caring role to other people because they feared a rejection or a negative response. After a time, they got tired of keeping quiet and started to be open about it, almost without exception the response was, 'I have someone in my family who has mental health issues too.' Many carers also feel that in not keeping quiet they are helping to educate other people about how it really is, which surely is no bad thing.

LGBTQIA+

The world of gay and transgender people is not one I know well, being old and straight. For those of us like myself that don't have much personal experience of these aspects of human nature it can be hard to understand what pressures there are. Certainly, like the stigma surrounding mental health, there has been a great deal of work done to break down the prejudice and ignorance that was so deeply ingrained in society for so long. Despite this hard work though, it appears that people from these groups can still live their lives facing more conflict and stigma than others. Some communities appear wonderfully supportive and others less so. Despite the progress there is still a big mountain to climb.

For younger people who are at the early stages of defining their identity, the discovery that you are not heterosexual or cisgender must still present some confusion and uncertainty, although younger people seem to have got a much healthier attitude to accepting the many variations found in the human population, at last.

Although the vast majority would describe ourselves as without prejudice we cannot always see how our responses may alter, however subtly, when someone says that they are gay or transgender or belong in a group that we cannot immediately identify with. This is particularly true within families; this information may cause barely a ripple or substantially change the whole family dynamic.

The reason why this section is in this book is because people from these communities seem to be more prone to mental health problems, particularly depression, self-harm and addiction. It's a strong possibility that these mental health issues originate in the anxiety caused by people experiencing – or anticipating experiencing –opposition or ridicule when this aspect of their identity goes public. This could be at school, at work or within family relationships. Until they find biological link between these life choices and depression it is a reasonable bet that it is the social aspect that is the root of the problem.

A family who finds that they have a member who identifies with the LGBTQIA+ communities faces coming to terms with a new expectation of their future and sometimes a different explanation of their past. A young person will now live a quite different life, maybe a complete contrast to family expectations. Confessions from a partner or parent can be equally complex and emotional. The person must be redefined, they were familiar and predictable but suddenly there is a side to them that has been a secret until now.

Reassurance and support from family will make a big difference of course, but not all close relatives may be able to offer that because of their own views. It wasn't that long ago that identifying as LGBTQIA+ was regarded as shameful, socially unacceptable and even criminal and had to be hidden at all cost. Those judgemental viewpoints still run deep in some families and in some communities.

Encouraging the person to speak to others who have been through a similar process may turn out to offer far more than even a well-meaning family member can, but indiscriminate online contact may not be helpful. This is something it isn't easy to prevent, however.

It someone has developed a mental health issue, even partially because of this new identity, it has to help if their family are well informed. A particularly useful aspect to understand might be what causes people to identify with these lifestyles, what could be the underlying reason? If the family can research around the science of the decision, then it could be helpful if they are ever forced to defend their choices against those who know little but say a lot.

Verbal abuse or discrimination might happen and therefore be worth preparing for. Number one coping strategy is to avoid a situation if possible and walk away. If not then stay calm, stay cool and have a few statements ready. Rehearsing what to say is helpful, especially with a younger person who is deeply affected by social media or peer group remarks. Assertiveness training can increase confidence and avoid resorting to insults in return, or getting emotional, both of which will increase the probability of the situation escalating. These are 'assertive' remarks:

'What your saying is just not true, and it is not OK to say that to me.'

'You have no reason to speak to me like that, I know I am far better than that.'

'What you are saying is unacceptable and untrue. I know who I am and that is all I need.'

I once worked with a transgender colleague who was going through a lot to make the change. It was a revelation to me to go out with her in public, noticing the looks and the occasional pointing and whispering. This was twenty years ago but I don't know that the world has changed that much, it is human nature to be curious or dismissive of things that can be a struggle to understand. It was a tough choice for her, and I admired her bravery – it must be acknowledged just how strongly a person must feel that their current identity is 'wrong' to go through that daily harassment.

Society is far more understanding nowadays and these communities have an accepted identity in public life. Despite this I have met carers in the last few years that were dealing with LGBTQIA+ issues in their family and this wasn't going well, possibly because of their own views or sometimes the opposition of close relatives who felt the situation should be dealt with 'firmly'. Typically, this would be the parent of a teenager who was wanting to start a gender reassignment process and was being told by other family members to prevent them from doing so. Carers may have to make a stand and take sides, at least for a while until the situation calms. That is not an easy option especially if they have their own uncertainty, so having accurate information from science and from others facing the same issues might be all they can call upon for support.

There follows a brief description of some of the recognised categories in this area of sexuality and gender identity in case it comes in useful and currently is not familiar territory.

L – Lesbian, homosexual female.

B – Bisexual, attracted to both female and male.

G – Gay, homosexuality generally but more usually applied to men.

T – Transgender or transsexual, people whose physical body doesn't fit with the gender they believe themselves to be.

Q – Queer/Questioning, a general term for non-heterosexual people and for those who are not yet ready to decide.

I – Intersex, unclear or indeterminate physical sexual characteristics.

A – Asexual, either a little or no sexual attraction to anyone.

+ – Any not already specified.

Additionally:

TRANSVESTITE – someone who likes dressing in the clothing of the opposite sex. This can be a very public flamboyant display (drag queen) or a very private hobby. It is important to note that this does not mean necessarily that the person is gay or bisexual or anything other than heterosexual.

PANSEXUAL – attracted to all sexual identities, they are attracted to a person rather than the fact they are male, female, transgender etc.

CISGENDER – someone who has no difficulty in accepting the physical characteristics they were born with.

GENDER fluid – a person who doesn't want to be labelled as male or female and prefers to be called 'they' rather than he or she.

There are quite a lot more!

It is a complicated world and maybe a confusing one too. If you are supporting someone who is moving towards one of these identities and they have developed a mental health issue as a result, then it may be a world that needs to become familiar, and fast!

FRIENDS AND FAMILY

Most carers that I have met find it hard to be overwhelmingly positive about all their closest social circle. When someone is diagnosed with a mental health issue there is a gradual process as the news goes out through family and friends, which then results in a range of reactions. These responses are sometimes supportive and therefore appreciated, sometimes they are infuriating and insensitive.

Unlike physical health problems which are more easily explained, mental health still has this air of uncertainty about it for many people. Is it a brain gone wrong, a weak personality or caused by indulgence in drugs? Relatives may also want to protect the rest of the family (including the carer) and view the situation largely from that perspective. This means they may challenge the person with the mental health issues more than is helpful.

'How can you do this to your poor mother?'
'You need to pull yourself together, you have (carer's name) to consider, you know.'

Insensitive responses can come from close family but may also bring people out of the woodwork that haven't been seen for a while. These could be people who really want to help, or those who love a bit of gossip, or who enjoy passing judgements on others.

In contrast, some respond to the news by muttering to themselves and to their immediate family, 'I expect they're really busy, best leave them alone for a bit,' which may possibly be interpreted as, 'Mental health? That could be dangerous, or catching, and I don't know what to say to them anyway.' It can be a good thing that they don't call round for coffee as making conversation could be painful – but they could manage an email or text surely?

Supportive friends are welcome of course, but sometimes they come with their ideas and these can sound suspiciously like a set of instructions on how this situation should be tackled.

'You should really get her to go back to the doctor, she doesn't seem any better to me.'
'You must sit her down and talk to her firmly, she can't carry on worrying you like this.'
'Why don't you just take all the sharp things out of the house?'
'He's putting it on, he just wants a bit of attention.'
'You have always let him get away with anything.'

These attempts at being helpful are frequently based on limited information and a scant knowledge of mental health, which is possibly what the carer started out with, but they have come a long way since then.

The most unwelcome 'help' could be those who come to the house wanting a word with the 'poor lad' with the aim of putting them straight. This can be well intentioned, but the not so subtle message frequently comes across as 'pull yourself together and stop this daft behaviour'. They offer to be a listening ear for the person's troubles but then proceed not to let them get much of a word in as they are too busy issuing instructions about what should be happening.

Even within the closest family, mental health issues can cause splits and tensions. Often it is the 'he/she needs to be looked after' school of thought versus 'he/she needs to get on with it, they won't get better without making a bit more effort'. It doesn't help that there isn't a right answer to this dilemma.

There are wonderful friends and relatives of course that become the source of much needed support. This could take the form of listening, without giving too much advice or judgement, or just coming round and mowing the poor neglected lawn. These people may come to be treasured; they can be a source of welcome support when it seems that the world just doesn't understand.

Those who want to help should not be dismissed easily, even if their views don't fit. People like to lend a hand, and it makes sense to use them according to their strengths. The carer may grind their teeth when they start on yet another lecture about how the person should be made to take their medication but this is the time for a quick interruption with a polite request to pick up the 'call and collect' shopping or take a parcel to the Post Office.

Sometimes a carer feels they are just using others; they

should do it all themselves and not take advantage of people's good nature. At this point it is worth considering how it feels to help someone else, (not the person with the mental health issue because they tend not to be appreciative a lot of the time). Helping someone or giving money away to a good cause makes people feel better about themselves, or else no one would do it. If someone offers support, and that offer is accepted, then they may feel positive as a result. If they are offended that their offer has been taken up then they may never be seen again, but that is probably not high on the carer's list of things to worry about.

Some people move closer in a family crisis and some move further away, possibly over the horizon completely. This seems to be a recognisable pattern, but many carers think it is just their family or friends that react in this way.

Being a carer, particularly in mental health, can be a very lonely job so keeping a relationship going, even if any touchy issues are avoided, could be worth the effort. If the carer has the energy it may be helpful to try to explain to those who are genuinely interested why things are as they are, or why certain decisions have been made. Sometimes it seems easier to offer a quick coffee and a talk about politics or gardening instead.

I once met a carer who said that she and her son had not been invited to the last ten family Christmas gatherings after one distressing episode when he didn't cope very well with the general jollity and had an anxiety-fuelled outburst. They spent the festive season alone together every year. This was certainly taking being mean to a whole new level, some families seem unable to be flexible.

When a group of carers are together talking about the reactions of family and friends it often provides a good laugh and maybe humour is the way to deal with it. However, it can also be very upsetting when choices need to be made, a previously important relationship is now creating bad feeling to the point where it cannot continue.

For a tired and worried carer finding people who do understand can make such a difference, so contacting other carers may be the only way. They will have stories about their lives that will be reassuring and help with the realisation that no one is alone with this.

OTHER CHILDREN

Any carer who has children at home at the time that they are supporting the person with the mental health issue will probably face family tensions sooner or later. Whether it is a partner, parent or a child that is requiring extra help this is going to shift the fair and equal distribution of time and attention, particularly to dependent children – and it will be noticed.

I have spoken to several carers who have been taken by surprise when their children have suddenly turned on them mid-argument and accused them of favouring the unwell person. This conversation seems to progress along these lines:

'You always had time for them no matter what. Whenever they called, there you were.'

'But you knew they had a mental health problem. You could see I had to help them.'

'You just spoilt them rotten and they played on you, they would turn it up because they knew you would come running.'

'Are you saying they weren't ill?'

'No, but you made all that fuss and it made it worse. When it came to the rest of us you would be too tired, or off to some appointment with them. We could have been dying and you wouldn't have noticed.'

'You said you understood. I tried to talk to you about it lots of times.'

'I didn't think there was a choice then, but I could see how you were being manipulated. You just cared more about them from the start.'

'That's not true!'

'Well it certainly looked that way to me.'

Can this conversation be avoided? Advice from carers who have been in this situation seems to be that it is important to talk to other family members, not just occasionally but frequently. They need to know that the carer is aware that they are neglecting them a bit, but that they are trying their best. This is not fool proof, although as the children mature they may be more accepting of the reasoning behind the carer's decisions.

Is there any way of involving the children more in the support of the cared-for person, bearing in mind their own needs and strengths? Do they have lots of age appropriate information about what a mental health issue is and how it affects people? It holds no certainties, but the aim is to try to avoid a split with the main carer and the unwell person on one side and the rest of the family on the other. Asking them for support might help or alternatively set aside a period of time every day which is theirs alone, barring real emergencies.

Getting people outside the family involved is also useful, maybe there is a relative or neighbour who would step up and do a bit more with the children. I have known of one senior nurse who took time out to explain to the (teenage) children what was happening with their father, which was much appreciated. Most areas have a 'Young Carers' organisation where children whose lives are affected by a family member's diagnosis could meet their peers and share moans about being ignored and maybe get some extra fun activities. Does school need to know if they are having disrupted sleep or a poor environment for homework?

The bottom line is that the carer cannot divide their time as they would in an ideal world. It is crucial to regularly monitor how much help the person with the mental health issue currently needs, and whether there is room to step back a bit. See the 'Am I doing too much?' section for more on this topic.

The situation can be even more worrying if the person with the mental health issue is aggressive or creates high risk situations in the house. This is particularly nerve-wracking if there are vulnerable people or younger children present who may not understand what is going on or protect themselves well. It is important that professionals and other trusted people are involved, both to give their advice and to support any choices that need to be made.

However, getting professional input may create another problem if it feels as though they might intervene and take direct action to protect any vulnerable children. This may effectively force the carer(s) to make very painful choices. Keeping a risky situation a secret is not a solution though, if it is that high a risk then it is unlikely to change without outside influence. If the person with the mental health issue is that disruptive or dangerous then there should be professional involvement and the police called whenever it seems necessary, if the family could fix it then it would probably have stopped, and it hasn't. It could end in a crisis with unimaginable damage.

The carer may simply have to choose between the unwell person and the rest of the family. This only happens in extreme circumstances, but I have known a couple of examples where the person with the mental health issue has been evicted to avoid the impact on others in the house. If the risky behaviour continues without improvement there may be a need to make these unpleasant decisions as a last resort.

This is particularly hard on the carer or people who are

facing that decision because there is always a sense of failure to make it right for everyone, even if the story ends well in time. It is one of those many moments when any individual can only say, 'I acted on the information I had at the time and did what I thought was best.'

SELF-PRESERVATION TACTICS

There are a range of suggestions dotted about in this book about how a carer can look after themselves, most of which will probably be ignored.

The bottom line is that if anyone is in this role for more than a few weeks and the person being supported is experiencing anything but the mildest depression or anxiety, then there is likely to be an increased level of worry and concern. The pressure could be considerable because there is no immediate solution, plus there is an emotional involvement that magnifies all the problems. There is no indication how long the situation will last or what the outcome will be.

The following list is a horribly negative one but realistic for a lot of people who find themselves in these caring roles for a lengthy period and coping with the more severe conditions:

- Family life will be disrupted, and other relationships tested
- Any social life, work or leisure activities may suffer
- It may cause financial hardship
- It may cause health problems, particularly 'stress related' conditions
- There could be a strong sense of loss, of bereavement,

because the person with the mental health issue is different now, and hopes for their future must be revised
- Feelings of guilt and apprehension are often exhausting
- The person's actions may cause shame or embarrassment
- Having to cope with their moods and behaviour can bring resentment
- Restrictions on the carer's personal freedom may result in feeling angry or bitter

This list is not intended to make carers feel worse but so these and other aspects of the role can be acknowledged and regarded as normal occurrences, the possible side-effects of the caring role.

These circumstances create what could be called 'unfair wear and tear'. Most people living in the rest of the world have no idea what is involved, what family carers need to cope with when someone develops a severe mental health issue.

Most carers do their utmost to say and do the best thing, possibly without any real guidance as to what that is, (and probably get it 'right' most of the time). They work to control a situation and keep it safe when realistically they have limited influence over how things work out – well that isn't strictly true. If the person co-operates with the treatment which is promptly made available by the mental health services, then family help is a vital part of the jigsaw and a huge source of support. If the person refuses any treatment and no one can get through to them, then the family's power to help is very much reduced.

The carer may well feel like the meat in the sandwich, between the person with the mental health problem and the services. The family will inevitably see the mental health teams as never be quite good enough because more will always be needed, more help, more quickly. The quality of the local service will vary considerably from place to place, in addition there is currently a serious lack of resources, which means fewer staff and a lack of time for them to spend face-to-face with people with mental health issues. On top of that there is a shortage of psychiatrists which will result in log jams in the system all over the place.

This is a gloomy picture, but the hope is that by seeing it set down people may recognise that this is a lot of pressure for anyone to be under. Giving over time and energy to support others will inevitably drain anyone's batteries and this shouldn't be ignored.

Most of the carers I have met have been cheery, capable sort of people who carry on like they did in the Blitz (or Corona Virus lockdown), because they have little choice. When several of them get together, especially for the first time, they cry a bit. This seems to be because they don't get to talk about their lives much, it's too upsetting and means facing up to their reality, which is often painful and distressing.

So as long as any carer can keep on keeping on what's the problem? Few would consider themselves a special case or seek any personal help until they feel their energy is nearly gone or their health is under threat.

Individuals with a mental health issue do better if they develop good self-management skills. If they plan ahead, they have ways of identifying when the stress levels are rising and have coping strategies in place to reduce this, as much as possible, then their quality of life will be much improved. They are vulnerable and may be overwhelmed by a demanding situation so having this combination of stress avoidance and resources to call on is beneficial for both their physical and mental health.

This statement also applies to carers - they could be a great role model.

WORK LIFE BALANCE

Caring is a (largely unpaid) job which often takes up a lot of time. Carers are probably thinking about what they just did or what they are going to do next, even when things are quiet.

This is a work/life balance quiz was drastically adapted to use in our carers' information courses. It is a quick snapshot of what is going on in life and whether there could be troubles ahead.

I never do quizzes or fill in little blank boxes in self-help books but this is the only one in this book and it will take less than five minutes except for the adding up, which can be done on a phone if necessary, so there is no excuse really.

Score 0 if it does not apply
Score 1 if it is true most of the time
Score 2 if it is true sometimes
Score 3 if it is true only very occasionally or not at all

1. I have control over my life as a carer, and my life outside of that role.
2. I have no difficulty relaxing at home.
3. I have time for quiet 'thinking time'.
4. I usually enjoy the way I spend my day.
5. I am able to enjoy weekends.
6. My family and friends understand why it is important that I look after myself.
7. My family and friends are supportive of me and help me take time out.
8. My caring role is satisfying and rewarding
9. The quality of what I do is generally good.
10. I find time for my hobbies, volunteer work, etc.
11. I can develop my skills and abilities.
12. I am generally able to choose when I can take a break.
13. I get enough sleep.
14. I do not have to 'care' unexpectedly on my planned days off.
15. I have a good circle of friends.

16. I usually have my evenings free to do as I wish.

17. I exercise regularly.

18. I can put my caring role out of my mind when I am 'off duty'.

19. I maintain a healthy and balanced diet.

20. I keep informed about topics I am interested in.

21. Most of the people I meet seem to like me.

22. My caring role does not interfere with my personal life.

23. I can pay attention to my spiritual needs.

24. My caring role allows me to be the kind of son/daughter/partner/parent I want to be with other family members.

25. I find time to handle urgent situations outside my caring role.

26. My personal life helps me keep going and recharges my batteries.

27. I feel part of my local community.

28. I do not abuse drugs, alcohol, or food.

29. I have at least one person with whom I can share my thoughts and feelings.

30. I feel good about myself.

If you score under thirty-two then you have a degree of balance in your life and it seems as though things are working well at the moment.

If you score thirty-two to sixty-four then there may be areas that need some attention, it is worth checking out if you can make any changes to give yourself a bit more of what you need.

Over sixty-four looks like things are out of balance and may impact on you in the long-term with either physical or mental health problems.

This quiz is not a scientific analysis of anyone's life, it is a very general guide to how things are currently working. Scoring a high number is not a reason to panic but it is a reason to start considering what can be done to ease the situation. Of course, the person being supported needs help and attention far more than anyone else does at the moment, but it would be good to be around to do that. Keeping on top of things means that the relationship will not suddenly collapse because of the carer's ill health. If that is the only reason that they will look after themselves then that is good enough.

THINGS TO TRY

Yoga, tai chi, chi gung and meditation (etc.) are some of the best self-preservation techniques available, they appeal to lots of people because they work. A response to the phrase 'why don't you try yoga' is sometimes a sort of internal cringe that means 'oh not that stuff again', or 'where do they think I would find the time?' or 'what a lot of old rubbish, how does bending my leg over my ear help me cope?' Mention meditation and the response is often 'my mind won't stop racing, it's a waste of time'. These things have to be tried and sometimes persevered with, but many people are being held together by using these techniques.

Mindfulness classes are very relaxing, no one is forced to tell their life story and with practice the methods can keep a person calm when all about them are losing it. It isn't a 'love yourself, tree hugging, hippie chanting' thing, it's far more practical than that. The underlying principle is that people spend a great deal of their time either ruminating on the past, usually the bits that didn't go right, or anticipating some dreadful event in the future. The only bit that is under anyone's control is this moment right now, so staying in the present greatly reduces the sense of being helpless. It doesn't mean that there is no forward planning or looking to the past to learn lessons but being completely 'there' in any situation creates more control and less emotional impact. It takes a bit of practice but our local NHS mental health trust holds sessions for their staff so they must be convinced it helps.

If these (mostly) ancient methods really don't appeal then they are not the only options but if there is a local class it could be worth a try, what have you got to lose? If it turns out to be unappealing then it is one option ticked off the list. There are also useful tasters and mini classes online that can be attempted in the privacy of one's own home.

A random list of other suggestions that might help carer survival include:

- Staying in touch with friends, but only friends that are a positive influence.
- Walking, running, gardening, playing footie, going to the gym, even doing the sex thing. Spend some time getting physically tired rather than just mentally exhausted.
- Painting a masterpiece, taking stunning photos, cleaning cupboards, whatever brings a sense of satisfaction.
- A voluntary job stroking cats or tidying up the park. Joining a 'knit and bitch' or a 'men and sheds' group. Or both.
- Eating well and staying hydrated, both can affect mood as well as health.
- Can sleep habits be improved? There are 'sleep hygiene' suggestions online or in GP surgeries.
- Forgetting that there is a 'to do list' with things like 'clean the car' or 'visit Auntie Annie'. The car is not going anywhere, it will rain soon anyway and unless Auntie Annie is a barrel of laughs, a great cake maker or an excellent listener, preferably all three, then she can wait too.
- When there is a bit of peace then carers or the whole family should have a rest or a treat, without any guilt whatsoever. Enjoying what used to be enjoyed and having some fun dammit!

How can positive things be made to happen and keep on happening? Is there a need for fun money and if so, is there a (legal) way to get it? Is it about picking up the phone and asking for something even if it seems scary? Is it about finding the energy and motivation to make some changes?

Doing these frivolous things may seem a waste of energy when there is little to spare, but they can be lifelines and could recharge a flat battery when required. This self-care is also setting an example for the person with the mental health issue, to get involved with whatever life has to offer, even though they may not appreciate the carer's increased 'me' time to begin with.

HAVING A PLAN

Number one on the list of making life a bit easier is therefore to get something going on which brings some sense of wellbeing or happiness. Number two is to have a plan which should cover:

- How to avoid emergencies / crises
- How to respond to the cared-for person's emergencies / crises
- How to respond to the carer's emergencies/crises
- How to make life as stress free as possible

This forms part of a Wellness Recovery Action Plan (WRAP planning) which is a tool used to help people with mental health issues as part of their recovery. There is a Carers' WRAP plan too, which may seem unnecessary because a carer is not a recovering patient, but a similar situation may develop where all the usual routines and 'coping with life' skills disappear for a while and need to be re-established. This plan may help to bring back some sense of control especially if life seems to be completely dictated by the state of mind of the person with the mental health issue.

Feeling prepared is important and if all the useful numbers are on all the possible phones, particularly those that would be vital in an emergency, then this will help. Having these contact details available and up to date is reassuring, it is one of the few things that can be done ahead of any problems arising.

Another important part of this plan would be about reducing the impact of the caring role. Are there people out there who have offered to help or who might if they are asked? This could be about increasing opportunities for social contact, even if certain topics might be off limits because there is a differing point of view? Perhaps they would just wash the car occasionally or take a load of stuff to the tip?

What can help a carer or family member most is suitable people to talk to. If there is a reliable and trustworthy source of advice, perhaps a professional or another carer or a friend, then is it possible to contact them more often? This might reduce feelings of being alone with all the decisions if that is a worry. The final choice is still the carer's, but it helps to have support while considering choices. The chances are that this backup will only be needed for a period while the situation is new, so it won't be a question of 'bothering' them for too long.

If what is needed is to offload anger or distress, rather than getting information or advice, then there are options other than family members or friends if these are either not available, or not very approachable. If the situation becomes overwhelming the Samaritans on 116 123 (UK) are always there, even at 3 am. It isn't just a service for people who feel suicidal. Talking to a stranger when there is a serious need to let off steam to can be really liberating. The alternative is to hang on for weeks feeling miserable or trying to shove the feelings to one side where they just lurk like a big black cloud. There may not be any answers from having a rant but then again there might be. At minimum, talking about the situation might lessen the emotional impact for a while.

There is also SANE line, this helpline specialises in mental health so, unlike the Samaritans, they will know much more about diagnoses and medication. This service can give out information and indicate how to contact local services etc. It is staffed by volunteers who are happy to talk to both carers and those with mental health issues themselves. I think they are great but then I used to work for them a long time ago. There may be other local helplines or 'pop in and have a chat' support available, those that offer support to carers can be especially valuable. The local Carers' Centre should have information, they may have their own services too.

If a carer gets into a state of emotional overload, and it isn't rare, then these alternatives are worth a try, the phone can always be put down if it's not helping. It's all anonymous and there are ways of withholding a number if the privacy aspect is important, although the only way a helpline would contact a caller back would be if they revealed that they were about to make a suicide attempt (or possibly a terrorist plot) and had given their number. It may also be important to ensure that no one can overhear the call, or walk in, if the hope is to have an opportunity to be totally honest. After all the call wouldn't be necessary if these feelings were easy to share.

Seeing a counsellor is something that a lot of carers have said they find tremendously helpful. Not because they are mentally unwell but because they then have a defined time to talk things through. A counsellor will not give advice on 'how to be a carer' but can help clear up some of the worries and hard to face issues that are often avoided just by offering a safe space to look at them. This could include thinking through past events, the story so far. This is a valuable exercise; it creates a narrative or explanation as to how this situation came to be. It is also a place to consider the future, it might lead to decisions about what is realistically possible and what changes could be made now to make life a bit easier.

The counselling process is one of 'letting go' but it also a demanding experience, it may be worth waiting until there is a calm patch where there is the opportunity for some self-care and time out. Carers can often get free or low-cost counselling to support them in their role, so ask at the local Carers' Centre if it might be of interest.

CBT is another real opportunity; this would focus on how the caring role could be thought about in a less overwhelming way and the most distressing aspects reframed. So perhaps if the carer had a frequent negative thought 'I can't cope,' despite the fact that they are managing well from day to day it may be possible to replace this anxiety with 'I do not know how this is going to turn out but so far I have coped with it.' The GP can refer anyone to the local CBT service if they consider that there are signs of anxiety or depression, these symptoms are not uncommon for those in caring roles.

The best support comes from other people who are in a similar situation. Some carers are reluctant to meet others, maybe because they don't want to hear even more troubles or fear that they will say too much themselves or get upset and embarrassed. Maybe they feel that their situation is uniquely awful or that they will be found out to be a pathetic excuse of a carer. These things are very rarely true.

For those who make the jump and meet others, there is usually a great sense of relief and of finding real support at last. If the opportunity presents itself then it is worth serious consideration, if it is disappointing then don't go again. There is nothing to lose but the sense of being alone with all this.

STAYING IN TOUCH WITH YOURSELF

Not everyone can find someone they want to talk to and even if they do all carers should talk to themselves on a daily basis as well.

A person with a mental health issue will most probably be encouraged to use coping strategies to resist being overwhelmed by their symptoms. They will also be supported to check whether their negative thoughts are in fact true, or just something they have come to believe for whatever reason. If they recognise how hard they are trying and celebrate when they win a victory, then they become their own support rather than their own critical judge.

Sounds useful? If a carer supports the person with the mental health issue to try these things, then they should be prepared to try it themselves. It also sets a great example if it is possible to share this experience with them and compare notes.

The situations that are faced as a mental health carer are far more testing than most people ever need to deal with in their lives. Even if it is a little calmer now because the most turbulent patch has passed there is a fair chance that the family are tired or less energetic than usual. If this description is inaccurate and everyone is bouncing through life like a bunny in spring, please feel free to stop reading this bit now.

Being aware of what is going on in your own head is important. I realise that sounds obvious, but I have been repeatedly puzzled by how many people do not tune in to their thoughts and just have them as background noise. Thoughts are important, they shape mood and behaviour, but they are not always a source of support. Surprisingly, we are not always our own best friends.

Everyone has an internal commentary going on. I believe that Buddhists call it the 'chattering monkey' but I prefer a term

I learnt recently, please excuse the vulgarity but isn't the 'itty bitty shitty committee' a useful phrase for the endless and often pointless debate that goes on inside people's heads?

The principle behind this listening in is to check what is being thought and if it is negative or pessimistic then to ask for evidence; are these ideas true? It may feel that these thoughts are hard facts, changing them is either trying to deny reality or is just a waste of time. Mental health issues don't usually come with hard facts though.

Suppose a carer felt guilty and ashamed because they were convinced that their son's problems were caused by smoking cannabis, this was something that had been accepted by the family as inevitable as all his friends were doing it too. But he 'should' have been stopped and then this awful mental health issue would not exist. This may feel like a hard fact, but some alternative viewpoints might be

A. His friends were all smoking weed too, so their parents didn't or couldn't stop them. How could he have been stopped?

B. The mental health issue might have been caused by this, or not. It might have developed anyway when a different trigger occurred.

C. The support that is being offered now by the family far outweighs any misjudgement that thousands of other parents have faced, and few have managed to avoid. The outcome of his behaviour was impossible to predict, the choices made were the only possible option at the time.

There are some areas which seem to produce guilt or worry for many carers, but which no jury would convict on. These sorts of thoughts can be wearing to live with; there is frequently a selection of constantly repeating ideas and memories which keep a person stuck but with little time or energy to think them through.

Another common feature of carers' internal rumination seems to be constantly anticipating the next relapse or re-running the last crisis time over and over, thinking about all the points at which it might have become even more catastrophic. This is about dwelling on the most stressful moments, then predicting that it is all going to happen again any minute now, only worse.

A carer is sitting at home waiting for her husband who has a diagnosis of PTSD; he is currently drinking a lot. He is out this evening and it's going to be hours before he walks through the door. Her thoughts are:

> 'He's got money, he's going to have a drink, he will come home and have a go at me again. I can't stand it. It was so awful last time. I am just so weak, why do I put up with it? He frightens me when he is ranting and raving like this but what can I do?'

Result is an evening of jumping at every sound, anxious and unable to concentrate on anything. Would it be possible to at least challenge these thoughts with something like this?

> 'I wonder how he will be when he comes home. He is scary when he's had a few but if I can stay calm, he will hopefully go to bed quite quickly, like he did last week. Whatever he does I have coped with it before and I'll undoubtedly cope with it this time too.'

If she is a little calmer when he does return she may make better choices in how she responds, if he does turn out to be belligerent.

Or perhaps a carer thinks:

> 'She's never going to get better; she is stuck like this
> for the rest of her life.'

This is a depressing thought, it will colour the relationship, the carer may stop trying to improve things. What evidence is there for this belief? Accepting that the outcome is not known is daunting, but surely more positive than presuming the worst.

> 'I don't know how all this will turn out and nor does
> anyone else. I can only focus on one day at a time and
> help where I can. So that's what I'll do.'

Rather than 'just knowing' that he is going to have a bad day the thought could be, 'I wonder how he'll be today?' 'I Wonder' is a useful phrase, because until there are clear clues it is often best to wait and see. Frequently it is not as bad as expected.

Another source of support is to remember the journey to this point, how much has been experienced and coped with. Any family that goes through these challenges has learnt a great deal and is better positioned to handle the future, whatever it may bring. They are better equipped, often much more than any professional in this individual's situation. They have skills and they have survived, (maybe with some collateral damage but they have survived).

Another useful exercise is to write a journal. Not everyone benefits from writing, but this isn't going to be checked for spelling or read by anyone else (as long as it is kept somewhere extremely well hidden, and I mean extremely).It is possibly the only place where there can be total honesty. This is not a diary of what the person with the mental health issue is doing (which is also useful) but a record of a carer's thoughts and feelings. The thing about writing is that it is a bit like a counselling session, new ideas and perspectives come into a person's head while they are writing if they just let it unroll to get it off their chest, rather than writing for an audience.

The carer needs to stay in contact with themselves during this time, especially when there are crisis episodes to get through. A useful tactic is talking to yourself, preferably out loud and preferably face-to-face; the bathroom mirror is ideal. My colleague, a carer for many years and a source of great inspiration, told me about this. If a carer looks themselves in the eye every morning and say, 'Hello gorgeous,' or better yet, 'How am I feeling right now?' then they will probably get an honest answer.

This self-monitoring can help to structure the day. If life is going well they can say 'Well done you!' If they are feeling depressed with little energy it is fine to prioritise these needs over the requirements of the person with the mental health condition. Yes, occasionally and in times of dire need, the carer come first. Assess the risk and if the worst possible outcome is one that can be coped with, then take the book to a café or the credit card to any large department store and leave them a cheese sandwich and a choc chip muffin.

Useful phrases to tell the mirror image that carers have told me they use when things are a bit rocky:

'This too shall pass.' – I am ashamed to say I picked this up from an elderly agony aunt rather than Buddha but they both agree. Everything is temporary and everything changes.

'I've done this before, we got through it before, we will get through it if it happens again.'

'I am doing the best I can. That is all anyone can do'

It sounds naff to say 'believe in yourself' but it isn't poor advice.

GRIEF AND GUILT

This sounds a negative and depressing title but there is nothing to gain by ignoring the strong emotional buffeting that mental health carers often experience. If this is a personal issue that maybe shouldn't be faced right now, then maybe read this a bit later. It is under the 'survival' section because it needs to be acknowledged and thought about at some stage. 'Turn around and face the dragon that is chasing you' as they say. But if this is not a good time then it can wait.

Guilt seems to be a fundamental part of most carers' thoughts.

- I made it happen
- I made it worse
- I haven't helped as much as I could have
- I hate them sometimes
- I occasionally want them to go away
- I hate that they have ruined my life
- It would have been better if I had never met them/they had never been born/ I had moved away
- I am not coping
- I should have got this sorted out and I haven't

This guilt is especially strong for parents but also seems to be there for any other relationship too. A truly guilt free carer is a rare occurrence, in my experience.

Logically, as an outsider, it is obvious that the situation is not of the carer's doing (nor the person with the mental health issue) and unless they are intentionally abusive and deliberately damaging then they are really just doing the best they can in a stressful situation. Of course, any carer wishes it hadn't happened and of course they sometimes have fleeting thoughts about putting lots of pills in their cocoa. That is normal after all. Me, or anyone else, saying that these thoughts are not unusual is probably not going to help. What might be more reassuring is to find a way to meet to other carers, preferably face-to-face. I have listened to quite a few YouTube clips of family carers talking about their experiences and they are wonderful and encouraging, but mostly seem to skirt round these less acceptable thoughts. Finding a gathering, preferably of only mental health carers, these issues often come to the surface – laughing at these negative thoughts together reduces their power considerably.

Strangely there seems to be a reluctance to go and meet other carers when the opportunity is there. There may be worries that the situation is more embarrassing or unacceptable than other peoples could possibly be, either because of how the person they support behaves or because they just feel they are doing everything wrong. All I can say to those ideas is that they are simply not true. I have been in many mental health carer groups and there are always shared experiences and common self-doubts.

If a carer feels guilty then this can be helped with a CBT approach. What hard evidence is there that the responsibility falls only on their shoulders or that the thoughts about escaping aren't a normal reaction to stress? Another test is to imagine that a friend told the exact same story as the carer's experience, with their innermost thoughts, then asked if it was their fault or if they were terrible people. What would the response be?

Grief is often left on the back burner because no one wants to go there and understandably so. When the first episode of the mental health story begins the family are far too busy to think about their own state of mind except in fleeting moments. Later they are either grateful that life is quieter or still preoccupied with coping day-to-day.

Why do family members feel grief? This isn't a death but a

loss, of the child that has been so important for so long, or the person that was chosen to be part of your life, the parent that offered so much support or an old friend who was so much fun a while ago. There is also a loss of the future that was planned and the life that seemed to be going OK. This is depressing stuff and I hope that it is not too much to think about.

If someone close dies, (sorry I can't use the term 'If you lose someone' because it sounds like an act of carelessness,) then it would be natural to expect to feel bereft, sad, a bit lost and tearful. All the people involved may look after each other a bit more carefully for a while.

This grief has a slower onset because there is always hope that things will get better and they frequently do. The new situation may still not be the one that was hoped for, for either the person with the mental health issue or those around them. They may be greatly restricted in what they feel able to do in their lives, and maybe this applies to some of the family too.

Grief has certain effects that are well recognised and the reason why this unhappy subject is included is because it may be helpful to consider if it is affecting the family's emotional state and ability to cope.

There are stages in reacting to loss, they can come together or mixed up so don't see this as a sequence.

DENIAL

'This isn't happening, they have got it all wrong. She will be fine once she gets back to her old self. This is still the effects of the last lot of cannabis, it won't last. It is just people being melodramatic, they want to turn every little crisis into a medical condition. She just needs a bit of rest because she has been overdoing it. I'll get her some St John's Wort and she'll be fine.'

The pause while the family process what is happening and recognise that the situation is more acute than it first appeared might delay the person getting help. It is a stage that is not easily missed out though; it is a hard truth to accept.

BARGAINING

'I will go back to church every Sunday if you will just make him better.'

'I will go and see the GP and explain what is going on properly this time and then she will sort it out.'

'If I can just make that psychiatrist realise what a complete idiot he is, then he will do something to fix this.'

'If I can just make his mother stop spoiling him and be a bit firmer then we will soon have this sorted.'

This stage can include a lot of 'if only' and 'why didn't I do that?' It might also include an element of 'it's all his mother's fault, her friend's fault, the GP's fault'. This is a frustrating period, this need to find the answers when in reality there are none, well none under anyone's immediate control at this early stage. Just a developing process that will take its own time.

ANGER

Anger may have a root in the 'why did this have to happen?' question and the 'it's not fair!' feelings. It can be directed at the carer themselves, or other family members, the world in general but is often directed at the NHS services. This is tricky because sometimes the mental health professionals do let people down, or fail to offer an appropriate response. This is not always a mistake on their part, they may just have had more experience and actually be following the best path. Perhaps there is a realisation at some stage that the nurse was right but at the time everything was just influenced by this overwhelming anger.

There must be somebody who can make this all right, there should be somebody surely. Maybe the carer has an idea about what should happen, and it isn't being offered. Tempers boil and are hard to control. Some carers don't hide their anger at the services, and this can influence the cared-for person. 'That mental health team are a load of idiots,' isn't a remark that is going to encourage trust in the only help available, even if there is a chance that the carer is right.

DEPRESSION

What's the point? Whatever is done doesn't seem to make any difference and the whole family is tired of trying. It's not fair (and it's not!). This is too much, there is no strength left in anyone. Every day presents the same brick wall. It is just a question of going through the motions now, there is no point hoping that anything will change.

ACCEPTANCE

This is the light at the end of the tunnel, I have witnessed several carers go through their own personal struggles and finally get there, but it's a long journey for most.

It involves realising at both a rational and emotional level that:

'This is really happening, to them and to me. It's not fair, it isn't what either of us deserve but it is happening, right now.' 'Although this person is important to me, I recognise that I can only do so much. I can help but only in certain ways, I cannot fix the whole thing or take responsibility for why it happened or how it works out.'

One carer said that she had spent months working out that she had a responsibility to help her son as much as she could but was not responsible *for* him. 'I cannot take responsibility for things I cannot control'.

Counselling can be useful for both guilt and grief issues; many areas have free or low-cost options for carers, ask the GP or local Carers' Centre for information. It is important to identify these feelings as being part of a widely experienced aspect of caring in this type of situation. When someone close develops any health condition there is always an emotional response. Mental health can be much more difficult to accept as there are few physical tests for it, no clear transition from being 'OK' to being 'not OK'. The more severe the symptoms the greater the emotional impact on the people actively involved.

This process of accepting that this mental health issue is part of the family's life now can be a slow one. This is a natural reaction to an unusually stressful situation and is best coped with by being supportive, understanding and compassionate to those involved, especially yourself.

THE GOOD ENOUGH CARER

The phrase 'a good enough parent' has been adopted in recent years to acknowledge that good enough is mostly as good as it gets. Perfect parents are few, the majority are just doing the best they can and on the whole that is absolutely fine, most children thrive. The same is undoubtedly true of being a carer within mental health.

What gets in the way for the carer is often that sense of guilt and the isolation, it can easily feel as though this is a totally unique situation that is not being managed well. There is not much in the media as to what life is like when there is someone in the house with a severe mental health issue. All there seems to be is the odd article where a celeb has pulled themselves out of depression through yoga and their loving partner. The person you support would laugh in your face if you suggested they do yoga and they often blame their family for causing their mental health issue. As a carer it is easy to feel that everyone else is on top of their situation, it's just you.

Whenever I found myself in a room with a number of carers in it there would always be that moment when the clouds lifted, people realised that their difficulties may be unique but these other people knew what it was like and weren't at all judgemental. Difficulty then was getting them to stop talking and go home at the end of the meeting.

Feeling alone with it all makes it a brave act to talk to others about what is going on, frequently including family and friends. Crucially the lone carer has no one to share decisions with. Even sharing the caring role with a partner or relative may produce different views as to how to approach it or result in taking out the inevitable frustrations on each other as a safe target.

How does a carer know if they are 'good enough'? If there is sufficient time and energy it is worth considering the points on this checklist, it is one method of reviewing the caring role. Some of the points may produce the response 'I am doing all I can' and some may be 'I could try and do that a bit differently'.

The carers' checklist

1. Do you have all the information you feel you need about the diagnosis, the medication, the treatment plan or anything else that might be going on? If not, who can you ask?

2. When the person is seriously agitated or distressed is there a preferred way to respond which has been developed through trial and error? Is this plan keeping things as calm as is possible for most of the time?

3. Are you doing more than you need to? Could you do less, particularly when they are having a good day? Is encouraging their independence the basis of day to day decisions?

4. Is it recognised that the only method that a carer has of changing the person's behaviour is to change their own behaviour, who they phone, what they say and what they do? There is no other way that is under the carer's control to make these changes happen.

5. If it is appropriate are there boundaries in place so both / all of you know where you stand, are these boundaries kept consistently?

6. Are you able to make time to really listen to this person and try to work out what their world is like for them?

7. Are you trying as best as you can to make a good working relationship with any professionals, making it clear what you believe to be important but also being aware of their job and time limitations?

8. Have you thought through what you might do if you ever feel completely overwhelmed and exhausted? What are your choices if this should happen?

9. Are you using any or all resources or options that will help you keep going? If you aren't getting what you need to recharge your batteries then are you working on making it happen (very soon)?

This is a basic summary of what this book is trying to say. If you have considered these points and are at peace with your plan, then that may be as good as it is going to get.

Last words.

What determines the outcome of any mental health situation?

- Finding the best treatment for that person
- The person's own attitude to what is happening
- The person's own ability to self-manage their symptoms
- Having a family that is calm(ish), non-judgemental and supportive
- Other sources of support such as professionals, peers or friends
- The opportunity to develop an identity or way of living that brings a sense of satisfaction and self-esteem.

Particularly with the more complex and severe mental health diagnoses 'I believe things will get better' is a powerful statement. It may not mean that all the difficulties completely disappear, but that there will be improvements and progress. These may well surpass all the bleak thoughts that happen on the darkest days. But no one can see how it will turn out and even though statistics are on the side of hope it may be down to the carer to keep that flame alive when things are at their worst by saying things like:

> 'You have such a struggle every day, not many people go through what you have to go through. It will be great when you can look back at this awful time and know that it's over.'

Some days this will be easier to believe than others, but it may be better to share your doubts with someone else or in a diary. Keeping positivity and some sense of optimism, even if it comes and goes, will contribute directly to their recovery. People with mental health issues need a degree of self-belief to tackle learning tasks and to maintain coping skills. People often say later that it was their family that gave them this strength, 'they believed in me'.

I have met so many carers who have said that life is so much better now than they ever could have imagined a while ago. Carry on holding the hope!

RESOURCES

Adfam – www.adfam.org.uk

Beat: Eating disorders – www.beateatingdisorders.org.uk/types

British Psychological Society – www.bps.org.uk

Carers UK – www.carersuk.org

LEAP Foundation (Dr Xavier Amador) – https://lfrp.org/home

Mind Mental Health Charity – www.mind.org.uk

Rethink Mental Illness – www.rethink.org

Royal College of Psychiatrists – www.rcpsych.ac.uk/mental-health/problems-disorders

Samaritans – www.samaritans.org *116123 or jo@samaritans.org*

SANEline – www.sane.org.uk

REFERENCES

Harty M.A. (2001) *'Mental Illness: A Handbook for Carers'* Eds. Rosaline Ramsay, Claire Gerada, Sarah Mars and George Smukler. London: Jessica Kingsley Publishers.

Carers UK State of Caring survey www.carersuk.org/news-and-campaigns/news/state-of-caring-report-2019years

'I Am Not Sick I Don't Need Help!: How to Help Someone with Mental Illness Accept Treatment'
(2011) Dr Xavier Amador. New York: Vida Press

ACKNOWLEDGEMENTS

I want to thank the many people that I have met over the years, both people who had mental health issues and family carers. Their insights taught me much and their personal courage was inspiring. I do hope you are all doing all right.

On the list specifically is my colleague of far too many years and partner in crime, Alan S, who walked the walk and talked the talk. He fought the battle for carers to be better supported for a long time; he won many of the skirmishes. I would also like to mention his wife Gill who still has to put up with him while I am retired to a relatively safe distance.

I thank Rachael R who actually read all this for me and politely told me about my serious lack of commas. She also helped me answer some awkward questions by listening to lengthy rants without interrupting. A rare skill.

I have learnt a great deal through Arvon writing workshops but would like to single out James Spackman for being a tutor who foolishly gave me his email address and then actually not only replied but also helped when I used it.

Thanks to Su and Em for their occasional positivity and especially to Steve for putting up with the hours of tapping on a keyboard and being grumpy, also for listening to one sided book related conversations that can't possibly have been of any interest. This has been most intense during the corona virus lock down when the poor soul had few means of getting away.

I would also like to express my thanks to the Book Guild for taking a chance on this book and being wonderfully supportive to someone new to the game.